D1426326

CLAUDIA HELLMANN · CLAUDINE WEBER-HOF

ON LOCATION 2

FAMOUS LANDSCAPES IN FILM

CONTENTS

FOREWORD · MOVIE LOCATIONS: A ROUND-THE-WORLD ADVENTURE 4

NORTH AMERICA
1 THE WEST · BIRTHPLACE OF FILM LOCATIONS 6
2 THE SOUTH · FROM THE SWAMPS TO THE SMOKIES 26
3 HAWAII · SURF & DINOSAUR TURF 36

CENTRAL & SOUTH AMERICA & THE CARIBBEAN
4 MEXICO · HOLLYWOOD SOUTH OF THE BORDER 42
5 PERU · WILD JUNGLES, MIGHTY RIVERS 46
6 ARGENTINA · A JOURNEY TO THE ANDES 48
7 THE CARIBBEAN · ISLAND PARADISE ON THE SILVER SCREEN 50

EUROPE
8   ENGLAND · LITERARY LANDSCAPES..62
9   SCOTLAND · HIGHLAND DRAMA 76
10 IRELAND · THE EMERALD ISLE IN FILM..82
11 FRANCE · BETWEEN SEDUCTION AND NOSTALGIA 84
12 SPAIN · THE SPAGHETTI WESTERN 92
13 GERMANY · FAIRY-TALE CASTLES & MAGIC MOUNTAINS 94
14 AUSTRIA · FROM SISSI TO THE SOUND OF MUSIC 98

15 SWITZERLAND · HOME OF THE MOUNTAINEERING FILM 100

16 ITALY · A LOVE AFFAIR WITH LOCATIONS 102

17 CROATIA · THE LEGEND OF KARL MAY 120

18 GREECE · ZORBA THE GREEK MEETS CAPTAIN CORELLI 122

AFRICA

19 MOROCCO · TINSELTOWN IN THE SANDS 126

20 TUNISIA · FILMING IN A DESERT OASIS 136

21 EAST AFRICA: KENYA AND TANZANIA · LOVE AND ADVENTURE IN THE SAVANNAH 138

22 CENTRAL AFRICA: RWANDA, THE CONGO, AND UGANDA · HEART OF DARKNESS ... 148

ASIA

23 INDIA · ON THE TRAIL OF AN EMPIRE 150

24 CHINA AND MONGOLIA · KUNG-FU FIGHTING & NOMADS' TALES 156

25 SOUTHEAST ASIA · FROM APOCALYPSE NOW TO THE BEACH 160

OCEANIA

26 AUSTRALIA · ON LOCATION "DOWN UNDER" 168

27 NEW ZEALAND · A CINEMATOGRAPHIC WONDERLAND 178

INDEX & CREDITS 188

FOREWORD

MOVIE LOCATIONS: A ROUND-THE-WORLD ADVENTURE

Have you ever been "on location?" If you have driven through the astonishing landscapes of the American Southwest, or to the United Kingdom's breathtaking north, then chances are you have. Movies like *Thelma & Louise*, filmed near Moab, Utah, and the *Harry Potter* films, shot in northern England and Scotland, use landscapes to embellish a story line. These places are portrayed so memorably in the movies that they begin to take on a life of their own. Moviegoers leave the theaters wondering just where in the world those deep canyons, vertiginous cliffs, golden beaches, or snowcapped mountains might be.

This book, a round-the-world tour of landscape locations in film, provides the answers. Entertainingly written essays use 450 selected films and their locations in 40 countries to provide you with the inspiration to book a flight or visit the local video store to plan your cinematic getaway. As in the first book of this series, *On Location: Cities of the World in Film*, stunning photographs, familiar film stills, and helpful maps provide a wealth of visual information to make sure you can find the movie locations you would most like to visit.

So go ahead and ask: Where exactly is *The Beach* from Leonardo DiCaprio's hair-raising Southeast Asian adventure? And what about those bamboo forests from the acrobatic kung-fu fights in *Crouching Tiger, Hidden Dragon*? The rolling hills of Ita-

ly enchanted many a moviegoer in *The Godfather* and *Under the Tuscan Sun*, the same effect the sand dunes of Morocco had on audiences in *The Sheltering Sky*. Who could ever forget the safari landscapes in *Out of Africa*, or Australia's outback in *Mad Max* and *The Adventures of Priscilla, Queen of the Desert*. Thanks to the success of Peter Jackson's *Lord of the Rings* series, New Zealand is now synonymous with the movies. Everyone wants to scale the slopes of Mount Doom!

As the birthplace of on-location filmmaking, America's landscapes have enchanted movie fans for generations. John Ford's classics like *Stagecoach*, the legendary *Easy Rider* road trip, *Dances with Wolves*, and *A River Runs Through It* are just a few famous examples. South America dazzled us most recently on the silver screen in *The Motorcycle Diaries*, just as it did decades ago in Werner Herzog's epic *Fitzcarraldo*. Some well-known locations, like the Austrian Alps from *The Sound of Music* or Lake Lure, North Carolina, from *Dirty Dancing*, have an enduring kitsch appeal that never fails to attract throngs of visitors. Lonely and remote, other landscape locations invite travelers to explore them free of crowds and souvenir shops – and to take goofy "action shots" as personal mementos of the famous films made there.

The authors of this volume have traveled widely to seek out their favorite landscape locations. The idea for the project originated in the United States when Anja Hauenstein and Claudia

Hellmann paid a visit to the Whistle Stop Cafe from *Fried Green Tomatoes*. The chance encounter turned their vacation in the American South into a location-hunting trip for films like *Forrest Gump, The Prince of Tides*, and *The Last of the Mohicans*. Curious to see where more cult movies were shot, the duo traveled to Vietnam to visit key locations from *Indochine* and to Morocco for *The Sheltering Sky* and *Kundun*.

Anja Hauenstein has also traveled extensively in Africa and the Far East, where the seasoned television journalist photographed several film locations. Luke Brighty has many years of experience in movie tourism as a writer and entrepreneur. He has organized movie tours in America and Australia, and more recently traveled to New Zealand to research and photograph locations for this book from films such as *The Piano, The Chronicles of Narnia, The Last Samurai,* and the *Lord of the Rings* trilogy.

Claudia Hellmann and Claudine Weber-Hof made numerous trips to Italy, France, Tunisia, the U.K., and the American Southwest, all of which inform the essays in this volume. David Weber went with them, taking many of the photographs that illustrate the book. Kate Cochran applied her extensive knowledge of France to her chapter on film in that country. Stephan Fuchs's travels in Central and South America shaped his chapters on Mexico, Argentina, and Peru. He and Claudia Hellmann also toured the Caribbean on the James Bond trail.

Verena Hertlein wove her U.S. expertise into the chapters on the American South and Hawaii, while Larissa Vassilian expressed her admiration of German-language film and Alpine vistas in her articles on Austria, Germany, and Switzerland. When she lived in Spain, Katrin Utzinger took every available opportunity to travel through Iberian landscapes brimming with film locations, a journey that inspired her piece on spaghetti Westerns. Thanks are due also to Greg Langley for his chapter on India, and Maggie Martin for her coverage of Greece.

The authors would like to thank Gerhard Grubbe of Bucher Publishing for his unwavering support of the *On Location* book series. To the photographers who have given freely of their resources and time to support the books, in particular Volkmar Janicke and David Weber, we are deeply grateful. We also extend our heartfelt thanks to Birgit Kneip, our talented editor at Bucher Publishing, and Peter Meredith, whose broad knowledge and uncanny ability to find errors greatly improved the manuscript. Marion Sauer and Johannes Reiner of the Vor-Zeichen studio in Munich, Germany, designed this book to be the visual celebration of films and places that it is.

Monument Valley (far left) in the American Southwest reigns as one of the world's most famous film locations. Claudia Hellmann (center) pedals past rice paddies on the trail of *Indochine* in Vietnam. Claudine Weber-Hof (right) on a visit to Tuscany's Sant'Anna in Camprena from *The English Patient*.

BIRTHPLACE OF FILM LOCATIONS

By Claudia Hellmann

No other part of the world has been immortalized on celluloid to the same degree as the American West. An entire genre, the Western, would be unthinkable without its characteristic landscapes. These are monumental, majestic vistas whose wide deserts, deep canyons, and high mountain ridges inspire deep respect. The West is a raw, untamed landscape governed by the laws of nature and the survival of the fittest. But it is also a landscape of yearning and promise in which true heroism and the pioneering spirit can prevail.

"Go west, young man, and grow up with the country," was a popular dictum in the nineteenth century, when land was ac-quired plot by plot and the frontier moved ever further west. But it might just as well have been the motto for the film industry when it relocated to California after its early years in New York – and not just because of the 300 days of sunshine that California promised each year. Hollywood offered an ideal situation, with a plethora of diverse landscapes on its doorstep just waiting to be captured on screen.

Westerns like *Sergeant Rutledge* made Monument Valley world famous.

Top landscape film locations

1. Banff National Park and surroundings, Alberta, Canada: **Legends of the Fall, The Edge, River of No Return**
2. Area near Canmore, Alberta, Canada: **Brokeback Mountain**
3. Glacier National Park, Montana: **Cattle Queen of Montana, Heaven's Gate**
4. Paradise Valley, Montana: **A River Runs Through It, The Horse Whisperer**
5. Grand Teton National Park, Wyoming: **The Big Sky, Shane**
6. Devil's Tower, Wyoming: **Close Encounters of the Third Kind**
7. Badlands National Park, South Dakota: **Dances with Wolves**

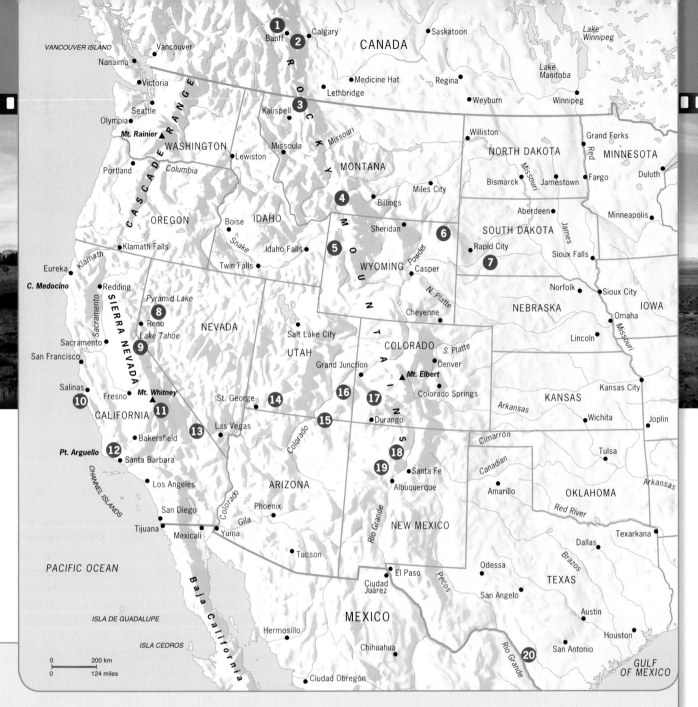

8. Pyramid Lake, Nevada: **The Misfits**
9. Lake Tahoe and Truckee, California: **A Place in the Sun, The Gold Rush**
10. Monterey Peninsula and Point Lobos, California: **Vertigo, The Sandpiper**
11. Mount Whitney and Lone Pine, California: **High Sierra**
12. Santa Ynez Valley, California: **Sideways**
13. Death Valley, California: **Zabriskie Point, Star Wars**
14. Zion National Park, Utah: **Butch Cassidy and the Sundance Kid, Jeremiah Johnson**
15. Monument Valley, Utah/Arizona border: **Stagecoach, The Searchers, Easy Rider**
16. Area near Moab, Utah: **Rio Grande, Thelma & Louise, Geronimo**
17. San Juan Mountains in Ouray County, Colorado: **True Grit**
18. Chama River Valley, New Mexico: **All the Pretty Horses, City Slickers, Wyatt Earp**
19. Zia Pueblo Reserve, New Mexico: **All the Pretty Horses, The Missing**
20. Alamo Village in Bracketville, Texas: **The Alamo**

The Southwest

America's Southwest is a barren, unwelcoming region – and yet its landscapes are extraordinarily alluring. Over the millennia, erosion and the heat of the sun have led to the formation of gigantic canyons, unique rock formations, and sandstone arches that are perfectly suited to be dramatic film backdrops. The road movie *Easy Rider* (1969) is inextricably linked with the landscapes of the Southwest. The film started out as a low-budget motorcycle flick but quickly achieved cult status for at least two reasons: It celebrated the ideal of freedom under America's endless skies while simultaneously underscoring the narrow-mindedness that fettered it. The combination epitomized the zeitgeist of the late 1960s. *Easy Rider* is a modern Western, with Wyatt (Peter Fonda) and Billy (Dennis Hopper) playing two stoned cowboys who ride through myriad landscapes from L.A. to New Orleans on their Harley Davidson choppers. Accompanied by music from Steppenwolf, The Byrds, and Jimi Hendrix, the camera follows the two antiheroes on their journey, long stretches of which follow the historic **Route 66** past the ghost town of **Ballarat** on the western edge of **Death Valley** – where Wyatt bids farewell to his wristwatch in a symbolic declaration of independence – and over the **Colorado River** at **Needles.**

Just north of **Flagstaff** in Arizona, the two adventurers pick up a hitchhiker and stop at the Sacred Mountain gas station, no longer in operation today. They ride on past the red rocks of the **Painted Desert,** reaching **Monument Valley** just as the sun sets. The camera pan over the evening sky shows a blaze of psychedelic color reaching out to the distant table mountains glowing faintly in the dusk, one of the most beautiful shots ever taken of this extraordinary landscape. They spend the night camping by the ruins of an old Anasazi pueblo dwelling in Monument Valley, and subsequently drop the hitchhiker at his commune, close to **Taos Pueblo** in Taos, New Mexico. To the south of Taos in **Las Vegas, New Mexico** (not to be confused with the famous gambling city in Nevada), Wyatt and Billy find themselves on

Born to be wild: In *Easy Rider,* Peter Fonda and Dennis Hopper motor through the Southwest on a search for the real America.

the wrong side of the law. In jail, they meet a lawyer named George (Jack Nicholson), who accompanies them on the rest of their trip. The journey continues from the wide open spaces of the West into the densely populated southern States, where the hippie duo meet with widespread mistrust.

Home of the Western: Monument Valley

What would John Ford be without Monument Valley? The bizarre rock formations in the middle of a Navajo reservation on the border between Utah and Arizona provided the famous director of Western movies with a unique backdrop. The sandstone monoliths, formed by centuries of erosion, stand out like mythic giants on a high plateau. The central group of three is instantly recognizable: The two Mitten Buttes rise up like a pair of gloves, with Merrick's Butte to their right. Countless Westerns have been filmed here, but none has captured the atmosphere of the place better than those directed by Ford. The camera was often placed on a particular rocky outcrop with an especially dramatic panorama view, a spot that has since been dubbed **John Ford's Point.**

A silent movie, *The Vanishing American,* was filmed here as early as 1925, but it was Ford who really captured the monumental greatness of this place in **Stagecoach** (1939). This seminal Western tells the story of a group of travelers thrown together on a risky coach ride through enemy Indian territory. The stagecoach rumbles forward on its lonely trajectory through the "Mittens" and across the seemingly endless expanses of Monument Valley. Seldom has nature appeared so overwhelming – or the people in its midst so lost and vulnerable. *Stagecoach* is also notable as the film that marked the breakthrough for the greatest Western actor of all time, John Wayne.

John Ford and John Wayne turned out to be a winning combination. In the years that followed *Stagecoach,* Ford shot many more Westerns with John Wayne in the starring role. Several were shot here and in the surrounding area, including *My Dar-*

With his 1939 movie *Stagecoach,* director John Ford made John Wayne into a star – and discovered spectacular Monument Valley as a film location.

ling Clementine (1946), *Fort Apache* (1948), *She Wore a Yellow Ribbon* (1949), *The Searchers* (1956), and *Sergeant Rutledge* (1960). In **She Wore a Yellow Ribbon,** Monument Valley was filmed in an especially dramatic fashion: Instead of the customary black-and-white shots, the *mesa* table mountains glow in full color, revealing gorgeous shades of red. A cavalry fort was constructed close to the Mitten Buttes especially for the film. Visually fascinating sequences – scenes that won the film an Oscar for Best Cinematography, Color – showcase John Wayne as Captain Brittles, a hardy officer leading his troops through Monument Valley as lightning flashes across the sky. Captain Brittles's small house still stands and is open to visitors behind the museum in **Goulding,** just across from Monument Valley. Goulding's trading post, a popular tourist stop today, was turned into a fort for the film.

By contrast, the dwelling where a family of settlers lives in **The Searchers** is a lonely little house that cowers in the shadow of the mighty Mitten Buttes, just below today's visitor center. John Wayne plays Ethan Edwards, a man obsessed with finding his niece (Natalie Wood). Edwards is intent upon killing the Indians who kidnapped her and massacred her family. The steep rocky needle known as **Totem Pole** appears in the scene in which John Wayne finally locates the Indian chief. Totem Pole and the **Three Sisters** are impressive rock formations that also provided the backdrop for Ford's 1960 drama **Sergeant Rutledge,** a contentious film about a black cavalry sergeant (Woody Strode), who is falsely accused of murdering the commander and raping his daughter.

Monument Valley became *the* classic Western backdrop and was closely associated with John Ford – but this did not prevent other directors from seeking out the unusual rock formations for their own projects. Some of the scenes for Stanley Kubrick's **2001: A Space Odyssey** (1968) were filmed here; **Forrest Gump** (1994) ended his marathon run across America between the colossal stones. Even the classic spaghetti Western **Once Upon a Time in the West** (1968), most of which was shot in Spain, includes some Monument Valley footage. Director Sergio Leone went so far as to have some of the location's characteristic red dust imported to the studios in Europe.

Round about Moab, Utah

A fascinating series of national parks unfolds along the Colorado River plateau in Utah, a fantastic set of landscapes just to the north of Monument Valley. Moviegoers will recognize many of these spectacular natural wonders from the silver screen, including Canyonlands, Arches, and Dead Horse Point. The ideal base for getting to know the area is the small town of Moab, a mecca for mountain bikers, jeep safari tourists, and film crews. Directors come here to shoot the wide variety of geological features, from bizarre rock formations, deep gorges,

The landscapes of the Southwest – such as Courthouse Towers near Moab, Utah – seem to hold the promise of freedom in *Thelma & Louise.*

and canyons, to great deserts, plateaus, and the snow-covered peaks of the La Sal Mountains.

With more than 2,000 sandstone arches, **Arches National Park** just to the north of Moab is a photogenic backdrop if ever there was one. Natural erosion has transformed the local stone into windows and arch formations with spans that can exceed 300 feet (90 meters) and colors that vary from sandy yellow to rust red. The opening scene of Wim Wenders's **Don't Come Knocking** (2005) shows a disillusioned cowboy galloping through **Landscape Arch,** one of the widest of these formations at 305 feet (93 meters). The arch is also one of the thinnest in the park, and consequently among the most fragile. Filming was strictly supervised so that arch and rider were shot separately and later edited together with the aid of advanced computer technology. The opening scene of **Indiana Jones and the Last Crusade** (1989), in which the young pathfinder Indy (River Phoenix) tries to save the Cross of Coronado from grave pillagers, was shot near the impressive **Double Arch.**

Not far from the visitor center at the south end of Arches National Park stands **Courthouse Towers,** a smooth, monolithic rock whose points rise up from the flat desert landscape. The atmospheric night shots in **Thelma & Louise** (1991) were filmed here, as was the scene in which the renegade friends, played

The *mesas* of Professor Valley on the Colorado River have appeared in many Westerns, such as *Rio Grande* with John Wayne as a cavalry officer.

by Geena Davis and Susan Sarandon, lock a policeman in the trunk of his car. The modern road movie about two women who take off for a weekend trip but end up being hunted as outlaws was shot largely in the area around Moab. The opening scene shows the **La Sal Mountains** viewed from the little town of La Sal, a location where some of the chase scenes were filmed. The dramatic finale, in which numerous police cars pursue the women across a plateau to the edge of a yawning precipice, was shot on Shafer Trail below **Dead Horse Point,** far above a narrow stretch of the Colorado River canyon.

Many films were made in and around **Professor Valley,** a pretty area situated opposite Arches on the other side of the Colorado River. Its pointed rocks, massive red sandstone table mountains, and broad plains lend it a certain similarity to Monument Valley – with the added advantage of being located on a wide river. The shallow fording area known as **Ida Gulch** has been the scene of many river crossings in films, such as the scenes of the cavalry and Indians charging into the water in John Ford's *Rio Grande* (1950). The center of the valley is marked by **Fisher Towers,** a group of rocks with cathedral-like spires, some 886 feet (270 meters) high. Prettily situated against a backdrop

The red sandstone of Professor Valley's Fisher Towers (left) in *Geronimo*.

of red rocks, **George White Ranch** is another popular film location whose extensive grounds served as the site of a cavalry fort constructed for *Rio Grande*. John Wayne plays Lt. Col. Kirby Yorke, an officer charged with protecting the frontier area from Indian attacks. The trouble starts when his teenage son turns up as a new recruit, followed by the colonel's argumentative wife, Kathleen (Maureen O'Hara). Several more Westerns were shot in this lovely area, including *The Comancheros* (1961), *Cheyenne Autumn* (1964), and *Rio Conchas* (1964). Ford used the area to particularly spectacular effect in one of his best and most personal films, **Wagon Master** (1950). The movie relates the saga of a wagon train of Mormons on a hazardous journey to Utah along the Colorado River.

Films such as *Geronimo* (1993) have featured this area in recent years, with breathtaking landscape shots a backdrop to stars such as Gene Hackman, Robert Duvall, and Wes Studi – a Cherokee actor who plays Geronimo. The epic centers on the life of the last Apache chief, his loyal warriors, and their final stand against ceding their land to the white man and being herded onto a reservation. The film was shot largely in the area around Moab, in **Professor Valley** in particular, near the sand dunes of **Behind the Rocks,** and at **Onion Creek** and **Needles Overlook** in **Canyonlands National Park** south of Moab.

Western City, Arizona

As with many Westerns, the makers of *Geronimo* needed a real Western town for some of its scenes. The most popular of these is **Old Tucson,** located a few miles west of the city of Tucson. This painstakingly constructed town – complete with saloon, railway station, blacksmith, and stables – is situated in the midst of **Tucson Mountain Park.** The park is surrounded by the **Sonora Desert,** with saguaro cactuses that can grow as tall as trees and low, brittlebush shrubs. The film town was built in 1939 as a gigantic set intended to represent the city of Tucson around 1860 in **Arizona** (1940). In just under forty days, more than fifty buildings were erected, many of which have survived to the present day. Old Tucson was rediscovered in the 1950s and developed into a popular film location for movies such as *Winchester '73* (1950), *Rio Bravo* (1959), *The Man Who Shot Liberty Valance* (1962), *El Dorado* (1966), and *Hombre* (1967). Today Old Tucson is a popular tourist destination, delighting visitors with a variety of stunt shows, dance routines, and carriage rides in post coaches.

Majestic Zion

The Mormons who settled in southwest Utah in the nineteenth century viewed the dome-shaped rocks and smoothly polished, tall red sandstone walls of the region close to the Arizona border as holy. They accordingly dubbed the place Zion, a

Paul Newman and Robert Redford as the legendary bandits *Butch Cassidy and the Sundance Kid*. Panned by critics when it first came out, the atypical Western filmed at Zion National Park went on to win four Oscars.

biblical name still borne by today's national park. The narrow canyons, colossal rock domes, wide plateaus, and petrified sand dunes also attract filmmakers. Some of the earliest films shot here in **Kanab Canyon** to the southeast of Zion and in the glowing **Coral Pink Sand Dunes** nearby include *The Deadwood Coach* (1924) with Tom Mix, one of cinema's first Western heroes, *The Big Trail* (1930), and *Buffalo Bill* (1944).

The movie that best showcases the variety of landscapes in and around Zion is ***Butch Cassidy and the Sundance Kid*** (1969). The Western, about two infamous outlaws – played by Paul Newman (Butch) and Robert Redford (the "Kid") – portrays the duo as likable antiheroes. The movie, which adroitly undermines many of the time-honored Western clichés, was shot largely in and around **Zion National Park.** Some scenes were filmed in the deserted but picturesque ghost town of **Grafton,** an old Mormon settlement that the filmmakers came across on the banks of the **Virgin River,** a tributary of the Colorado. The film centers on a half-hour chase scene in which Butch and the Sundance Kid try to elude their pursuers with a wild ride over wide plains, mountain ridges, and petrified dunes. The scene was shot in the **St. George, Virgin,** and **Zion** region. The culmination of the sequence – a liberating leap into a river flowing at the bottom of

a canyon – was shot in **Las Animas River Gorge** near Durango, Colorado, also the scene of the film's **Durango Silverton Narrow Gauge Railroad** train robbery.

Robert Redford returned to Zion some years later to play the lead in Sydney Pollack's melancholy Western ballad ***Jeremiah Johnson*** (1972), the story of a man who retreats into the lonely mountain wilderness of Utah in the mid-nineteenth century. Instead of a remote idyll, Jeremiah finds himself facing a hostile tribe of Crow Indians. The breathtaking mountain world of Zion is captured here in tranquil images of snowed-in landscapes.

The Deserts of Nevada

The gambler's paradise of Las Vegas has always attracted filmmakers, but it is the bleak beauty of the desert that distinguishes the landscape of Nevada. The effects of the sun and wind are especially manifest in the north of the state, with its bleached, bone-dry vistas. John Ford filmed his silent classic ***The Iron Horse*** (1924) in the middle of the **desert near Pyramid Lake,** roughly 30 miles (50 kilometers) from Reno. By contemporary standards, making the movie about the construction of the Union Pacific and Central Pacific railroad lines was a difficult and costly undertaking. A film made almost forty years later

The scene in which Butch and Etta take a bike ride to the Oscar-winning song "Raindrops Keep Fallin' on My Head" was filmed in the ghost town of Grafton.

would again bring the Nevada landscape to the forefront of the public's attention: John Huston's melancholy drama *The Misfits* (1961). Playwright Arthur Miller wrote the screenplay and tailored the role of Roslyn to fit the alluring figure of his wife at that time, Marilyn Monroe. By the time shooting started, their marriage was on the rocks. The remote locations, scorching heat, and Monroe's habit of turning up late on the set made for a very difficult shoot – but the film is considered a masterpiece.

The story starts in **Reno,** where the disillusioned and recently divorced Roslyn meets the aging cowboy Gay Langland (Clark Gable) and the pilot Guido (Eli Wallach). Both men are enchanted by the buxom blonde, and persuade her to travel out to Guido's homestead with them. Shooting took place on the **Quail Canyon Ranch** to the west of Pyramid Lake. In **Dayton,** they pick up the young rodeo rider Perce (Montgomery Clift) and decide to hunt wild horses together. When Roslyn realizes that they intend to sell the horses for slaughter – and ultimately for dog food – she desperately tries to stop them. The scene in which the mustangs are rounded up was filmed on salt flats at the **Pyramid Lake** Indian reservation. Tragically, *The Misfits* turned out to be the last film Monroe and Gable would ever make: Gable died the year of the film's release, and Monroe succumbed to a drug overdose on August 5, 1962.

The Misfits was the last film Marilyn Monroe and Clark Gable would ever make. Director John Huston shows how to round up mustangs on the salt flats of Pyramid Lake.

Deserts, Rivers, and Pueblos: Texas and New Mexico

The rough-and-ready western corner of Texas has achieved special prominence as a film location: This is where *Giant* (1956) was filmed, a family saga about a Texan cattle rancher and his rival that received ten Oscar nominations. The crew constructed the set of Reata Ranch, managed by beef baron Bick Benedict (Rock Hudson) and his wife Leslie (Elizabeth Taylor), in the desert town of **Marfa,** west of Alpine and close to the Mexican border. A fight begins to brew when ranch hand Jett Rink (James Dean) strikes oil and begins to show a romantic interest in Leslie. The set collapsed in the 1980s, but its ruins are still standing on Ryan Ranch to the west of Marfa, and can be seen from Route 90. Wim Wenders chose the tiny town of **Marathon,** the gateway to the Big Bend National Park about an hour's drive east of Marfa, to shoot the memorable opening scenes of his road movie *Paris, Texas* (1984). The movie tells the tale of Travis (Harry Dean Stanton) – a lonely figure wandering through the desert – and his eventual return to everyday life with the help of his brother Walt (Dean Stockwell). The view stretches from the Marathon Motel and RV Park, where the brothers spend the

The flat land stretches out to the mountains of Big Bend National Park just outside of Marfa, Texas, where *Giant* (1956) starring James Dean was filmed.

The filming of *The Alamo*, especially its extravagant set, brought John Wayne to the brink of ruin. The set appeared in later films and television shows such as *Bandolero!* from 1968 with James Stewart and Dean Martin.

night, into the seemingly endless expanse of desert to the **Chisos Mountains** in the distance.

The most famous film location in Texas is **Alamo Village** in **Bracketville** near the border town of Del Rio. What is said to have been the largest film set ever built outside Hollywood was constructed here for the three-hour epic ***The Alamo*** (1960), which John Wayne directed and also starred in. The film is based on a legendary chapter in Lone Star State history: the 1836 stand taken by handful of soldiers to defend the Texan Mission of Alamo against the massive Mexican army. Builders needed two years to complete a realistic copy of the Alamo, an effort as costly as it was ambitious.

More Texas lore hit the silver screen some years after *The Alamo* in ***Bonnie and Clyde*** (1967). Faye Dunaway and Warren Beatty play the notorious Texan outlaws Bonnie Parker and Clyde Barrow who, with their gang of thieves, robbed countless banks, shops, and gas stations in the 1930s. Despite being criticized for presenting a romanticized picture of crime, as well as for the gratuitous use of graphic violence, the film was nominated for ten Oscars and rapidly achieved cult status. Shooting took place at real locations from the duo's past in the **Dallas** area. For the bank robbery scenes, director Arthur Penn used the banks that Bonnie and Clyde had robbed in the little towns of **Pilot Point, Ponder,** and **Red Oak.** Bonnie and Clyde perish in a hail of bullets in a bloody finale filmed at **Lemmon Lake** in the Joppa Preserve, a gathering place for African Americans after the Civil War that today is a protected wetland biotope.

Billy Bob Thornton filmed Cormac McCarthy's novel ***All the Pretty Horses*** (2000) in New Mexico. In the mid-nineteenth century, two young cowboys, John Grady Cole (Matt Damon) and Lacey Rawlins (Henry Thomas), make their way from Texas to Mexico. On the route south, they pass through jagged rock formations, deep canyons, and meandering rivers – landscape scenes that were filmed on the **Zia Pueblo Indian Reservation** at the southern tip of the

Jemez Mountains. The mighty Rio Grande that they cross in the film is actually the **Chama River** near Abiquiu, New Mexico. John and Lacey have high hopes for a better future on the other side of the border: Once in Mexico, they find work taming wild horses at a well-to-do hacienda. The problems start when John falls in love with Alejandra (Penélope Cruz), the horse breeder's daughter. The hacienda scenes were shot on **Hill Ranch** to the west of San Antonio, Texas, near the little town of Helotes. Further

Faye Dunaway and Warren Beatty are the gangsters *Bonnie and Clyde.*

scenes were shot on ranches located close to Las Vegas, New Mexico: **Ruby Ranch** stood in for Rawlins's hometown in Texas while the **Charles R. Ranch** was the scene of the dramatic

The Chama River near Abiquiu (right), New Mexico, is an important location in the film *All the Pretty Horses* starring Matt Damon and Henry Thomas.

Would-be cowboys and real pioneers: *City Slickers* with Billy Crystal and *The Missing* with Tommy Lee Jones and Cate Blanchett are just two of the many movies that have been filmed at Ghost Ranch near Abiquiu, New Mexico, once the home of artist Georgia O'Keeffe.

shooting. The campfire sequences and John's grandfather's funeral were filmed at **Bonanza Creek Ranch,** a farm to the south of Santa Fe also seen in ***The Man from Laramie*** (1955) starring James Stewart.

One of New Mexico's many pleasant monikers is "the Land of Enchantment." The deserts and the mountains as well as the unusually bright light have attracted numerous artists, including the photographer Anselm Adams and the painter Georgia O'Keeffe. Inspired by the dramatic landscape in the north of New Mexico, O'Keeffe worked in her studio on the extensive grounds of **Ghost Ranch** near Abiquiu from 1929 onwards. The **Chama River Valley** where Abiquiu is situated is a particularly picturesque location, with its mountains, broad plains, ochre-colored earth, spectacular rock formations, and numerous water courses. Westerns such as ***City Slickers*** (1991) and ***Wyatt Earp*** (1994) were filmed at Ghost Ranch.

The Missing (2003), an up-to-date Western, features the splendor of New Mexico's startling landscape diversity. Cate Blanchett plays the pioneer Maggie, whose daughter has been kidnapped by Indians and taken to Mexico. She embarks on an odyssey to find her daughter, traveling from the pine forests near her farm to the dusty deserts and baked canyons of the frontier lands. She is accompanied by her father (Tommy Lee Jones), who had abandoned his family to spend his life with Indians. Maggie's cabin, originally built for the film *Lucky Luke* (1991) with Terence Hill in the title role, is situated in the **Valles Caldera** in the highlands north of Santa Fe. This broad valley is actually the center of a volcanic crater that collapsed in prehistoric times. Some of the most beautiful shots were filmed on the **Zia Pueblo Reserve,** a landscape characterized by steep red cliffs, snow-white limestone tablelands, and dense pine forests, as well as at **Ghost Ranch.**

The beauty of the Chama River Valley unfolds all around Ghost Ranch. Filmmakers come for the landscapes drenched in New Mexico's famous light.

California and the Coast

It is no coincidence that the cradle of the movie industry is located in California. Hollywood's filmmakers found an endless variety of landscapes here, right on their doorstep – deserts, snowy mountain peaks, vineyards, towering redwoods, canyons, and the Pacific coast. Not all were such spectacular sites: Consider the legendary scene from Hitchcock's **North by Northwest** (1959), in which Cary Grant is chased by a low-flying airplane across the no-man's-land of fields and plains to the south of **Bakersfield.**

Wine Country

One film can make an overnight success of a region – as was the case with the tragicomic movie **Sideways** (2004). Tourists made a pilgrimage of following in the footsteps of the friends Miles (Paul Giamatti) and Jack (Thomas Haden Church), with

Director Alexander Payne chose the vineyards of the Santa Ynez Valley to star in *Sideways,* attracting tourists to follow the film's trail to the idyllic landscapes near Santa Barbara, California. Napa Valley's vineyards (right) served as the setting for *A Walk in the Clouds.*

the vineyards of the **Santa Ynez Valley** to the north of **Santa Barbara** their new pop-culture holy land. The highlights of the tour include the **Kalyra Winery** in **Santa Ynez** where Jack falls in love with Stephanie (Sandra Oh) during a wine-tasting; the picturesque vineyards of the **Andrew Murray Winery** near **Los Olivos** that Jack and Miles drive past in their cabriolet; and the **Sanford Winery** in **Buellton,** where oenophile Miles introduces his friend to the niceties of wine-tasting. Buellton is also the home of the **Hitching Post** restaurant, where Miles gets to know the waitress Maya (Virginia Madsen).

Images of sun-kissed vineyards also dominate the kitschy drama **A Walk in the Clouds** (1995). Keanu Reeves plays a soldier who returns home from World War II only to find adapting to daily life more difficult than imagined. All semblance of workaday normalcy disappears when he agrees to take on the role of husband to the pregnant daughter of a local vineyard owner for just one day. The idyllic scenes were shot at vineyards in the **Napa Valley,** including the Mayacamas Vineyards and the Mount Veeder Winery in Napa, the Haywoods Vineyards in Sonoma, and Beringer and the Duckhorn Vineyards in Saint Helena.

The Sierra Nevada

In the **Alabama Hills** to the west of Lone Pine, wind and weather have spent thousands of years polishing the rust-red sandstone into rounded stone formations – an ideal backdrop for Westerns and sci-fi movies. Some of the more famous films shot here

A Place in the Sun: Elizabeth Taylor and Montgomery Clift soak up the rays at Lake Tahoe.

include **Hop-Along Cassidy** (1935), the first of several dozen popular cowboy films with William Boyd as "Hoppy," **Maverick** (1994) with Mel Gibson and Jodie Foster, and **Star Trek V: The Final Frontier** (1989), in which **Owens Dry Lake** became the planet Nimbus III. Visitors trek along Movie Road to **Movie Flats Plain,** where numerous scenes have been shot and sites named after movie stars like Gary Cooper Rock and Lone Ranger Canyon bear witness to great productions in film history.

The 370-mile (600-kilometer) long mountain ridge of the **Sierra Nevada** rises up majestically behind the Alabama Hills. One of the earliest directors to defy the snow-covered mountains near **Truckee,** north of Lake Tahoe, was Charlie Chaplin in **The Gold Rush** (1925). Chaplin filmed an impressive scene at **Chilkoot Pass** with the help of some 600 extras, most of them vagrants transported to the set in trains from Sacramento. In this sequence, hordes of gold-diggers struggle through the snowdrifts that impede their progress up **Mount Lincoln.** Most of the filming took place at a set built to look like a small gold mining town in a depression known as **Sugar Bowl.** Despite blizzard-like conditions, Chaplin directed the cameras to roll to capture Big Jim (Mack Swain) heaving his sled through deep snow. These images were supplemented by Hollywood studio sequences in which chicken wire, sackcloth, and tons of plaster and flour were used to recreate the vast winter landscapes.

Charlie Chaplin shivers in the mountains of the Sierra Nevada.

High Sierra (1941), for which John Huston wrote the screenplay, was shot in the hills behind Lone Pine at the beginning of the 1940s. Humphrey Bogart starred as Roy "Mad Dog" Earle, a hard-nosed gangster with a soft heart, and the role made him a star. Many of the outside shots were filmed close to **Mount Whitney** with its spectacular peak of 14,435 feet (4,400 meters). Some of the scenes were filmed close to Hollywood in the **San Bernardino Mountains,** near **Cedar Lake,** and in **Arrowhead Springs.** But for the key sequences, it had to be the Sierra Nevada. The dramatic chase was shot on **Whitney Portal Road,** and Earle seeks refuge in the mountains above **Lone Pine** during the thrilling finale. The film version of Hemingway's Spanish Civil War drama **For Whom the Bell Tolls** (1943) was also filmed in the Sierra Nevada in the area close to the **Sonora Pass.** This is where the freedom fighter Robert Jordan (Gary Cooper) joins a group of partisans to blow up a strategically important bridge, and loses his heart to Maria (Ingrid Bergman).

Lake Tahoe, situated at an altitude of roughly 6,500 feet (2,000 meters) in the Sierra Nevada, offers some 193 square miles (500 square kilometers) of deep blue waters framed by dense forests and snow-capped mountains – features that have not escaped the notice of filmmakers. What a pity that **A Place in the Sun** (1951) was filmed in black and white, denying moviegoers the lake's brilliant natural palette. In all other respects, the drama, based on Theodore Dreiser's novel *An American Tragedy*, was an all-out success: Montgomery Clift plays George Eastman, a young man forced to work his way up from the bottom at his wealthy uncle's factory. He caddishly dumps his factory worker girlfriend Alice (Shelley Winters) when he falls for Angela (Elizabeth Taylor), a dazzling debutante. But Alice is pregnant and insists they get married. Disaster looms during a boat trip on a lonely lake where George once spent a carefree day with Angela, a scene filmed on **Cascade Lake** close to Lake Tahoe.

A star is born: Humphrey Bogart in *High Sierra*.

Death Valley is a multifaceted backdrop in the movies, from the strange cliff formations at *Zabriskie Point*, where Daria (Daria Halprin) and Mark (Mark Frechette) find one another on the run, to the sand dunes at Stovepipe Wells, where several scenes in *Star Wars* were filmed.

Death Valley

It is no coincidence that this part of the Mojave Desert bears such a macabre name. **Death Valley** is one of the hottest places on Earth, where summer temperatures can easily exceed 120 degrees Fahrenheit (50 degrees Celsius). But spectacular desert landscapes attract film teams to this inhospitable region despite its extreme conditions. Sand dunes and multicolored rock formations are as indigenous here as volcanic craters and dry salt lakes. When director Erich von Stroheim insisted on filming the scenes from his silent movie **Greed** (1924) in Death Valley at the height of a hot summer, just getting to the locations in the August heat proved an almost insurmountable

challenge. Stanley Kubrick filmed the Sicilian scenes from **Spartacus** (1960) in Death Valley, and Michelangelo Antonioni shot the key sequences for **Zabriskie Point** (1970) – a road movie that was derided for its anti-Americanism – amid the bizarre, eroded landscapes for which the film is named, also located in Death Valley. A perfect location for science fiction flicks, Death Valley appears in **Star Wars** (1977) when Obi-Wan Kenobi (Alec Guinness) and Luke (Mark Hamill) look out over the planet Tatooine from **Dante's Peak.** The sand dunes of **Stovepipe Wells** also served as a scenic backdrop in the film. Today, conditions imposed by nature preservation authorities have severely curtailed filmmaking in the area.

Hemingway's Spanish Civil War drama *For Whom the Bell Tolls* with Gary Cooper and Ingrid Bergman was filmed over three months in the Sierra Nevada.

The Pacific Coast

Alfred Hitchcock learned to appreciate the cinematic charm of the north Californian Pacific coast when he shot the jagged cliffs of Point Lobos for **Rebecca** (1940) and the area between Carmel and Big Sur for **Suspicion** (1941). His love affair with California landscape locations would extend to his later master-pieces as well. In **Vertigo** (1958), Scottie (James Stewart) and the enigmatic Madeleine (Kim Novak) leave San Francisco for a ride down **17-Mile Drive,** motoring south along the ocean to the mission at **San Juan Bautista.** They share a kiss at **Cypress Point,** and Madeleine admires the towering redwood trees in the **Big Basin Redwoods Park** – not in Muir Woods, as mentioned in the film. Hitchcock chose the San Francisco Bay area again as the setting for his thriller **The Birds** (1963) in which a small coastal town – in fact, the neighboring towns of **Bodega** and **Bodega Bay** – is terrorized by feathery attackers. Hitchcock selected the two towns for their sequestered location and dependably foggy weather. As luck would have it, filming took place under a cloud-less sky. John Carpenter's horror movie **The Fog** (1980) was also shot in Bodega Bay, and also required the aid of special-effects fog for the requisite atmosphere.

The California coast showed its picturesque side in **The Sand-piper** (1965), a dramatic love story directed by Vincente Min-nelli. Elizabeth Taylor plays a single mother who begins an affair with a married Episcopalian priest (Richard Burton), a doomed

The lone cypress on 17-Mile Drive, where Madeleine (Kim Novak) and Scottie (James Stewart) share a kiss in *Vertigo*. Alfred Hitchcock also filmed *The Birds* on the California coast, in the towns of Bodega and Bodega Bay.

The Sandpiper with Elizabeth Taylor was filmed on the California coast near Big Sur.

situation underscored by the rocky coastlines of **Big Sur** and **Point Lobos State Reserve.** Point Lobos and the **Monterey Peninsula** also served as locations in *Anna Karenina* (1935) starring Greta Garbo, *Lassie Come Home* (1943) with the male collie Pal in the title role, and *One-Eyed Jacks* (1961) with Marlon Brando.

The Rocky Mountains

The Rocky Mountains constitute the western chain of massive North American mountains that run from Alaska to Mexico in a series of parallel ranges. Great rivers such as the Rio Grande, the Missouri, and the Colorado have their sources here, amid land-

in Indian territory. His lengthy journey from Kansas westwards was filmed in the **Sage Creek Wilderness Area** of the **Badlands National Park.** The "Badlands" rise like an island from a sea of prairie, a high plateau marked by deep valleys and strange, multicolored rock formations.

If *Dances with Wolves* showed the world one thing, it was that there were impressive landscapes in South Dakota other than Mount Rushmore. Scenes featuring herds of buffalo were filmed at Triple U Standing Butte Ranch. John Dunbar's (Kevin Costner) westward journey was shot in Badlands National Park.

scapes as beautiful as they are varied. Its wilderness brims with rugged mountains cleaved by deep gorges, crashing waterfalls, dense pine and aspen forests, as well as extensive grasslands and prairies that gallop off to the horizon. No wonder this region resounds with the myths of hardy pioneers, intrepid trappers, unstoppable gold-diggers, and hard-as-nails cowboys.

A single film can bring visitors by the busload to an otherwise remote region – and what **Dances with Wolves** (1990) did for South Dakota is a classic instance of film-inspired tourism. Kevin Costner both directed and starred in the modern Western, playing the part of the highly decorated Civil War soldier John Dunbar. Dunbar decides to get to know the West before it disappears and volunteers for duty at a lonely frontier post deep

When Dunbar arrives at a deserted outpost, a lone wolf pays him a visit. Members of the neighboring Lakota Sioux tribe materialize, and Dunbar becomes fascinated with the Indian way of life. When he alerts them to the long-awaited arrival of buffalo, he secures their friendship and begins to overcome the barriers of language and culture. Subsequent images of the buffalo hunt gave audiences a rare glimpse of how the vast herds once roamed the prairies. The scenes featuring numerous galloping buffalo were shot at the **Triple U Standing Butte Ranch** to the north of **Pierre,** a farm whose 2,000 buffalo comprise the largest private herd in the world. Many scenes were shot on the ranch's 77 square miles (200 square kilometers), with further sequences shot on the **Belle Fourche River.** The Lakota set up

True Grit with John Wayne was filmed amid the San Juan Mountains in Ouray County, Colorado. The True Grit Café in Ridgway (left) bears witness.

Darby) to find her father's murderer, Tom Chaney (Jeff Corey). Together with a Texas Ranger (Glen Campbell), the trio set off on a dangerous journey into Indian territory, where the killer is hiding out with a gang led by Ned Pepper (Robert Duvall). The film was shot in southwest Colorado, mostly in **Ouray County** before the spectacular backdrop afforded by the **San Juan Mountains.** The striking summits that can be seen in the opening scene and dominate the mountainous scenery throughout the film

their winter quarters to the north of Roughlock Falls at **Spearfish Canyon** in the **Black Hills National Forest.**

Colorado

Some of the most beautiful parts of the Rockies are situated in Colorado, the highest state in the nation with a mean elevation of 6,800 feet (2,070 meters). While ski resorts such as Aspen and Vail have made the region a must for devotees of winter sports, filmmakers find themselves drawn by the mountain world in all seasons.

Many of the old silent Westerns starring cowboy hero Tom Mix were filmed on the Arkansas River and in Glenwood Canyon. In the charming Western ***True Grit*** (1969), Colorado appears almost idyllic with its craggy mountain ranges and stands of bright yellow aspens silhouetted against a clear blue sky. John Wayne received the only Oscar of his long career for his outstanding performance as the gruff old codger Rooster Cogburn. The unconventional sheriff is hired by the resolute Mattie (Kim

are the **Wilson Peaks** near Telluride. Mattie's family ranch, a quaint old farmhouse, is still located on the **Lost Dollar Road,** a dirt route that branches off from Highway 62 about 10 miles (15 kilometers) to the west of Ridgway near the so-called Dallas divide. The town where Mattie tries to recruit Cogburn is **Ridgway,** now a pilgrimage site for John Wayne fans who come for a meal at the **True Grit Café.** The tiled wall

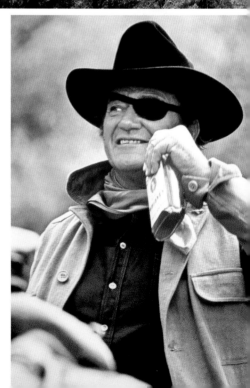

Roy (Richard Dreyfuss) can hardly believe his eyes: A UFO lands on Devil's Tower, Wyoming, in *Close Encounters of the Third Kind.*

The Big Sky starring Kirk Douglas and Elizabeth Threatt was filmed on the Snake River at the foot of the majestic Grand Teton mountains.

of the haberdashery shop where Cogburn rents a room is still visible in the dining room. The courthouse scenes were filmed to the south in the little town of **Ouray.** The **Cimmaron Range** mountain peaks and **Owl Creek Pass** also feature in the film: Mattie, Cogburn, and the ranger set up camp here between a stand of aspens and a stream; Cogburn and Ned Pepper's gang shoot it out in a clearing surrounded by aspens below **Chimney Peak.**

Wyoming

After Alaska, Wyoming is the least populated of all the United States. The "Cowboy State" boasts two of the country's most beautiful national parks, Grand Teton and Yellowstone, both of which have provided filmmakers with numerous scenic backdrops. Off to the northeast of Wyoming, the 1,266-foot (386-meter) stone mass of **Devil's Tower** rises from the wide prairies like a giant tree stump, visible for miles around. The landmark is the subject of many Indian legends, but movie fans know it best as where the spaceship landed in Steven Spielberg's ***Close Encounters of the Third Kind*** (1977).

The craggy peaks of **Grand Teton National Park** emerge to the north of the broad valley of Jackson Hole to rise some 13,800 feet (4,200 meters) above the meandering curves of the Snake River. John Wayne's film career took off here in a movie entitled ***The Big Trail*** (1930), the saga of a wagon train on its way to Oregon. Filming took place at **Spread Creek** in the western part of the valley, with dramatic scenes showing the hardy settlers using ropes to lower their wagons from a rocky outcrop down into the dales of **Jackson Hole.**

The Big Sky (1952) starring Kirk Douglas and Dewey Martin – a movie version of the Pulitzer Prize-winning novel by A.B. Guthrie – was also filmed in this region. The story of a band of brave men who take their keelboats 2,000 miles (3,220 kilometers) up the Missouri River against the current – and fighting wild animals and hostile Indians – was shot on the **Snake River** near Menor's Ferry.

One year later, another film based on a novel by A. B. Guthrie would be filmed here and become the movie most closely associated with the region. In ***Shane*** (1953), Alan Ladd plays an enigmatic hero who helps a family of settlers fight a nasty group of established ranchers. The weathered wooden cabin where the decent settler folk live still stands on the **Antelope Flats** behind the town of Kelly. It can be viewed along with a row of similarly fragile-looking buildings known as **"Mormon Row."** Just like the original Mormon settlers, the film's protagonists reach their homestead after crossing the Snake River on the old ferry at **Schwabacher's Landing.**

Montana: Big Sky Country

In Robert Redford's poetic film *A River Runs Through It* (1992), the narrator reflects on the Montana of his youth as "a world still fresh with dew." It is precisely this sense of untrammeled nature that filmmakers have sought and found in Montana. No wonder "Big Sky Country" is the state motto: People say that here the horizon stretches farther into the distance than anywhere else in the country. Prairies, forests, rivers, and mountains make it a landscape lover's paradise. Although events in Norman Maclean's autobiography actually take place on the Big Blackfoot River, Redford chose **Paradise Valley** in the south of Montana as the setting for his film. *A River Runs Through It* tells the story of Norman (Craig Sheffer) and Paul (Brad Pitt), sons of a strict Presbyterian minister. Conscientious Norman plans to follow in his father's footsteps, but Paul is drawn to the fun side of life, which includes drinking and gambling. What unites the disparate siblings is a passion for fly-fishing. The angling scenes were shot in the countryside close to **Bozeman** and **Livingston,** as well as on the **Gallatin**, **Madison** and **Yellowstone Rivers.** More filming took place on **Mill Creek,** a tributary of the Yellowstone River. All

are excellent fly-fishing areas. The little town of Missoula was reconstructed on **Livingston's Callender Street,** and the scenes that take place in the idyllically situated Maclean household were filmed west of Bozeman. Five years later, Robert Redford returned to southern Montana to shoot *The Horse Whisperer* (1998). The story of Annie (Kristin Scott Thomas), a sensitive horse trainer, is based on the novel by Nicholas Evans and was filmed in the lush green foothills of the **Absaroka** and **Beartooth Mountains.** Annie's daughter Grace (played by the thirteen-year-old Scarlett Johansson) loses her best friend and part of her leg in a riding accident; her horse is also severely injured in the tragedy. Annie decides they must face the consequences together: They load up the spooked horse in a trailer and drive from New York City to Montana to engage the services of the famous "horse whisperer" Tom Booker (Redford).

Both the horse and the girl rediscover their will to live in the nature-infused, down-to-earth surroundings of Double Divide Ranch. The producers inspected more than 300 ranches before they chose a beef cattle farm to the south of **Big Timber** on the **Boulder River** as their film location. They set up their own

The historic barns of "Mormon Row" (left) and the Grand Tetons in Wyoming provided a marvelous backdrop in *Shane*. Robert Redford as *The Horse Whisperer*, filmed in the Montana foothills of the Absaroka and Beartooth Mountains.

farm – including stables and horse pastures – on a specially selected spot directly on the riverbank.

Montana revealed some of its most dramatic scenery in the action thriller **The River Wild** (1994). A wild water rafting trip turns into a life and death fight for Gail (Meryl Streep) when the two men she and her family meet during their vacation turn out to be dangerous gangsters. The dramatic white-water rafting scenes were shot on the Middle Fork section of the **Flathead River** and on **Kootenai River** near Libby in northwest Montana.

Glacier National Park in Montana's northwest at the border with Canada is popular as a film location where prairies transition to mountain terrain. Many varied movies have been shot here, including Westerns such as **Cattle Queen of Montana** (1954) starring Barbara Stanwyck and Ronald Reagan – filmed on the Blackfeet Indian Reservation near East Glacier – and the tearjerker **What Dreams May Come** (1998) with Robin Williams. Michael Cimino's Western epic **Heaven's Gate** (1980), possibly the most spectacular flop of all time, was also filmed here; the movie recouped only a tenth of its $44 million production budget at the box office. The somber Western, which chronicles the fight

between big landowning farmers and Eastern European immigrants, uses impressive images to express views critical of society. Shooting took place in **Kalispell,** the gate to Glacier Park, and on the shores of **Two Medicine Lake.**

Glacier National Park (above) appeared in *Heaven's Gate*. *A River Runs Through It* was filmed in southern Montana on the Yellowstone River (left).

Nature Untouched: The Canadian Rockies

Some of the most isolated and primitive parts of the Rockies are situated over the Canadian border. Many a movie set in the American West was actually filmed in Canada, such as Clint Eastwood's **Unforgiven** (1992), shot in the area around Calgary and Banff. **Brokeback Mountain** (2005), based on the short story by Annie Proulx, was filmed in idyllic landscapes **south of Alberta.** Two young cowboys, Jack Twist (Jake Gyllenhaal) and Ennis Del Mar (Heath Ledger), spend a summer in the early 1960s herding sheep on Brokeback Mountain. Haunted by the stigma of homosexuality in cowboy culture, the two young men

Brokeback Mountain as such does not exist: Director Ang Lee found the ideal landscapes for his film in the region near the Three Sisters mountain in southern Alberta. Some scenes were shot in the small towns of Cowley and Fort Macleod near Canmore.

are surprised to find that they are falling in love with one another. At the end of the summer, each of them returns to a "normal" life: Ennis weds Alma (Michelle Williams) and has two daughters with her, while Jack works as a rodeo rider before he, too, gets married. But when the former lovers meet up again some years later, their feelings for each other cannot be denied. And yet living together is out of the question, at least for the taciturn Ennis. The clandestine couple meet up for occasional "fishing trips" to secluded Brokeback Mountain, a forbidden pleasure that becomes a necessity as time goes by.

Brokeback Mountain as such does not exist: Most of the images depicting the lonely, pine-forested idyll were filmed in the **Three Sisters** mountain region close to the little town of **Canmore,** some 45 miles (70 kilometers) west of Calgary. Some shooting was done near **Fortress Mountain** and on **Moose Mountain** in **Kananaskis Country,** a picturesque valley to the south of Canmore. The scenes in Ennis and Jack's campsite were also shot in Kananaskis – on **Upper Kananaskis Lake,** on **Canyon Creek, Mud Lake,** and near **Elbow Falls. King Creek,** where Ennis encounters a bear at the start of the film, is also close by.

Canada's broad landscapes at the foot of the Rocky Mountains stand in for Montana in *Legends of the Fall* with Brad Pitt and Anthony Hopkins.

The two famous national parks to the north at Banff and Jasper are also popular with moviemakers. The romantic family saga ***Legends of the Fall*** (1994) luxuriated in captivating landscape shots filmed in this area. The epic tale of three brothers who fall in love with the same woman (Julia Ormond) is set in Montana but was filmed in the foothills of the Rockies to the west of Calgary. The remote ranch where Colonel William Ludlow (Anthony Hopkins) lives with his sons Samuel (Henry Thomas), Tristan (Brad Pitt), and Alfred (Aidan Quinn) was shot near **Ghost River,** between Calgary and Banff National Park.

Anthony Hopkins returned to the Alberta region some years later to make the hair-raising film ***The Edge*** (1997). After a plane crash leaves them marooned in the wilds, the aging millionaire Charles (Hopkins) and the fashion photographer Robert (Alec Baldwin) – who is having an affair with Hopkins's young wife – fight to survive in the wilderness. When a bloodthirsty Kodiak bear starts to track them, they are forced to forget their rivalry and focus on staying alive. The wonderful images of snowy mountain ranges and glaciers, pine forests, and crystal clear mountain lakes were filmed in **Banff National Park,** in the region around **Canmore** and **Edmonton,** as well as on **Fortress Mountain.** Other segments were shot on **Mount Assiniboine** and in **Yoho National Park** in British Columbia.

Hollywood started coming to the Canadian Rockies in the 1950s, when CinemaScope technology and its new widescreen format made it possible to better capture the wide open spaces on screen. Anthony Mann directed ***The Far Country*** (1954) in **Jasper National Park** and on the Saskatchewan glacier in neighboring **Banff National Park.** James Stewart plays a cowboy accompanying a female saloon owner (Ruth Roman) to the Klondike goldmines: Once again, Alberta stood in for Alaska. Otto Preminger shot ***River of No Return*** (1954) in this area at roughly the same time. In this film, Marilyn Monroe plays Kay, the girlfriend of an unscrupulous gambler (Rory Calhoun) who steals a horse and gun from farmer Matt Calder (Robert Mitchum). When Indians attack the farm shortly thereafter, Matt is forced to flee with his son and Kay on a raft. Without the benefit of firearms, the three of them have to ward off attacks by Indians, bandits, and wild animals, as well as negotiate river rapids. The opening scenes were shot east of Jasper on the banks of the **Snake River,** in the **Devona Flats,** and on the **Maligne River.** Preminger filmed the close-ups of his stars in the area around Jasper; most of the waterborne action was filmed with stunt doubles on the **Bow River near Banff.** Back in L.A., new takes of some of the raft scenes featuring Monroe and Mitchum were shot on a hydraulic stage in front of screen images of a roaring river. Fifty years on, these scenes seem quaint. But when it opened, audiences went crazy for the film: A star-studded cast and awe-inspiring landscape shots – all in the newest cinemascope technology – was a big hit at the box office.

When Marilyn Monroe twisted her ankle during the filming of *River of No Return*, the press claimed she had been injured during a white-water rafting shoot. The real story? She slipped while walking along the Maligne River. The waterborne action scenes were filmed with stunt doubles on the Bow River (right).

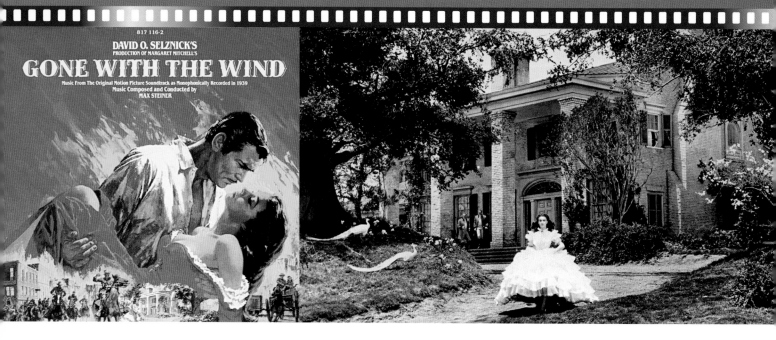

FROM THE SWAMPS TO THE SMOKIES

By Verena Hertlein

The American South as represented in film is far more loaded with cultural symbolism than the mere attractiveness of its landscapes might imply. The region is synonymous with an outlook and with certain traditions, as well as with particular historical events and cultural developments. Alongside the West, the South is the most strongly mythologized landscape of the United States.

The different types of Southern landscapes frequently mirror the central themes in individual films. Dark, labyrinthine swamps often symbolize a place where a crime will occur, as in

Mississippi Burning (1988), *Down by Law* (1986), and *Adaptation* (2002). In movies such as *Fried Green Tomatoes* (1991) and *Forrest Gump* (1994), small towns romanticize the quaintness of daily life and sincerity of family values, while simultaneously shedding light on the inevitable limitations and restrictions of society. Vast forests provide refuge for baddies, the persecuted, and outsiders, as in *Deliverance* (1972) and *Nell* (1994). The seaside is used to represent freedom, inner silence, and deep yearnings, as exemplified in *The Prince of Tides* (1991). Fields and meadows stretching into the distant horizon are reminiscent of the era when large plantations depended upon slave labor. The history of slavery and the Civil War as well as the controversy surrounding racism that is deeply rooted in the South are central themes in films such as *The Color Purple* (1985) and *Mississippi Burning*.

The "Deep" South in Film

Historically, the "deep" South is defined first and foremost by its economic dependence on cotton and the slavery that was associated with it. The South includes the states of Louisiana,

Scarlett O'Hara's estate of Tara in *Gone With the Wind* was a Hollywood set (above). To show Atlanta going up in flames, sets from King Kong and other films were torched in the studio. The famous bench from *Forrest Gump* starring Tom Hanks now enjoys pride of place in the Savannah History Museum.

Top landscape film locations

1. Tallulah Falls, Georgia: **Deliverance**
2. Fontana Lake, North Carolina: **Nell**
3. Chimney Rock Park and Lake Lure, North Carolina: **The Last of the Mohicans, Dirty Dancing**
4. Blue Ridge Parkway, North Carolina: **The Last of the Mohicans, The Fugitive**
5. Ansonville, North Carolina: **The Color Purple**
6. Ross Barnett Reservoir, Mississippi: **Mississippi Burning, O Brother, Where Art Thou?**
7. Juliette, Georgia: **Fried Green Tomatoes**
8. Beaufort, South Carolina, with Fripp and Hunting islands: **Prince of Tides, Forrest Gump**
9. Swamps near Slidell, Louisiana: **Down by Law**
10. Wakulla Springs, Florida: **Creature from the Black Lagoon**
11. Everglades, Fakahatchee Strand State Preserve, Florida: **Adaptation**

Mississippi, Alabama, Georgia, South Carolina, and Florida. Together with North Carolina, Tennessee, Arkansas, Virginia, and Texas, these states joined to form the Confederation in 1861. Strictly speaking, the boundary states of Kentucky and West Virginia are also considered part of the South.

The historic split from the North, the Civil War, and the abolition of slavery are dominant events in the history of the South and central motifs in many films. No other film exemplifies these themes better than the South's film par excellence, **Gone With the Wind** (1939). This dramatic love story between Scarlett O'Hara (Vivien Leigh), for many the original Southern belle, and Rhett Butler (Clark Gable), is set in Atlanta during the Civil War and features the splendid white mansions typical of the South. Film buffs will search in vain for Scarlett's legendary estate of Tara in Georgia, however: The film was shot in the former Selznick Studios in Culver City near Los Angeles. Nevertheless, the legend of the film is still very much alive in the deep South. Numerous hotels are named after Tara, several museums have been dedicated to the movie, and Southern belles dressed in

sweeping hoop skirts offer guided tours of mansions, plantations, and old slave quarters.

Paddle steamers on "Ol' Man River," the eerie swamps of Louisiana, cotton fields, flowering meadows dancing in the breeze, Georgia's mansions, the sleepy towns of Alabama, God-fearing folk who believe in family and hospitality – this the classic cliché of the South. Writers such as Mark Twain, Tennessee Williams, and William Faulkner were at home here, and faithfully recorded the world of the American South in their work. Not unlike the region's novelists, filmmakers love nothing more than to place the pleasant, popular caricature of Southern culture into contrast with a cruel or even brutal social reality.

Mississippi: Between Comedy and Tragedy

Infamous for its cruel racial policies, Mississippi occupies a solid position in the cinematic history of the South. In **Mississippi Burning** (1988), director Alan Parker created a memorial to a tragic event that took place in 1964. The film about solving the murder of three civil rights activists is based on scrupulous research. At the time, three members of the American civil rights movement disappeared on a drive through Mississippi, and the FBI stepped in to investigate. The bodies of the missing activists were found in a swampy area just two months later. Three white men were tried and found guilty in the case – not for murder, but for civil rights abuses. In the film, Gene Hackman and Willem Dafoe engage in a struggle for truth and justice at historical locations. The stark contrast between the violence of the events and the colorful backdrop of lush green trees, glittering lakes, and the luminous blue of the Southern sky make the telling of this story

A Southern odyssey: In *O Brother, Where Art Thou?*, three inmates make a break from a chain gang and run across the fields of rural Mississippi.

all the more powerful. Most of the locations were in Mississippi: in **Vicksburg, Vaiden, Bovina,** and in the vicinity of **Jackson. Cedar Hill Cemetery** in **Vicksburg** appears as the location for the burial of one of the civil rights activists. The **Ross Barnett Reservoir** northeast of Jackson, a fertile landscape punctuated by numerous bodies of water, served as a backdrop for several of the exterior shots.

Not all films made in Mississippi relate tragic events. In a loose adaptation of Homer's epic poem *The Odyssey*, Ethan and Joel Coen created a quirky comedy about the escape of three convicts from a prison colony in the 1930s. **O Brother, Where Art Thou?** (2000) starts with the unlikely trio bound together by chains and dressed in striped prison garb. Everett (George Clooney), Pete (John Turturro), and Delmar (Tim Blake Nelson) make a break for it, and flee their captors across rural Mississippi en route to where the loot from Everett's last robbery is hidden. Countless hardships stand in the path to freedom and riches: seductive sirens, a blind prophet, the Ku Klux Klan, and John Goodman as a one-eyed Bible salesman. The South of the Depression era comes alive in outlandish characters, old houses and churches, cotton and tobacco fields, and forlorn country roads. The film is perfectly scored with outstanding music from numerous contemporary bluegrass greats.

Film locations included **Vicksburg, Jackson,** and **Valley Park, Yazoo City.** The latter is home to the bank that is robbed in the film, which is located on the town's main street. The small city of **Canton** features in a dinner scene in *O Brother, Where Art Thou?* and in several other movies, including the bank robbery scene from the gangster film *Thieves Like Us* (1974) and the cinema sequence in *My Dog Skip* (2000). Its historic houses make for the perfect backdrop. The movie version of John Grisham's novel *A Time to Kill* (1996) starring Sandra Bullock and Matthew McConaughey was also largely shot in Canton.

Tom Waits, John Lurie, and Roberto Benigni try their luck in the jungle-like swamps outside of New Orleans in *Down by Law*.

Louisiana: Swamplands and "The Big Easy"

Who doesn't associate the state of Louisiana with its moss-hung swamps? The alluvial land crisscrossed by numerous bayous is vast and labyrinthine. Reeds, swamp cypresses, ash trees, and ancient oaks create a vibrantly living contrast to the deeps of the dark bog. Water snakes and turtles don't mind the heavy, humid heat, nor the alligators that lurk in the waters, ready to pounce on Hollywood beauties. In the past, escaped slaves and prisoners found refuge in such swamplands; director Jim Jarmusch painted a vivid image of what such an escape might have been like in *Down by Law* (1986). Zack (Tom Waits), Jack (John Lurie), and Roberto (Roberto Benigni) escape from prison in **New Orleans** and make their way through the jungle-like swamp in the environs of **Slidell**. Black-and-white cinematography creates a powerful impression of the danger that characterizes this region, despite comic relief offered in the form of humorous dialog.

Director Jim McBride immortalized New Orleans's nickname for filmgoers with *The Big Easy* (1987). The movie starring Dennis Quaid and Ellen Barkin was shot exclusively in and around the city, tragically changed forever by the recent ravages of Hurricane Katrina. Famous for its cool and easygoing lifestyle, the city shows its dark side in the legendary film ***Easy Rider***

Easy Rider takes viewers from the deserts and canyons of the West to the lushness of the South.

(1969). The lightheartedness evoked by the title has little in common with the film, a road movie that is anything but easy to watch. While celebrating the beauty of the American Southwest, the film also delivers a scathing critique of society. Dennis Hopper directed and also starred as Billy, one of the two main protagonists. He and Peter Fonda in the role of Wyatt play bikers on a quest for a freedom that must remain illusory in an America that has grown intolerant and brutal.

The bikers' first encounter with hostile Southerners takes place in a café in **Morganza** on the Mississippi River, a tiny town some 30 miles (50 kilometers) from Louisiana's capital at

Baton Rouge. Wyatt and Billy incur the wrath of rednecks by flirting with their women, a provocation that brings out the worst the locals have to offer. Again and again, the vastness and virginity of nature stand in contrast to the bigotry and intolerance of a society that has no use for long-haired hippies – and especially not for their ideas about freedom or their taste for drugs. Mardi Gras scenes toward the end of the film seem carefree until an acid trip goes bad in the **Old St. Louis Cemetery.** The extreme contrast between the joyful celebrations in the city and the morbid mood between the graves peaks when the carnival masks take on a ghostly appearance, and the party deteriorates into a nightmare.

At the end of the film, Wyatt and Billy, "born to be wild," as the famous title song goes, are killed by a redneck on a country road to **Krotz Springs.** In the final frame, the camera pans up from the burning motorcycle wreck in the ditch to the broad waters of the **Mississippi River** and the distant horizon.

Georgia: Nature Unspoiled

The state of Georgia is notable for the variety of its scenery; it only seems fitting that the films that have been shot there are just as disparate. The 1972 thriller *Deliverance* contains what are perhaps the most stunning landscape shots of Georgia ever captured in a feature film. Most of the action was shot in

Jon Voight and Ned Beatty (above) face the mighty Tallulah Falls in *Deliverance*.

Rabun County in the northeast of the state. Four city guys travel to the back country to embark on an adventurous rafting trip down the **Chattooga River.** The river and the spectacular **Tallulah Falls** symbolize the search for freedom and adventure, but the central theme of the film is violence. Nature's allure is soon overlaid with the ugliness of the events that unfold. The film is nothing if not an invitation to reflect on man's increasing alienation from the natural environment. This conflict is reflected at the end of the movie when nature succumbs to "progress" through the construction of a dam. The city dwellers' luck is no better than Mother Nature's: Their adventure takes a horrific turn when two of the group are brutally beaten and their friend Lewis (Burt Reynolds) kills the perpetrators. From that moment forward, the apocalyptic story runs its course, and the film ends with a bleak look at the future of man and nature.

Georgia is shown in a more romantic light in *Fried Green Tomatoes* (1991). Although the story of two Southern women and their road to emancipation is set in the Alabama of the 1920s, director Jon Avnet shot most of the movie in **Juliette,** Georgia. The small town framed by fields and forests lies some 60 miles (100 kilometers) southeast of Atlanta. The famous **Whistle Stop Cafe,** run by Idgie (Mary Stuart Masterson) and Ruth (Mary-Louise Parker) in the movie, is a real eatery at 443 McCrackin Street. Filming also took place near the old mill and at the **reservoir** on the **Ocmulgee River.**

The Carolinas: Nature's Expanse

Numerous films have been shot in North and South Carolina, states that attract filmmakers with fields and meadows, forests and mountains, lakes and rivers, and beaches and the sea.

The Whistle Stop Cafe in Juliette, Georgia, from the 1991 film *Fried Green Tomatoes*. Order the dish that gave the movie its name – it's on the menu.

North Carolina offers a particularly broad variety of landscapes as evidenced in many memorable movies.

Based on the Pulitzer Prize-winning novel by Alice Walker, **The Color Purple** (1985) relates the story of Celie, an African-American woman who survives life in the American South at the beginning of the twentieth century. As well as being a tale of mistreatment and degradation, the narrative also details Celie's successful journey to freedom. Critics were divided in their opinions of director Steven Spielberg's film adaptation. However, the still relatively unknown actress Whoopi Goldberg shone in the main role, and was promptly put up for an Academy Award, one of eleven Oscar nominations for the film.

Although the story is set in rural Georgia, film locations were concentrated in North Carolina, not far from Charlotte. Chief among them were the small country towns of **Ansonville, Lilesville,** and **Marshville,** and their rural surroundings, places where time seems to have stood still for decades. The farm houses found here are typical of the South, complete with the ubiquitous porch where much of the drama of daily life is played out. Wheat fields dancing in the wind, glorious flower meadows, and enchanting lakes form the picturesque backdrop for a variety of scenes. The glorious, screen-filling purple flowers employed in the film as a symbol of hope, life, and the fortitude of the women – they gave the book its title – make an impression not soon forgotten. And yet it is the contrast of this idyllic landscape against the brutality of life in the region that lends the tale its poetry.

In *The Color Purple*, the fields of North Carolina frame the story of Celie, brilliantly played by Whoopi Goldberg. The film was nominated for eleven Oscars.

The outside shots for *Nell* (1994) were also filmed in North Carolina; the cabin where Jodie Foster's character grows up cut off from civilization is located on **Fontana Lake.** The film opens with exquisite landscape images shot from a bird's-eye perspective: Viewers are treated to a flight across the sun-dappled lake and the forests on the southern edge of **Great Smoky Mountains National Park.** The two principal locations were the sprawling **Nantahala National Forest** and the small town of **Robbinsville,** where the forest-dwellers venture to purchase provisions. Foster excels under the direction of Michael Apted, applying her formidable acting talents to become a "savage" who gradually helps scientists to understand the beauty of her remote existence. Her close relationship with nature and the spiritual strength she derives from it are the envy of all "civilized" folk. Visitors wishing to experience this relatively unspoiled natural paradise may rent one of the many cabins available near Asheville in the Smoky Mountains for a weekend retreat.

Jodie Foster as *Nell* at the edge of Fontana Lake.

Not far from this idyll are the locations from *The Last of the Mohicans* (1992) with Daniel Day-Lewis, shot exclusively in the mountains and forests of the Carolinas. Although James Fenimore Cooper's story is set in New York State, the film team found what they needed in the foothills of the **Smoky Mountains:** dense forests, rugged cliffs, and thundering waterfalls. The film tells the story of a struggle between the French and the English for colonial power in eighteenth-century America, a conflict that took a heavy toll on the local settlers and natives. Privately-owned **Chimney Rock Park** east of Asheville provides the backdrop for the dramatic action in the film. **Chimney Rock** juts out from the middle of deciduous forests; from its peak, the view sweeps across a vast canyon with waterfalls, the Smoky Mountains, and **Lake Lure** in the distance. This lake is perhaps best known as the location for the famous scene from *Dirty Dancing* (1987) in which Johnny (Patrick Swayze) and Baby (Jennifer Grey) practice their lifts in the water. The dramatic closing scenes in *The Last of the Mohicans* were shot on the **Cliff Trail,** a steep path leading up to Chimney Rock and to the **Hickory Nut Falls.** In the movie, Fort William Henry is located on **Lake James,** while the set for the British headquarters was built in **Asheville.** Various exteriors were also shot along the legendary **Blue Ridge Parkway,** which runs through wide valleys and forests from the Great Smoky Mountains National Park to Virginia. Scenes from *The Fugitive* (1993) starring Harrison Ford were also filmed here.

The Last of the Mohicans was filmed in the forests of Chimney Rock Park.

Lake Lure in North Carolina, *the* location in *Dirty Dancing.*

North Carolina also gets its due in ***Forrest Gump*** (1994), in particular when the simple-minded southerner (Tom Hanks) makes a dash through the countryside. When a gang of boys teases him on their way home from school, Forrest's childhood sweetheart, Jenny, calls out a warning that changes his life. He hears "Run, Forrest, run!" and takes off, his leg braces falling from him as he sprints. Even as an adult, he keeps on running his

Scenes from *Forrest Gump* were shot near Beaufort, on the grounds of Biltmore Estate, and at Bluff Plantation.

own private marathon past famous landmarks such as the Hollywood billboard and Monument Valley. North Carolina is showcased when he passes wheat fields and a pretty lagoon, featured at **Biltmore Estate** in **Asheville,** with 250 rooms the largest private estate in the United States. This spectacular location also appears in several other films, including *Patch Adams* (1998), *Hannibal* (2001), and *The Clearing* (2004). As the sun sets in one scene, Forrest also runs by **Grandfather Mountain** in **Linville,** located on the **Blue Ridge Parkway.**

South Carolina also features in *Forrest Gump*: Old-timey **Varnville** stands in for Forrest's hometown in Alabama. Both Jenny's house and the Gump residence with its large, sheltering oak tree are located on **Bluff Plantation** southeast of Yemassee, near Beaufort. The movie's Vietnam scenes were shot on the islands off the coast of Beaufort. The war was filmed on **Fripp** and **Hunting** islands, where director Robert Zemeckis had discovered an almost Asian landscape replete with lagoons, palm trees, and reeds. Gump's friend Bubba (Mykelti Williamson) moves into his new home at **Lucy Creek** on **Lady's Island,** with some of the water scenes shot on the **Coosaw River.** The famous bench where Forrest perches as he tells the story of his life was erected for the film on **Chippewa Square** in **Savannah,** Georgia. Today it is part of an exhibit at the Savannah History Museum.

The historic houses near Beaufort, South Carolina, provided a dreamy setting for *The Prince of Tides*.

with **Botany Bay Plantation** on **Edisto Island** near Charleston a favorite among filmmakers. The island is characterized by salty marshland, an oak forest, and deserted beaches – some stretches are almost jungle-like in appearance. Parts of *Ace Ventura – When Nature Calls* (1995), *The Patriot* (2000), and a scene in *Cold Mountain* (2003) – the beginning of Inman's fateful journey – were shot here.

Florida's Swamps

In addition to the long sandy beaches on the east and west coasts, and the Caribbean flair of the Florida Keys, the dark swampland of the **Everglades** is a landscape highlight of the state that often finds its way to the silver screen. Movies that have made use of this untamed natural environment often seek to convey an image of horror or, conversely, a sense of unspoiled paradise. *Adaptation* (2002) succeeds in combining both sensibilities. Orchids are the leitmotif of this film, in which Charlie Kaufman (Nicolas Cage) desperately tries to adapt the novel by Susan Orleans (Meryl Streep) about the delicate plant into a screenplay. Nocturnal excursions in search of the perfect specimen of a rare species feature in the film, with shooting taking place in the **Fakahatchee Strand State Preserve,** famous for its abundance of wild orchids. The dark water and dense reeds help to create an ominous atmosphere for scenes such as the swamp chase when a hunter is devoured by an alligator.

Another film team found ideal locations close to where, a few years later, *Forrest Gump* would be filmed. **The Prince of Tides** (1991) opens with the breathtaking images of a flight across the picturesque **marshlands** between **Beaufort** and **Lady's Island** at sunset. Red, pink, and orange hues bathe the countryside in a dreamy light. The historic homes of **Beaufort** and **Charleston** serve as sets for the home of Tom Wingo (Nick Nolte) and his sister. When Tom's sister tries to kill herself, psychiatrist Dr. Susan Lowenstein, played by director Barbra Streisand, asks the unemployed football coach to travel to New York City to give her a detailed account of his sister's childhood. The differences between life in the North and the South become one focus of the film, a study in contrasts underscored by the melodic Southern accent that Nolte masters for the movie.

The lonely islands off the coast of South Carolina have served as settings of complete isolation in several movies,

The mangrove swamps of the Everglades provide an eerie backdrop for the showdown scenes in Martin Scorsese's

Chris Cooper is the orchid hunter John Laroche in *Adaptation*. His desire to find a rare flower takes him deep into the swamps of the Everglades.

psycho-thriller **Cape Fear** (1991). The remake of the 1962 film of the same name that starred Robert Mitchum, Gregory Peck, and Martin Balsam masterfully replays the tale of two men locked in mortal battle – as well as including cleverly thought-out minor roles for Mitchum, Peck, and Balsam. This time, Robert De Niro plays convicted rapist Max Cady, and Nick Nolte steps into the role of Sam Bowden, his lawyer. The heavily tattooed and highly intelligent criminal is desperate to take revenge on Bowden, who was the public defender in his court case. He is convinced that his attorney could have prevented him from spending time behind bars.

After serving his fourteen-year sentence, Max goes on the warpath, terrorizing Sam in an effort to destroy his life and the lives of his loved ones. Filming took place near **Fort Lauderdale,** with the dramatic closing sequences shot in the swamps of the **John U. Lloyd State Park** in the south of Port Everglades, not far from Fort Lauderdale, a lush region that stood in for Cape Fear River in North Carolina. It is here that Bowden and his wife (Jessica Lange) and their daughter (Juliette Lewis) famously hide out on a houseboat, only to be stalked by Max.

Exquisite shots of the Everglades feature in scenes from **Wild Things** (1998) when teacher Sam Lombardo (Matt Dillon) sets off on an excursion in his inflatable boat. The mood of the film grows stranger by the minute, with the story unfolding to reveal numerous unexpected evil surprises – alligators being the least of them. In the classic horror flick **Creature from the Black Lagoon** (1954), Florida's swamps stand in for the Amazon. The fantastic underwater scenes were shot in the north of the state, near Tallahassee, in the deep waters of **Wakulla Springs.** To this day, the Tallahassee Film Society hosts the annual "Creature-fest" in honor of the famous monster. Scenes of the early Tarzan movies were also shot on location in the **Wakulla Springs State Park.** In *Tarzan's Secret Treasure* (1941) and *Tarzan's Adventure in New York* (1942), alligators lurk at every corner in a tropical landscape setting – here in the Sunshine State.

In *The Truman Show,* ignorance is bliss: Jim Carrey doesn't know that his life in the happy city of Seaside on Florida's Gulf coast has been scripted.

The perfectly manicured lawns of Florida's recreational areas and private clubs provide a civilized contrast to the untamed swamplands of the Everglades. Nonetheless, the cult golf comedy **Caddyshack** (1980) gave audiences an eyeful of how wild life on the fairways could be despite the patina of privilege. Chevy Chase is Ty Webb, the resident golf pro who teaches wealthy wives how to hold a golf club, while Rodney Dangerfield plays the overbearing millionaire Al Czervik, offering up a performance that lampoons the leisured life of the obscenely rich. But none of the film's antics can hold a candle to Bill Murray as Carl Spackler, a gopher-obsessed groundskeeper. Filming took place at the Rolling Hills Golf & Tennis Club, now called the **Grande Oaks Golf Club,** in Davie, near Fort Lauderdale. Some scenes were shot in **Boca Raton** at the **Boca Raton Resort & Country Club.**

The image of Florida as the "Sunshine State" – complete with golden beaches and pastel-hued villas – is perfected in **The Truman Show** (1998), filmed at Seaside in Florida's panhandle. The town, built to be a model beach community, served as the seemingly perfect world of Truman Burbank (Jim Carrey), whose life, without his knowledge, has been broadcast on television as an unending reality show starting with the day he was born.

The classic horror flick *Creature from the Black Lagoon* was filmed in Florida's Wakulla Springs, one of the largest freshwater sources in the world.

3

HAWAII

SURF & DINOSAUR TURF

By Verena Hertlein

It is surprising how many filmmakers are drawn to Hawaii, despite its remote location in the Pacific Ocean. The various climate zones and the evolutionary history of the individual islands offer an astonishing variety of landscapes. A total of eight principal islands – Oahu, Kauai, Maui, and Hawaii (Big Island), as well as Molokai, Lanai, Niihau, and Kahoolawe – form the least contiguous of the United States. In addition to countless beaches and turquoise-hued lagoons, Hawaii also boasts high mountain ranges with peaks shrouded in clouds, volcanoes in a surreal lunar landscape, green slopes, dense rainforests, waterfalls, and vast pineapple plantations. Filmmakers love to train their cameras on the islands of Oahu and Kauai: Their extraordinarily varied and lush landscapes provide a backdrop for everything from romantic comedies and dramas to adventure, war, and surfer films.

Dinosaurs in an Island Paradise

Steven Spielberg's blockbuster **Jurassic Park** (1993) showcases what are perhaps the most fascinating landscape shots of Hawaii, most of which were taken on the "garden island" of Kauai. Studio work and computer animation played a key role in this film, so adding footage of the natural landscape provided a necessary balance. To adapt Michael Crichton's bestseller for the screen, Spielberg chose Kauai as a stand-in for Isla Nublar,

Jurrassic Park's fictitious home off the coast of Costa Rica. With its rugged shores, deep gorges, waterfalls, and rich green valleys, the oldest of Hawaii's main islands offers an especially primitive appearance.

In 1992, the film team arrived at the **Olokele Canyon** in the south of **Kauai,** one of the most humid regions in the U.S A towering electric fence was erected to depict the enclosure for the dangerous raptors in the movie. Locations were scouted across the entire island with the goal of capturing the entire spectrum of landscapes. Many of the locations are difficult to find and even more difficult to reach. The waterfall where John Hammond's (Richard Attenborough) helicopter lands is so inaccessible that the production team had to erect a landing pad especially for the shoot at the **Manawaiopuna Falls** in **Hanapepe Valley.** From the air, a breathtaking view of waterfalls and valleys in the interior of the island opens up. The entrance to the Jurassic Park visitor center – a monumental set – was also located inland, at the edge of the **Blue Hole** canyon, several hours' trek from the east coast.

Hurricane Iniki destroyed parts of Kauai toward the end of shooting, so the team relocated to the island of **Oahu** for the

Film editors used the rugged coasts and green valleys of Oahu and Kauai to produce the fictitious Isla Nublar in *Jurassic Park*. Oahu's Kaaawa Valley hosted the impressive scenes of vast herds of dinosaurs in motion.

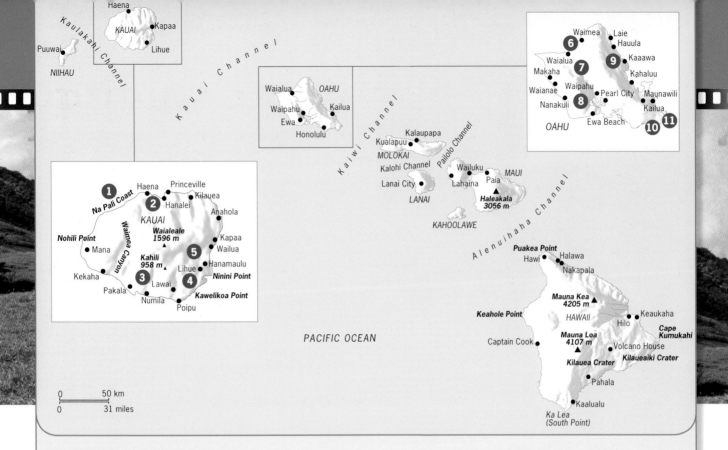

Top landscape film locations

1. Na Pali Coast, Kauai: **The Lost World: Jurassic Park, King Kong, Six Days Seven Nights**
2. Lumaha'i near Hanalei Bay, Kauai: **South Pacific**
3. Hanapepe Valley, Kauai: **Jurassic Park**
4. Menehune Fishpond, Kauai: **Raiders of the Lost Ark**
5. Wailua River, Kauai: **Jurassic Park III**
6. North shore and Waimea Bay, Oahu: **Point Break, Blue Crush**
7. Dole Plantation, Oahu: **50 First Dates**
8. Pearl Harbor, Oahu: **Pearl Harbor, Tora! Tora! Tora!**
9. Kaaawa Valley and Kualoa Ranch, Oahu: **Jurassic Park, Godzilla, 50 First Dates**
10. Hanauma Bay, Oahu: **Blue Hawaii**
11. Halona Cove, Oahu: **From Here to Eternity**

Steven Spielberg used computer animation and lifelike models of dinosaurs.

final scenes. The tropical beauty of **Kualoa Ranch** in **Kaaawa Valley** features in the scene where a huge herd of dinosaurs wanders across the plain, observed from a safe distance in the shelter of a large tree by Dr. Alan Grant (Sam Neill) and the children. The same valley also appears in **Blue Hawaii** (1961) and in the opening scenes of Roland Emmerich's **Godzilla** (1998), when the footprints of the giant lizard are shown.

The sequel would return only briefly to the Hawaiian locations featured in the original film. Shooting took place on the rugged **Na Pali Coast** on **Kauai,** but the majority of *The Lost World: Jurassic Park* (1997) was shot at locations ranging from San Diego to New Zealand. Before being completed at studios in California, filming for the final release of the trilogy, *Jurassic Park III* (2001), also began on Oahu and Kauai. The team set up

Oahu's Halona Cove: the site of Burt Lancaster and Deborah Kerr's famous surfside love scene in *From Here to Eternity.*

tents at the **Dillingham Airfield** in Mokuleia on **Oahu,** and sought out the **north coast** and the dense forests in the **Manoa Valley** as picturesque backdrops for the jungle scenes. On **Kauai,** the production crew shot the surroundings in **Hanalei Valley** and the landscape along the **Wailua River.** The cliffs of **Molokai's northeast coast** are also visible in some of the aerial sequences. These images convey a sense of endless expanse, a quality important to capture since the dinosaurs would be incorporated into the landscape during post-production work using state-of-the-art computer technology.

Hawaiian Romance: the ´50s & ´60s
On-screen romance, too, gets its due in this honeymoon paradise. Especially in the 1950s and 1960s, Hawaii was a dream destination for romantics of all kinds, and it was during these decades that the first famous films were shot here.

From Here to Eternity rattled the box office with its immense popularity in 1953 and includes a famous screen kiss in the

In *South Pacific,* the soldiers get hula fever while waiting to be sent into action. They pass the time with a few songs – and shimmies – on the beach.

surf that is associated with Hawaii to this day. The passionate love scene with Burt Lancaster and Deborah Kerr was filmed on the beach at **Oahu's Halona Cove,** located at the foot of the **Koko Crater.** This popular destination at the southeastern tip of Oahu has since been nicknamed "Eternity Beach." Another location from the movie is **Schofield Barracks,** the Army base at the heart of the island where Sergeant Warden (Burt Lancaster) is stationed and falls in love with the wife of the company commander. En route to the famous beach, the lovers pass by the famous landmarks of **Waikiki Beach, Diamond Head,** and **Hanauma Bay.**

Picturesque **Hanauma Bay** is even better known from another film: Elvis Presley stood in front of the camera on the shore by these emerald waters during the shoot for **Blue Hawaii** (1961). The **Coco Palms Hotel,** located on the easterly **Coconut Coast** in Kapaa, is where Elvis weds his Hawaiian bride in the movie. The hotel, which closed in 1992 due to severe damage from Hurricane Iniki, is scheduled to reopen in 2008. Elvis returned to Hawaii to film the comedies *Girls! Girls! Girls!* (1962) and *Paradise, Hawaiian Style* (1966), but the highlight everyone remembers would come a few years later. The first live satellite transmission of a concert worldwide was *Aloha from Hawaii,* Elvis's legendary 1973 concert in Honolulu.

Another famous scene from the history of film was shot on **Kauai** in the late 1950s. On the beach at **Lumaha'i** in the north of the island, not far from Hanalei Bay, Mitzi Gaynor sang "I'm Gonna Wash That Man Right Outta My Hair" in the classic musical **South Pacific** (1958). Tourists who visit the beach today can continue eastwards along the coast to **Princeville,** where "that man," Rossano Brazzi, cast a spell on Gaynor with his song.

Modern Romantic Comedies
Director Peter Segal wanted to embellish **50 First Dates** (2004) with authentic Hawaiian flair, and scouted the perfect setting

for this charming romantic comedy on the island of **Oahu.** Since the beautiful Lucy (Drew Barrymore) suffers from short-term memory loss, Henry (Adam Sandler) has to "remind" her that he has already won her heart. Day in and day out, Henry meets her over breakfast at the café, and uses what he learns about her from the previous day to woo her yet again. The fictitious Hukilau Café was filmed at **Kualoa Ranch** in **Kaaawa Valley,** where a fishpond, lush vegetation, and mountain backdrops provide a charming setting. Nearby is the location used to film Lucy's family home, with its long dock providing a glorious view of the ocean and the coast.

One day, Lucy sits on the pier and recalls the accident that robbed her of her memory. Suddenly she realizes that her life is stuck in a holding pattern. After Henry's daily farewell, the viewer accompanies her over dusty roads into the interior of the island at **Waialua** and **Wahiawa,** the pineapple groves of the **Dole Plantation,** and **Sandy Beach** and **Halona Cove** in the south. **Sea Life Park** in **Waimanalo** at the extreme southeast of the island also makes an important appearance: Henry proposes to Lucy by the dolphin lagoon and the sea lion pool where he works as a veterinarian.

Hawaii's movie connection continues with Johnny Depp as *Don Juan DeMarco* (1995), also filmed on Oahu. Bathed in the pink light of a sunset, Oahu's beaches form the backdrop for the film's enchanting love scenes. The narrative centers on a young man who is checked in to a psychiatric clinic after a suicide attempt. He claims to be none other than Don Juan, the greatest lover in the world, and tells his psychiatrist Dr. Jack Mickler (Marlon Brando) of his erotic exploits. Mickler knows that he should guide "Don Juan" back to reality, but is nevertheless increasingly fascinated by his adventurous tales. Near the end of the film, Don Juan, Mickler, and the doctor's wife (Faye Dunaway) kick up their heels on the beach, a sequence captured on the **north shore of Oahu** in the inlet off of **Turtle Bay Resort.**

Oahu's Kualoa Ranch served as the backdrop to the comedy *50 First Dates.*

Heroes on Kauai

Steven Spielberg sought out the southeastern coast of **Kauai** for scenes in *Raiders of the Lost Ark* (1981) of a trek through the jungles of South America. Part one of the adventure trilogy begins with a chase across the fields near **Nawiliwili Harbor** down to the **Huleia River.** Harrison Ford grabs a rope and swings across the river, ultimately escaping his pursuers in a seaplane that takes off from **Menehune Fishpond.**

Blue Hawaii lives from its music and the exotic setting on Oahu's Hanauma Bay. Johnny Depp (right) finds paradise on this island in *Don Juan DeMarco.*

In *Six Days Seven Nights*, Harrison Ford and Anne Heche are stranded on a remote island in the Pacific – in reality, Kauai.

In **Six Days Seven Nights** (1998), Harrison Ford returns to Kauai in the role of a gruff pilot, Quinn, accompanied by Robin, a New York sophisticate (Anne Heche). The island stood in for French Polynesia, where their adventures take place after an emergency landing. The images of the rugged **Na Pali Coast** in the northwest of the island – home to **King Kong** in John Guillermin's 1976 cinematic version – are stunning. Other locations include **Lihue Airport** and **Nawiliwili Harbor** in the southeast, **Papaa Bay** in the northeast, and the **Waimea Canyon**, also known as the "Grand Canyon of the Pacific," in the interior.

Battleground Oahu

In addition to romance and adventure, Hawaii is also inextricably associated with World War II, first and foremost because of the Japanese attack on Pearl Harbor on December 7, 1941. Several films have adapted the historic event for the screen. The two best known are the Japanese-American coproduction **Tora! Tora! Tora!** from 1970 and Michael Bay's **Pearl Harbor**

Nurse Evelyn (Kate Beckinsale) falls in love with Rafe (Ben Affleck) in *Pearl Harbor*. The bombing of Pearl Harbor was filmed at the historic locations of the attack, as seen in the sweep of Japanese fighters over Kolekole Pass.

(2001) starring Ben Affleck and Kate Beckinsale. Both movies reconstruct the bombing at the historic locations of **Pearl Harbor** and **Ford Island.** *Pearl Harbor* is especially impressive for its breathtaking aerial shots of the harbor and the coast. The exteriors of the hospital, showing how the wounded are tended to after the attack, were shot on the **Palm Circle** of **Fort Shafter,** the oldest military base on Oahu. **Wheeler Army Airfield** near Schofield Barracks is featured as a location for combat scenes in both films. The Japanese levied a surprise attack on the airfield in 1941 to knock out the American Air Force's ability to defend Pearl Harbor. **Kolekole Pass** also appears in both films, although embarrassingly so in *Tora! Tora! Tora!*: When the Japanese fighter planes navigate the Kolekole Pass en route to Pearl Harbor, viewers can see the monumental white cross that was erected *after* the attack as a memorial to the fallen soldiers.

The dramatic scenes of the attack on Pearl Harbor won the 1970 film *Tora! Tora! Tora!* an Oscar for best special effects.

Surfer's Paradise

Hawaii is a surfer's paradise. Especially in winter, towering waves form along **Oahu's** famous **north shore,** attracting the world's finest wave-riders to take part in daredevil competitions. Director Don Taylor shot parts of his classic surfer flick *Ride the Wild Surf* (1964) on Oahu's **Waimea Bay.** Scenes from *The Endless Summer* (1966), a documentary on the surfing life, were also shot on the **north shore.** The famous coast even lent its name wholesale to another classic surfer movie: *North Shore* (1987) treats audiences to spectacular shots of surfers riding waves as high as houses.

In *Point Break* (1991), Keanu Reeves plays an undercover FBI agent hoping to unmask a gang of bank-robbing surfers. Although the story is set in Los Angeles, the beach scenes were shot in Hawaii on **Pipeline Beach, Sunset Beach,** and **Waimea Beach,** all located on Oahu's north shore. Reeves's character takes a lesson from a pretty surfer in how to ride the waves in the waters off of Sunset Beach. Oregon's beaches make an ap-

pearance towards the middle of the film, but the gigantic waves that Patrick Swayze's stunt double rides at the end of the film crashed onto the sands at **Waimea Bay.**

Another film that shines the spotlight on Oahu's beaches is *Blue Crush* (2002). The story of three young surfer girls living on Oahu's **north shore** and struggling to compete in the male-dominated world of surfing is notable less for its story line than the impressive shots in the water. Anne Marie (Kate Bosworth) trains for the Pipeline Masters in the towering waves of the **Banzai Pipeline.** North shore locations **Kawela Bay** and **Waimea Falls** also make appearances. In the movie, the girls earn a living at the upscale **JW Marriott Ihilani Resort & Spa** in **Ko Olina** on Oahu's west coast.

Keanu Reeves and Patrick Swayze surf the waves in *Point Break*, filmed on Oahu's famous north shore.

4

MEXICO

HOLLYWOOD SOUTH OF THE BORDER

By Stephan Fuchs

In Mexico, the line of Pacific Ocean beaches stretches from Baja California via Acapulco to Puerto Escondido in the south. The Central American nation also has the longest coastline on the Caribbean, as well as a mountainous hinterland and historical sites that have witnessed Aztec empires, Spanish conquistadors, and revolutionary heroes. Best of all for film-makers, all of this location splendor unfolds just a few hours south of Hollywood.

Director Wolfgang Petersen sought out Mexico's shores when the war in Iraq disrupted the filming of his epic **Troy** (2004). The crew had started shooting the Greek fleet's arrival in Morocco when producers voiced concerns about unrest in the region. One of the production assistants knew the perfect beach in **San José del Cabo** in southerly **Baja California,** and the whole film team moved to Mexico. More bad luck lay in wait: Back-to-back hurricanes devastated the movie set and razed the house where actor Brad Pitt lived when he wasn't playing the Greek hero Achilles. Less complex productions have taken advantage of Mexico's natural beauty and rich history as well. Jeff Bridges, Rachel Ward, and James Woods star in **Against All Odds** (1984), a film famed more for its Oscar-nominated title song by Phil Collins than for its plot. The script is happily obscured by splendid backdrops afforded by the Mayan ruins of **Chichén Itzá** and **Tulúm,** and the island of **Cozumel.**

Hollywood's fascination with Mexico is almost as old as the movie industry itself. Film production was still in its infancy in the early twentieth century, and largely immobile owing to the heavy cameras. Although American moviemaking really got its start in New York City, California seemed a better place to establish permanent studios: The weather was good and there were more hours of sunlight. Proximity to another country was an additional reason to relocate – frequent arguments over copyright made it convenient for filmmakers to cross the

In *The Night of the Iguana*, Ava Gardner and Richard Burton meet in the secluded bay of Mismaloya (above) and fall in love.

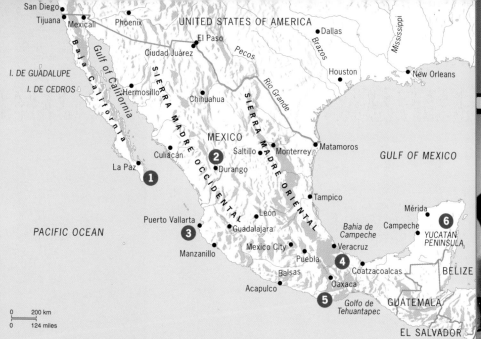

Top landscape film locations

1. San José del Cabo beach: **Troy**
2. Durango: Westerns like **The Wild Bunch, The Magnificent Seven**
3. Puerto Vallarta and Mismaloya: **The Night of the Iguana**
4. Laguna Catemaco: **Medicine Man, Apocalypto**
5. Puerto Escondido and the beaches of Oaxaca: **Y tu mamá también**
6. Chichén Itzá: **Against All Odds**

Brad Pitt is god-like as Achilles. The Greek hero leads his men into battle against *Troy* in Wolfgang Petersen's screen adaptation of Homer's *Iliad*. Several scenes were filmed at the southern tip of Baja California.

Fred Dobbs (Humphrey Bogart) suspects that someone is after his gold in *The Treasure of the Sierra Madre.*

border into Mexico to evade the long arm of the law. Technical progress in the 1940s made shooting more mobile, and it wasn't long before the first outside shots were being filmed in the hills around Hollywood and at locations farther south.

John Huston was especially enthusiastic about making movies in Mexico, and shot **The Treasure of the Sierra Madre** (1948) south of the border with Humphrey Bogart as Fred C. Dobbs, Tim Holt as Bob Curtin, and Huston's father, Walter, in an Oscar-winning role as Howard. Huston, who would win Oscars for Best Director and Best Screenplay for the film, extended his stay in Mexico beyond the originally planned two months to half a year despite the fact that many scenes had already been filmed near Los Angeles, on Iverson Ranch, and in the mines of Kernville. But the sequences shot in Mexico compensated both for the delay and the enormous budget of over $2 million – ten times the money usually spent on movie productions in the late 1940s.

Huston managed to shoot part of the movie at locations mentioned in the novel of the same name by B. Traven. The enigmatic author had been living in Mexico for some time and offered Huston his support in the form of letters detailing his opinions on everything from casting to script. Rumor had it that he turned up on the set disguised as an agent. Filming took place at the Gulf of Mexico port of **Tampico** and near the spa town of **San José Purua** in **Michoacán Province** farther west, mostly in the village of **Jungapeo**. Native Indian extras were hired for certain sequences, such as the famous scene in which Howard resuscitates a local boy after a swimming accident.

Pacific Ocean and Gold Coast Beaches

Filming *The Treasure of the Sierra Madre* in Mexico taught Huston that actors behave differently when they are removed from the glitz of Los Angeles. When he began work on **The Night of the Iguana** (1964), an adaptation of a play by Tennessee Williams, he decided to station cast and crew on Mexico's Pacific coast for the entire shoot. Richard Burton is the disillusioned preacher Lawrence Shannon, who takes on a job as travel guide to make ends meet. On a trip to Mexico, he finds himself hopelessly entangled with three women, young Charlotte (Sue Lyon), boring Hannah (Deborah Kerr), and a hotel owner named Maxine (Ava Gardner).

Cast and crew took up quarters in the little town of **Puerto Vallarta.** Each morning they would boat over to the set a few miles away in **Mismaloya.** Most of the action took place in Maxine's hotel, a set constructed in Mismaloya, with little contact with the outside world. The story's many emotionally fraught situations placed a heavy burden on everyone there, a problem exacerbated by the presence of Elizabeth Taylor, whom Burton married in March 1964. Huston, known for his macabre sense of humor, used the tension on set to his own ends: He gave every main character as well as the jealous Taylor a pistol and bullets inscribed with the other actors' names, and encouraged them to shoot one another if things got too tense. Happily, no shots were fired. Burton and Taylor were so pleased with Puerto Vallarta that they bought the villa they'd been staying in. The town later served as a film set for other productions, some less ambitious, such as *Caveman* (1981) with Ringo Starr and Dennis Quaid and *Predator* (1987) with Arnold Schwarzenegger.

The landscape near the seaside resort of Acapulco proved to be even more popular as a film location: Orson Welles's *The Lady from Shanghai* (1947), Elvis's *Fun in Acapulco* (1963), and

the Bond flick *Licence to Kill* (1989) were shot here. The beautiful region south of Acapulco had to wait a little longer for its film debut. Local director Alfonso Cuarón – later known for *Harry Potter and the Prisoner of Azkaban* (2004) and *Children of Men* (2006) – chose the heavily touristed area as a setting for **Y tu mamá también** (2001). In the Oscar-nominated film, the director sends two teenagers, Tenoch (Diego Luna) and Julio (Gael García Bernal), on a road trip with a beautiful Spanish woman named Luisa (Maribel Verdú) in the summer before they start college. The boys take a circuitous route starting in **Mexico City,** heading southwest to the dream beaches of **Oaxaca Province.** The movie was shot mainly in **Santa Cruz Huatulco** and on the nearby beaches of **Playa Cacaluta** and **Playa La Entrega.** Some sequences were shot in the coffee port and former hippie hangout of **Puerto Escondido,** now a destination for yuppie backpackers. In the film, they avoid Puerto Escondido for this very reason – even though the movie was shot there. Assisted by great performances, Cuarón portrays Mexico's contrasts with humor and warmth, from the pulsating metropolis to stretches of sleepy countryside and lonely coastal bays.

Mexico's Gulf coast has attracted filmmakers for its coastal towns and mountainous hinterland. **Veracruz** replaced Verona

Mexican actor Gael García Bernal (left) made his acting breakthrough as Julio in the 2001 film *Y tu mamá también*. On a roadtrip with the beautiful Luisa, the friends Tenoch and Julio find the dream beach "Boca del Cielo" – but in reality, it's Playa Cacaluta in the bay of Huatulco.

Director Mel Gibson shot *Apocalypto* in the rain forests of Catemaco and Las Tuxtlas, as well as at the Eyipantla Waterfall.

in Australian director Baz Luhrmann's modern adaptation of **Romeo + Juliet** (1996), in which Leonardo DiCaprio and Claire Danes play Shakespeare's star-struck lovers. Beautiful **Laguna Catemaco,** an inland lake in south-central Veracruz Province, is surrounded by verdant hills that still convey an impression of dense rainforests – despite the fact that vegetation here is relatively sparse these days. The area provided locations for films such as **Medicine Man** (1992), with Sean Connery as the

constructed to look like a typical Western town, is still open to the public, as is the village of **Chupaderos,** discovered by none other than John Wayne. More than 120 films have been made here, including classics such as **The Tall Men** (1955) with Clark Gable; **Big Jake** (1971) and **The Train Robbers** (1973), both starring John Wayne; **A Man Called Horse** (1970) with Richard Harris, loved by children of all ages as Albus Dumbledore of Harry Potter fame, and **The Mask of Zorro** (1998) with Anthony Hopkins in the title role.

The Wild Bunch (1969) is perhaps the most grueling Western to have been filmed in this area. Some view it as a masterpiece of blood and dust, while others consider the film by Sam Peckinpah to be abusively misogynous. The movie was shot to the northeast of Durango in **Parras de la Fuente** where the 400-year-old **Hacienda Cienega del Carmen** is situated. The film's final massacre took place under the vineyard's famous aqueduct. Some ten thousand blanks were shot over the eleven days it took to film the sequence. In addition to the extreme noise levels,

With its deserts, grasslands, and craggy peaks, the landscapes of the Durango region look a lot like the American Southwest. No wonder so many Westerns were filmed here, including classics like *The Wild Bunch* with William Holden (left) and *The Magnificent Seven* with Yul Brynner (right).

aging hippie researcher who finds a cure for cancer in the secretions of wood ants, but cannot prevent a road construction team from making the insects extinct.

Mel Gibson's **Apocalypto** (2006), a drastic comparison of the downfall of Mayan culture to the decline of contemporary society, was also filmed in Catemaco, even though Mayan ruins were never found here. The set features a colorful mixture of elements from 1,500 years of Mayan architectural history that left archeologists crying in the aisles.

Westerns in Durango

Most movie fans are familiar with Mexico as a backdrop in Westerns. The dusty desert region around the small town of **Durango** has been a popular movie location since **White Feather** (1955), starring Robert Wagner, was filmed here. **Villa del Oeste,** a set

the main actors were required to wear their costumes until the clothing literally fell apart. Each was supplied with seven identical sets of clothes, but not one costume survived the making of the film.

The Magnificent Seven (1960), inspired by Akira Kurosawa's *Seven Samurai* (1954), seems almost lighthearted by comparison. John Sturges's film draws its strength from a star-studded cast. Yul Brynner and Steve McQueen could never quite decide who the better Western hero was, and considered the German actor Horst Buchholz to be totally miscast in his role as a Mexican farmer. The fictitious border town was constructed in Durango and in a Mexican village not far from **Cuernavaca** to the southwest of Mexico City. It is here that the magnificent seven make their stand against the bandit Calvera (Eli Wallach) on behalf of the villagers.

5

PERU

WILD JUNGLES, MIGHTY RIVERS

By Stephan Fuchs

Three very different kinds of landscape comprise Peru's image: the coastal lowlands, the Andes, home of the Incas, and the vast upper reaches of the Amazon's tributaries to the west, a region that extends down into the mighty river's basin. Despite its diverse nature, Peru attracts few international film projects. Logistics are one reason: Scenes set on beaches or in jungles are far easier to shoot in Mexico, where Western standards of technical support and convenience are easy to come by. Terrain is another: The Andean highlands and the still largely inaccessible Amazon basin are difficult locations for equipment-laden film crews to operate in and capture for the screen. A few brave souls have tried it nonetheless, such as Dennis Hopper, who filmed *The Last Movie* (1971) in the remote mountain town of **Chincheros** and in **Cuzco.**

The fact that most cineastes are familiar with Peru and its contrasting landscapes can be attributed to the efforts of one man: director Werner Herzog. In 1972, the twenty-nine-year-old Munich native shot his spectacular film *Aguirre: The Wrath of God* in the Andean highlands. Although the movie initially confused critics and viewers alike, today it is considered a great landscape film. *Aguirre* also marks the beginning of the troubled yet fruitful partnership between Herzog and the actor Klaus

Kinski, who plays Aguirre. The film is based on an expedition searching for El Dorado that disappeared without a trace from the jungles of Peru in 1561. Using spectacular shots of remote landscapes, the movie portrays a delirious obsession with gold and power. In its long-drawn-out opening sequence, the conquistadors trek across a mountain crest, scenes filmed in the **Urubamba Valley** near Machu Picchu. Aguirre instigates a coup in a camp situated on the **Rio Huallaga,** and the allegorical final scene, which shows Aguirre drifting alone in circles on his river raft, was filmed on the **Rio Nanay.**

Herzog returned to Peru a few years later to film his most spectacular movie ever, *Fitzcarraldo* (1982). The film, set during the heyday of the rubber barons in the early twentieth century,

With the same mania as the music-obsessed *Fitzcarraldo* (above), Werner Herzog insisted his crew pull a ship up a mountain in the wilds of a rain forest.

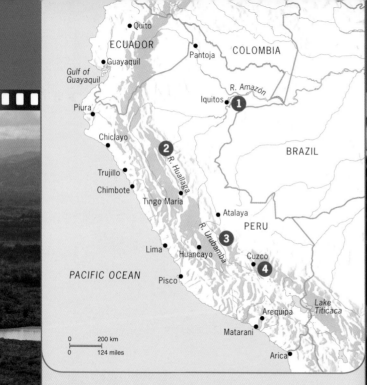

Top landscape film locations

1. Iquitos: **Fitzcarraldo**
2. Rio Huallaga: **Aguirre: The Wrath of God**
3. Rio Camisea and Rio Urubamba: **Fitzcarraldo**
4. Urubamba Valley: **The Last Movie,**
   Aguirre: The Wrath of God

Klaus Kinski lends his typical intensity to the title role of *Aguirre*. Scenes from the 1972 movie were filmed on the Rio Huallaga (left). The film uses spectacular shots of remote landscapes to tell the tale of an expedition that disappeared without a trace while searching for El Dorado.

was shot primarily in the Amazon basin. A brief newspaper account that Herzog had stumbled across inspired the project: A riverboat crew had dismantled a ship and transported it part by part over a mountaintop in an attempt to access the upper reaches of a non-navigable river. This was all the inspiration he needed for the story of the Irish opera buff, Brian Sweeney Fitzgerald (Fitzcarraldo), and his obsession with building an opera house in **Iquitos** to attract the famous tenor Enrico Caruso to perform in Peru. Brazilian **Manaus** would serve both as model and location for the memorable opening scenes.

"Ecstatic landscapes and ecstatic characters" were the words Herzog later used to describe the jungle shoot in Peru and his work with actors Kinski and the ever congenial Claudia Cardinale. Yet Kinski, allegedly Herzog's "best friend," was the director's second choice for the part of Fitzcarraldo. Half the movie had already been shot with Jason Robards as the star when the American actor fell ill. Robards's doctors blocked him from participating in further film work in Peru, so Herzog invited Kinski to take the part. Scenes that had originally been shot with Mick Jagger in a brilliant supporting role had to be scrapped, too: Delays in filming conflicted with the dates of the Rolling Stones's world tour. To make matters worse, war broke out on the border between Peru and Ecuador, and Her-

zog had to relocate the entire shoot. Undaunted by the challenging topography, he insisted they film farther south in the Andean highlands, where a slope of land separated two rivers. Rubber baron Carlos Fermín Fitcarrald had actually spent time here in the late nineteenth century, a fitting coincidence for the film.

The story of the shoot, itself the subject of a documentary by Les Blank entitled **Burden of Dreams** (1982), is no less bizarre than the film. To turn the tale of a ship on a mountain into movie reality, Herzog arranged for 450 Kampas natives to drag a 360-ton ship up a 40-degree incline. They moved it from one river to another – from the **Rio Camisea** to the **Rio Urubamba** – using nothing but winches. Not once did the director consider using a model or special effects, not even when the boat's ride through the **Pongo de Mainique** rapids, called the Pongo das Mortes in the film, presented a considerable risk to the actors and crew.

Shooting took more than two years and was beset by further jungle adventures: The Amahuaca natives mounted attacks with poison arrows to try to drive the crew out from their territory; deadly snakes and piranhas also put in appearances. Herzog's diary of the shoot, *Eroberung des Nutzlosen* ("Conquering the Useless"), reveals his unflagging enthusiasm for the project as well as his great love for the very jungle landscapes that made making *Fitzcarraldo* such a monumental challenge.

6

ARGENTINA

A JOURNEY TO THE ANDES By Stephan Fuchs

From the ice deserts of Tierra del Fuego and Patagonia in the south to the broad expanses of the Pampas and jungles and the towering peaks of the Andes, Argentina is nothing if not a land of astonishing diversity. One such story is narrated in **The Motorcycle Diaries** (2004), based on the book of the same name by Ernesto "Che" Guevara. As a young student of medicine, Che (Gael García Bernal) and his friend, Alberto Granado (played by Rodrigo De la Serna, a cousin – once removed – of Che himself), traveled from Argentina to Venezuela from January to July 1952. Their journey, the first part of which was completed on a 1939 Norton 500 motorbike, covered a grand total of 8,100 miles (13,000 kilometers).

The movie was filmed on location, and the camera follows the two protagonists as they trace Che and Alberto's original itinerary. The journey kicks off in **Córdoba** in Argentina, Alberto's hometown, then moves on to **Rosario,** Ernesto's birthplace, and shifts from there to **Buenos Aires** and points farther south. The two young men visit Ernesto's first love, Chichina (Mía Maestro), who lives close to the picturesque little coastal town of **Miramar,** and then follow a southwesterly route through the **Pampas** to **San Martín de los Andes.** In **Bariloche** they catch a ferry across the high-altitude waters of **Lago Frías.** Once they've reached the other side, they disembark and leave Argentina behind, traveling on to Chile, where they soon lose their motorcycle in a collision with a herd of cows. The duo hitch rides in cattle trucks, on Amazon ferries, and on foot, and in doing so come

Tibet in the Andes: Jean-Jacques Annaud filmed *Seven Years in Tibet* in Argentina's Uspallata Valley. Brad Pitt stars as an Austrian mountaineer.

into closer contact with the people of Latin America and the extreme poverty they are forced to endure. A strenuous hike forces them to brave subzero nighttime temperatures while crossing the dusty **Atacama Desert** before arriving at the copper mines of **Chuquicamata.** They cross the Andes to **Cuzco** and the ruins of **Machu Picchu** and to Lima, then continue on to the Peruvian Amazon basin to **Iquitos** and the nearby leper colony of **San Pablo,** where Che undergoes a personal transformation – or revolution.

Argentina's border with Chile winds its way through 2,300 miles (3,650 kilometers) of the Andes, and boasts the highest

In 1952, Ernesto "Che" Guevara set out with a friend to discover the South American continent. *The Motorcycle Diaries* follows their incredible journey of 8,100 miles across Argentina, over the Andes, and along the Chilean coast from the Atacama Desert to the Amazon basin of Peru.

Top landscape film locations

1. Waterfalls at Iguazú: **The Mission**
2. Uspallata Valley: **Seven Years in Tibet**
3. Lago Frías: **The Motorcycle Diaries**

peak of the western and southern hemisphere: the **Cerro Aconcagua,** about 60 miles (100 kilometers) west of **Mendoza,** nearly 23,000 feet (7,000 meters) high. In addition to scenes from *The Motorcycle Diaries,* parts of *Seven Years in Tibet* (1997) were shot here, with director Jean-Jacques Annaud choosing the **Andes** to stand in for the Himalayas. Brad Pitt is the Austrian mountaineering legend Heinrich Harrer. He escapes from a POW camp at the start of World War II and takes refuge with the young Dalai Lama in Tibet before history catches up with him in 1951, when China annexes Tibet. Annaud began filming

Jeremy Irons as the zealous Jesuit Gabriel in *The Mission.*

in India, but was forced to relocate to Argentina when his shooting permit was rescinded. He admitted two years after the film's premiere that his crew had been filming secretly in occupied Tibet. Some twenty minutes of this material was integrated into the final cut alongside sequences filmed in the mountainous landscapes of Argentina.

It took the crew more than eighteen months to reconstruct the Tibetan capital of Lhasa in the **Uspallata Valley** between Mendoza and the Chilean border. Twenty-five yaks were imported for authenticity on the set, and each animal required its own passport complete with nose print to enter Argentina. The Tibetan monks who arrived to work as extras were moved to tears when they saw the replica of their holy city of Lhasa after years of exile. Even the Dalai Lama's sister, Jetsun Pema, played a part, appearing in the film in the role of their mother.

The fantastic waterfalls at **Iguazú,** located in the border region shared by Argentina, Brazil, and Paraguay, are the world's largest and as such are practically predestined to become a backdrop for film scenes. Roger Moore's James Bond made an appearance here in *Moonraker* (1979). Movie fans will remember the unforgettable opening scenes of Roland Joffé's *The Mission* (1986), in which a missionary becomes the victim of his own converts' zeal: Nailed to a cross, he hurtles down the face of the falls. In the film, Jeremy Irons plays the Jesuit priest Gabriel while Robert De Niro is the Spanish mercenary and slave dealer Rodrigo Mendoza, who kills his brother in a jealous rage and tries to atone for his sins by becoming a monk.

7

THE CARIBBEAN

ISLAND PARADISE ON THE SILVER SCREEN By Claudia Hellmann

There's no way around the clichés: palm-fringed beaches, turquoise waters, and lush, tropical vegetation. No wonder the Caribbean is such a popular destination. Paradise-like landscapes can be found everywhere in the Caribbean, from the Bahamas off the coast of Florida down to Trinidad & Tobago close to the northern shores of Venezuela. The Caribbean archipelago stretches across the ocean on a parabolic curve of some 1,490 miles (2,400 kilometers), allowing each of these islands to have its own geographic and cultural characteristics. Initially it was the Caribbean's unusually vibrant underwater world that attracted filmmakers to visit the islands.

Its long coral reefs, the variety of its tropical fish, ideal water temperatures, and exceptional water clarity are all factors that have made the Caribbean popular with divers – and with underwater filmmakers.

Jamaica: Tropical Diversity

The rugged Blue Mountains, tropical rainforests, impenetrable swamps, spectacular waterfalls, and long, sandy beaches make Jamaica one of the prettiest and most diverse islands in the Caribbean. Place names such as Blue Lagoon, Glistening Waters, and Dolphin Cove conjure images of a magical, tropical

The Round Hill Hotel and its superb view over Montego Bay was the setting for the romantic comedy *How Stella Got Her Groove Back*. In the film, Stella (Angela Bassett) falls for Winston (Taye Diggs), a much younger Jamaican man.

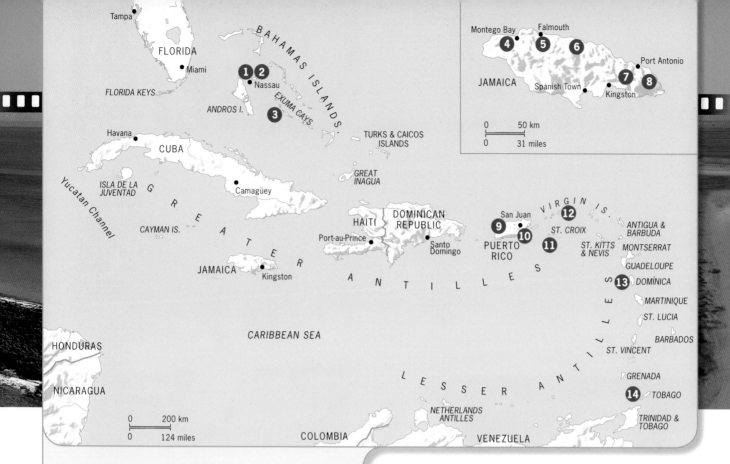

Top landscape film locations

1. Reefs and shipwrecks off the southwest coast of New Providence Island, Bahamas:
   20,000 Leagues Under the Sea, For Your Eyes Only, Thunderball
2. Ocean Club, Paradise Island, Bahamas:
   Casino Royale
3. Golden Grotto, Staniel Cay, Exumas, Bahamas:
   Thunderball
4. Montego Bay, Jamaica: **How Stella Got Her Groove Back**
5. Swamps near Falmouth, Jamaica: **Dr. No, Papillon**
6. Beach at Laughing Waters, Jamaica: **Dr. No**
7. Blue Mountains, Jamaica: **Wide Sargasso Sea**
8. Reach Falls, Jamaica: **Cocktail**
9. Observatory in Arecibo, Puerto Rico: **GoldenEye, Contact**
10. Vieques Island, Puerto Rico: **Lord of the Flies**
11. St. Croix, U.S. Virgin Islands: **The Island of Dr. Moreau**
12. Wreck of the *Rhône* off of Salt Island, British Virgin Islands: **The Deep**
13. Indian River, Dominica: **Pirates of the Caribbean: Dead Man's Chest**
14. Tobago Cays and Union Island, Grenadines: **Pirates of the Caribbean: The Curse of the Black Pearl**

landscape. Jamaica has fired the global imagination more than any other Caribbean location, and film has done more than its fair share to reinforce its cliché-ridden image. The idea that Jamaica is synonymous with rum, reggae, and Rastafarians does little justice to its rich heritage, a history particularly shaped by slaves from Africa.

The streets of the capital, Kingston, often serve as a backdrop for local films that handle topics such as crime and music, such as *The Harder They Come* (1972) with reggae star Jimmy Cliff, *Smile Orange* (1976), and *Rockers* (1978). Foreign directors, on the other hand, see the luxuriant natural surroundings as representative of an exotically sultry atmosphere, a backdrop ideal for romance and adventure. Films such as **Wide Sargasso Sea** (1993) capitalize on this impression. Thanks to images of the **Blue Mountains,** waterfalls, and colonial plantations, many filmgoers regard the movie version of Jean Rhys's novel as one of the most beautiful Jamaican films ever made. Their admiration is usually limited to the scenery, however: Jamaican writer Michelle Cliff decried *Wide Sargasso Sea* as "a soft-porn romp through the tropics." Australian director John Duigan may be guilty of squeezing the Jamaica cliché for all it's worth – and yet the story has a certain charm: After the emancipation of slaves in Jamaica in the 1840s, impoverished young plantation owner Antoinette (Karina Lombard) is married off to the English aristocrat Edward Rochester (Nathaniel Parker). The arranged marriage develops into a brief but passionate love that ultimately founders on cultural differences and prejudice. Even if the sumptuous exotica and erotica are riddled with clichés, the landscapes remain breathtaking.

Michelle Cliff would doubtless have levied an even more biting attack on *How Stella Got Her Groove Back* (1998). The film, almost universally panned by critics, developed a fan base among women who still visit the island in search of a tropical paradise and a flirtation with younger Jamaican men. The film really is a kitschy love story that centers on Stella (Angela Bassett), an attractive single mother and successful Wall Street broker about forty years of age who takes a holiday on Jamaica with her best friend, Delilah (Whoopi Goldberg). She falls head over heels in love with strapping Winston (Taye Diggs), who is half her age. The film is based on the successful, semi-autobiographical novel by Terry McMillan, and shows Jamaica from its sunniest side. The movie was shot near **Montego Bay,** a seaport in the northwest of the island that depends on tourism for its livelihood. The fifties era **Round Hill Hotel** nestles in the hills a few miles outside of "MoBay," and visitors who want to relive Stella's romp at the resort should rent one of the luxurious bungalows. Stella lived in

The swinging beach bar on Dragon Bay in *Cocktail.*

Cottage 11, which commands a fantastic view over the bay. Filming also took place in the gardens, at the pool, and on the hotel's seaside terrace.

The Jamaica scenes in the flashy Tom Cruise vehicle *Cocktail* (1988) are just as cliché-addled. Yet again, the fantastic landscape shots manage to hold the viewer in thrall. Cruise plays barman Brian Flanagan, who learns his trade in New York with old hand Doug Coughlin (Bryan Brown) before decamping to Jamaica to earn the cash he needs to open up his own bar back in the Big Apple. Once again, Jamaica plays the role of holiday paradise where dreams can come true. Cruise mixes cocktails in a beach bar on **Dragon Bay** outside **Port Antonio.** During filming, the straw-thatched bar belonged to **Dragon Bay Beach Resort.** The auberge has since been bought up by the Sandals hotel group, which has big plans for renovating the premises.

Between bouts of margarita making, Brian falls in love with the enchanting Jordan (Elisabeth Shue), and they ride along the

Honey Ryder (Ursula Andress) bewitches James Bond on the beach at Laughing Waters. Her *Dr. No* bikini fetched $61,500 at an auction.

beach to the sounds of a reggae version of "Run for the Shelter of Your Love." The love scene takes place under a waterfall in the middle of dense rainforest, filmed at the **Reach Falls** in the **John Crow Mountains** in the northeast of the island, the point at which the Drivers River cascades into a turquoise limestone basin. Famous as the location from this romantic scene, the idyllic falls have attracted considerable tourist attention. Nature has been given a helping hand for the visitors' benefit: A whirlpool was installed in one of the three small caves behind the waterfall to enhance the romantic ambience.

Port Antonio is conveniently situated amid other famous film locations on Jamaica's northeastern coast. The town was once a popular meeting place for Hollywood's high society, but its former glamour has long faded. "Porty" has film star Errol Flynn to thank for its brief prosperity. Flynn moored his yacht here in 1947 and was instantly beguiled by the town's natural beauty. He bought a house, a hotel, and a little offshore plot of land in Port Antonio known as Navy Island. In the 1940s and '50s, Flynn's legendary parties brought many Hollywood stars to town. One of his neighbors on the island was Ian Fleming, formerly of the British secret service and author of the famous James Bond novels, all fourteen of which he wrote in Jamaica. After the war, Fleming purchased a remote bit of country not far from **Oracabessa,** literally the "golden head" of the north coast, intending to winter here. He built a low bungalow with glass-free, open windows. **Villa Goldeneye** remains the centerpiece of today's eponymous luxury resort.

Fleming's spy achieved real fame only as a film character – and Jamaica played an important role in his cinematic apotheosis. In **Dr. No** (1962), the secret agent 007 (Sean Connery) is sent to Jamaica to investigate the mysterious disappearance of the head of the Kingston office. He quickly discovers that the pokerfaced Dr. No and his plan to take over the world are behind the trouble. With the help of a Jamaican contact called Quarrel (John Kitzmiller) and the beautiful Honey Ryder (Ursula Andress), Bond sets out to find Dr. No's secret fortress on the fictitious island of Crab Key. When Bond surreptitiously lands on the island, he spies the bewitching Honey rising from the waves like Venus and wearing only a cream-colored bikini and diving knife strapped at her hip. The cult scene was shot

Let Die (1973). Jamaica stood in for the fictitious Caribbean island of San Monique, where Bond is ordered to investigate the murder of several agents – likely at the hand of the dubious dictator and drug baron Dr. Kananga (Yaphet Kotto). Agent 007 uncovers Kananga's plan to gain control of the American drug market. In real life, Bond's hotel was the **Sans Souci Hotel in Ocho Rios,** where the crew stayed during shooting. The chase scene with the double-decker bus was filmed on the **coastal road between Montego Bay and Lucea.** Location scouts had discovered a sign bearing the threat "Trespassers will be eaten" close to Falmouth, and subsequently stumbled across the crocodile farm belonging to Ross Kananga, a sometime stuntman. Thus the spectacular scene was born in which Bond – doubled by Kananga – saves his own skin by jumping over the heads of crocodiles lurking in the water below. Today, the crocodile farm, which covers slightly less than two square hectares of

Hidden away from the world at remote Villa Goldeneye, Ian Fleming wrote spy novels about Agent 007, James Bond. Right: Roger Moore with Jane Seymour in the Bond film *Live and Let Die.*

on the beach at **Laughing Waters** to the west of Ocho Rios, now known as **James Bond Beach.** Ian Fleming, whose villa was close by, visited the set several times during shooting, and insisted on dishing out well-intended advice to Connery. Pursued by Dr. No's security personnel and their tracker dogs, Bond and Honey escape into the island's interior via the river near **Dunn's River Falls.** The island's most famous waterfalls are located close to Ocho Rios in the middle of a dense rain forest, where water cascades spectacularly down a series of limestone terraces. Dr. No sends his "dragon" after them, a fire-breathing variety of armored tank that repeatedly foundered in the **swamps around Falmouth,** much to the director's dismay. Eleven years later, 007 returned as Roger Moore in **Live and**

mangrove swamp, is called **Swaby's Swamp Safari.** The scenes in the Kananga Cave were filmed in the **Green Grotto Caves** and the **Runaway Caves** between Falmouth and Ocho Rios.

In *Live and Let Die*, it wasn't much of an imaginative leap from the real Jamaica to the fictitious Caribbean Island of San Monique. Other films have shown, too, how well Jamaica's varied landscapes can double for other countries. The scenes from **Legends of the Fall** (1994) in which Brad Pitt struggles through Africa were filmed near **Ocho Rios.** In **Instinct** (1999), the **Roaring River** and the **rain forest around St. Ann** are entirely credible as the Rwandan jungle where Anthony Hopkins lives with a band of gorillas.

One of the best films ever made in Jamaica, one that showcases the island's diverse landscapes, is **Papillon** (1973). This time Jamaica poses as an infamous penal colony off French Guiana where Henri Charrière, a.k.a. Papillon (Steve McQueen), and Louis Dega (Dustin Hoffman) are sent to serve life sentences in prison. Papillon is innocent and begins planning his escape from the very first day of his incarceration, when he requests permission to work with the labor gangs in the swamps. The penal colony was painstakingly reconstructed near **Falmouth,** but the swamp scenes were filmed in **Paradise Park,** a plantation on the west coast near Ferris Cross. Here

Indian tribe whose village lies in a cove – actually the beach near **Ocho Rios.** It is only on the third attempt, however, that Papillon finally manages to flee the aptly-named Devil's Island.

Underwater Adventure: The Bahamas

"The scent of flowers and trees wafted over the land so sweetly that there seemed to be nothing more beautiful in all the world." Christopher Columbus spoke these words as an early visitor to the islands more than 500 years ago. Even if they do not, strictly speaking, belong to the Caribbean, no other group of islands in the region is so popular with filmmakers. Hollywood is particularly drawn to the Bahamian underwater realm. With one of the largest coral reefs in the world and crystal clear waters, the Bahamas constitute the world's foremost underwater location. The coral archipelago consists of some 700 islands and more than 2,000 small and miniature islets, or cays. The Bahamas derive their name from the Spanish term "baja mar" or "shallow sea." Most of the islands rise no more than 100 feet (30 meters) above their snow-white or powdery pink beaches. The beaches dip gently into the crystal clear sea and extend well out into the water before dropping off suddenly into the depths at the reef's edge. Depending on the water's depth and the structure of the reefs, the water around the island shimmers

In *Papillon*, Steve McQueen is a prisoner who risks his life time and again to escape from a penal colony. After one attempt, he hides out with an Indian tribe whose village is in a cove, filmed on the beach near Ocho Rios. Meanwhile, his friend Dega (Dustin Hoffman) resigns himself to a life of wearing stripes.

the Sweet River flows into the sea framed by a landscape of grasslands and dense scrub punctuated by mangrove and palm groves. Although the first escape attempt fails and Papillon is sentenced to a year's solitary confinement under horrendous conditions, his desire for freedom remains unbroken. His second escape attempt is initially successful: After wandering about the island for some time, Papillon finds refuge with an

in a thousand different hues, from emerald green to turquoise to deepest midnight blue.

Film history was written in the Bahamas in 1916 when John Ernest Williamson, a pioneer of underwater film photography, filmed Jules Verne's **20,000 Leagues Under the Sea** in the island's waters. The story of the megalomaniac Captain Nemo and his submarine *Nautilus* was shot despite alarming weather

Not much is left of the Vulcan fighter plane from the James Bond film *Thunderball*, where several underwater scenes where filmed. And yet the wreck off the coast of New Providence Island is very popular with divers.

conditions off the **southwest coast of New Providence Island.** The location has remained popular with filmmakers over the years, and continues to attract film crews to this day, including those shooting the underwater scenes in *For Your Eyes Only* (1981), *Splash* (1984), and *Cocoon* (1985). Divers call this first-class underwater area **Elkhorn Gardens** for its plethora of colorful corals and tropical fish. Another spectacular diving spot to the south has become so popular that it is now known as the **Hollywood Bowl.** A maze of Elkhorn corals branches out from a depth of a few feet below sea level, almost piercing the water above the broad, sandy depression and crisscrossed by a multitude of fish, plus small sharks and turtles.

Today, it is Williamson's underwater camera equipment itself that takes on the look of a futuristic piece of equipment from a Jules Verne novel. To film under water, the photographer used a five-foot-wide observation chamber with glass sides to shoot footage through an extendable tube some 250 feet (75 meters) in length. The spectacular underwater scenes taken from his "photosphere" were a hit with audiences, and *20,000 Leagues Under the Sea* became a big success. Walt Disney produced a remake of this underwater classic in 1954, investing so heavily in the film that it almost drove the studio into bankruptcy. The cast was new, starring James Mason, Kirk Douglas, and Peter Lorre, but the locations were the same as those used in 1916. Filming took place off the **southwest coast of New Providence** and close to **Lyford Cay** in the extreme west of the island. Although New Providence, only 21 miles (34 kilometers) long, is one of the smaller islands, it is home to the capital city of Nassau, where two thirds of the Bahamian population lives. Film enthusiasts can visit a wealth of underwater locations off the coast, including real shipwrecks and those constructed by film crews as sets and left behind to the delight of divers.

The world's favorite spy proved that there was plenty of action on land as well: In **Thunderball** (1965), Sean Connery variously strolls through Nassau's luxury hotels and casinos in a bespoke suit and chases evildoers while sporting bathing trunks or a diving suit. In the fourth James Bond movie, the dashing secret agent is sent to Nassau in pursuit of SPECTRE,

a group of criminals who have kidnapped a fighter plane armed with two nuclear warheads to blackmail NATO states. Agent 007 makes contact with Domino Derval (Claudine Auger), who takes him by motorboat to **Paradise Beach** in the northwest of **Paradise Island.** Clearly their meeting is not coincidental: Domino is not only the sister of the pilot who kidnapped the plane, but also the mistress of shady millionaire Emilio Largo (Adolfo Celi). Largo resides in the splendid beach villa Palmyra, known as **Rock Point** in

reality and situated on a small promontory on the **north coast of New Providence** off the coastal road of West Bay Street. Largo, whose eye patch makes him into a caricature of a villain, keeps his pool full of sharks for tossing enemies into. In an attempt to get rid of the tiresome 007, Largo puts an ice-cold killer on his trail. Bond shakes her off his trail in the hustle and bustle of the Junkanoo Parade in Nassau. The popular carnival celebration traditionally takes place immediately after Christmas and was reenacted especially for the film.

Bond and Domino get to know one another better on a beautiful palm beach after he has removed a poisonous thorn from her foot and eliminated Largo's killer Vargas (Philip Locke). The north New Providence location is known, appropriately enough, as **Love Beach.** While on a reconnaissance flight over the islands, Bond finally spots the camouflaged wreck of the Vulcan combat bomber: It is submerged under water. The wreck was built for the film and lowered to a depth of approximately 45 feet (15 meters) into the waters near **Clifton Wall,** off the western tip of New Providence. All that remains today is a steel skeleton encrusted with sponges and other ocean plants such as soft corals. The wreck of the sunken freighter *Tears of Allah* lies nearby in a large sandy depression, an important location in the *Thunderball* remake *Never Say Never Again* (1983).

Although *Tears of Allah* was severely damaged by a hurricane a few years ago, both of the well-known "Bond wrecks" still draw numerous tourists. The long fight scene toward the end of *Thunderball,* in which a crowd of agents in diving suits takes on Largo's frogmen in what looks like an elaborately choreographed underwater ballet performed with harpoons, was also filmed close to Clifton Wall. Some sixty divers – actors and camera crew – romped across the ocean floor for this scene. The **Golden Grotto,** also known as **Thunderball Grotto** for its

Only a real fan could love the Beatles' film *Help!* The bizarre story follows the Fab Four from the Alps to the beaches of the Bahamas.

appearance in the film of the same name, is a further location highlight. This wonderful underwater cave is situated near **Staniel Cay** on the **Exumas,** an island chain that extends like a string of pearls south from New Providence. Here Bond is rescued by a CIA contact: 007 dangles dramatically from a helicopter after being pulled out through an opening in the cave's roof. The sunlight filtering through the openings in the roof and glancing off the water makes this an attractive spot in real life as well.

Sean Connery was not the only British star to bring the Bahamas to the attention of enthusiastic fans in the spring of 1965. Just prior to his visit, the Beatles had been in Nassau to film scenes for their surreal comedy **Help!** on **New Providence** and **Paradise islands.** The locals came to marvel at the eight-armed goddess who was supposed to rise dramatically from the waves, but kept toppling over. The filmmakers lost their patience and decided to strike the scene. Non-swimmer Ringo Starr would doubtless have been happy to have skipped this part of the film

Sean Connery in the unofficial Bond film *Never Say Never Again* two decades after *Thunderball.* Stuart Cove's divers work with sharks during a shoot.

schedule completely: In one scene, he was required to jump from a boat into the ocean fully clothed.

Today, would-be divers hoping to conquer their fear of the water can apply to veteran **Stuart Cove** for help. Most divers and filmmakers end up in Cove's **Dive Center** near **Adelaide** in the southwest of New Providence Island. The diving center itself was turned into a film set some years ago when construction managers built a quaint little fishing village here for the remake of *Flipper* (1996), starring Paul Hogan and Elijah Wood. Film fans can still visit the set today. Cove's talents as a shark wrangler are coveted in Hollywood: His first gig was in *For Your Eyes Only*, for which he enticed sharks to swim in front of the camera using bait attached to the end of a spear. The *Thunderball* remake also features a breathtaking shark scene: The unofficial Bond film ***Never Say Never Again*** (1983) showcases the 53-year-old Sean Connery as more than equal to his job alongside Kim Basinger. After Fatima Blush (Barbara Carrera) has lured Bond to the **wreck of *Tears of Allah*** on the ocean floor, he only just manages to escape the jaws of a trio of bloodthirsty tiger sharks.

Cove was also heavily involved in the production of the fantastic shark scenes in the diving drama ***Open Water*** (2003). The low-budget production tells the story of a young couple who get left behind in the open seas after a diving expedition and fall prey to poisonous jellyfish, hungry sharks, and rising panic. Shots taken with a camera that hovered over the water's surface made the threat seem omnipresent and immediate to the viewer. The waters of the Caribbean have seldom seemed so fraught with danger. The remarkably realistic scenes were shot with the help of shark suits – diver's suits intended to protect the wearer from shark attacks, a bit like a bulletproof vest for the sea – a camera cage, and considerable quantities of tuna fish to keep the reef sharks at bay.

The Caribbean is fraught with danger in the diving drama *Open Water*.

James Bond returned to the Caribbean in 2006 with ***Casino Royale*** – this time, in the person of Daniel Craig. The breathtaking opening scene, in which Bond chases a terrorist over

a construction site, was actually filmed in **Coral Harbour** on New Providence Island. The Bahamas shows its glamorous side, too, as Bond sets out to investigate the terrorist Alex Dimitrios (Simon Abkarian) from his bungalow at the swank **Ocean Club** on Paradise Island. He joins a game of poker in the hotel and wins Dimitrios's sports car. The scene was shot in the lobby of the luxury hotel, whilst Bond himself lived at **beach villa 1085.** Dimitrios and his sultry girlfriend Solange (Caterina Murino) reside in the equally deluxe **Albany House** in the southwest of New Providence.

The tried and true recipe for a James Bond adventure: beautiful women and exotic settings like the Ocean Club in the Bahamas in *Casino Royale*.

The 2003 film *Pirates of the Caribbean* was a hit at box offices worldwide. Why? Because no one could resist Johnny Depp as the swashbuckling weirdo Captain Jack Sparrow. The odd outlaw steps casually from the tip of the mast of his sinking ship onto the pier at Port Royal, in reality St. Vincent's Wallilabou Bay.

The Lesser Antilles

Natural beauty and exclusivity characterize the Lesser Antilles, a chain of islands in the eastern Caribbean that stretch from the Virgin Islands to the coast of Venezuela. The island of **St. Vincent** and its little sisters, the **Grenadines,** were hardly known to tourists and filmmakers until a few years ago; visitors were mostly divers and sailors. But sometimes one film is enough to attract the limelight. In this case, it was the blockbuster ***Pirates of the Caribbean: The Curse of the Black Pearl*** (2003), a tongue-in-cheek spectacle that breathed new life into the moribund genre of the pirate film, and made more than $650 million at the box office.

When Elizabeth (Keira Knightley), the beautiful daughter of the Governor of Jamaica, is kidnapped by the dastardly Captain Barbossa (Geoffrey Rush) and his crew, young blood Will Turner (Orlando Bloom) and the eccentric Captain Jack Sparrow (Johnny Depp) take up the chase. Will wants to rescue the girl he loves while Jack's only interest is to save his beloved ship, *The Black Pearl*. The simple story is enlivened by spectacular special effects and a marvelous Johnny Depp, who steals the show with the help of some black eyeliner, rasta braids, and wonderfully campy acting. Producer Jerry Bruckheimer mixed a cocktail of adventure story, turquoise blue seas, and white beaches that proved irresistible to audiences everywhere. Filmmakers resurrected the eighteenth-century version of Jamaica's Port Royal in **Wallilabou Bay** on **St. Vincent,** constructing a lavish set with wooden landing stages and warehouses.

Some of the film's most beautiful landscape scenes were filmed on **Union Island,** in the nature reserve on **Tobago Cays** (not to be confused with the Island of Tobago, which belongs to Trinidad), and on the island of **Dominica.** The scene in which Elizabeth and Captain Sparrow are abandoned on a lonely island by Barbossa was filmed on **Petit Tabac,** one of the most remote islands in Tobago Cay. The beaches' bright white sand and countless coconut palms make the crescent-shaped island a true Caribbean paradise. The two sequels to the pirate movie

In *Pirates of the Caribbean: Dead Man's Chest,* Jack Sparrow stays ahead of a hoard of hungry cannibals on Dominica's Hampstead Beach.

(*Pirates of the Caribbean: Dead Man's Chest* and *Pirates of the Caribbean: At World's End*) were filmed back to back on **St. Vincent** as well as on the Bahamas (**Grand Bahamas** and the **Exumas**) and on the island of **Dominica,** also known as the Caribbean's "Nature Island" for its dense rain forests, water falls, and volcanic hills. Dominica's jungle, with its huge trees, lianas, and streams, served as a perfect setting for the eerie rain-forest scenes in *Pirates of the Caribbean: Dead Man's Chest* (2006). Sparrow and his crew follow the **Indian River** to pay the mysterious fortune-teller Tia Dalma (Naomie Harris) a visit in her treehouse. The cannibal village was built on the southwest coast of Dominica, while the memorable scenes involving a rolling waterwheel, as well as Jack Sparrow's rough and tumble flight from the cannibals, were filmed on **Hampstead Beach** in the island's north.

What was the woman thinking? Elizabeth (Keira Knightley) starts a fire on the tiny isle of Petit Tabac using, of all things, Jack's precious stores of rum.

The Island of Dr. Moreau (1977), based on the novel by H.G. Wells, was filmed in the same year on **St. Croix,** the southernmost of the Virgin Islands. A shipwrecked passenger is brought to an island only to fall into the hands of the crazed Dr. Moreau (Burt Lancaster), who is experimenting with the possibility of turning beasts into men. The lush tropical landscape of **Davis Bay** in the northwest of the island provided the setting for this science fiction classic. Director Luc Besson also shot several scenes for the film *Le Grand Bleu (The Big Blue)* (1988) on St. Croix. **Smuggler's Cove,** a little-known beach on the northwestern tip of the island **Tortola,** recently attracted international attention as the location for a TV film version of Hemingway's classic *The Old Man and the Sea* (1990), starring veteran actor Anthony Quinn as the fisherman Santiago.

Jack pays a visit to fortune-teller Tia Dalma (Naomie Harris) in her jungle treehouse. These scenes from *Pirates of the Caribbean: Dead Man's Chest* were filmed on Dominica's Indian River. The West Indies isle is a jewel of the Caribbean, known for its lush flora, high mountains, and impenetrable rain forests.

One of the most famous diving films ever made was **The Deep,** the most successful movie of 1977 after *Star Wars*. A mustachioed Nick Nolte and a tantalizing Jacqueline Bisset play a couple of amateur divers. While exploring an historic shipwreck, they discover morphine ampoules – which also happen to be of interest to an unscrupulous band of gangsters. Shooting also took place on Bermuda, where the story actually takes place, but the fantastic underwater images, which account for more than half the film, were shot on the **wreck of the *Rhône*,** off the **British Virgin Islands.** The royal mail packet ship sank off the southwest coast of **Salt Island** during a hurricane in 1867 and remains a favorite destination for divers to the present day. Further filming took place at the Peter Island Yacht Club.

The underwater scenes in the *The Deep* with Nick Nolte and Jacqueline Bisset were shot on the wreck of the *Rhône* off the coast of Salt Island.

The 1839 rebellion of African slaves on board the *Amistad* inspired Steven Spielberg to make a movie about the historic events. The fortresses of El Morro and San Cristóbal in San Juan, Puerto Rico, served as film locations.

Puerto Rico: More than Beaches

Thanks to its varied landscapes, from volcanic mountain ranges to long, sandy beaches and dense jungle, as well as its Spanish and African heritage, Puerto Rico has often stood in for other countries – in particular for Cuba, off limits to Hollywood filmmakers because of the U.S. embargo. In Woody Allen's **Bananas** (1971), the island was the setting for the fictitious banana republic of San Marcos. Steven Spielberg used the mighty fortresses of **El Morro** and **San Cristóbal** in San Juan as a location for **Amistad** (1997).

One of the most unusual shooting locations is doubtless the **observatory in Arecibo** on the northern coast that appeared in the James Bond film **GoldenEye** (1995). With its vast parabolic antenna with a depth of over 980 feet (300 meters), the second largest radio telescope in the world can receive radio waves from outer space. Situated in a valley where it is framed by green hills, it seems to hail from another world – and it provided a perfect setting for **Contact** (1997), in which Jodie Foster plays a scientist intent on proving the existence of extraterrestrial civilizations.

In **Lord of the Flies** (1963), filmed largely on **Vieques Island** off the east coast of Puerto Rico, the normally paradisiacal surroundings of the island suddenly take on a threatening aspect. The film version of William Golding's novel sets a group of English schoolboys down on a lonely island following a plane crash.

William Golding's novel *Lord of the Flies* is a terrifying tale of castaway savagery. The 1963 movie was filmed largely on Vieques Island near Puerto Rico.

Not just beautiful beaches, as below: Puerto Rico also offers directors some unusual film locations, too. The Arecibo radio telescope observatory with its gigantic dish appears in the James Bond film *GoldenEye,* and in *Contact* starring Jodie Foster.

Here, in the middle of the jungle, bitter power struggles are soon underway and archaic rituals reassert themselves – all filmed in sharply contrasting black and white. The scenery is also portrayed as varying dramatically, from the broad coves of **Sun Bay** outside Esperanza in the south of the island and **Half Moon Bay** situated further east to dense undergrowth and rugged cliffs. Director Peter Brook shot the film in the hilly area of western Vieques, with its deep gorges and lush mountains, as well as in the **El Yunque mountain region** in the east of Puerto Rico. The fight scenes in which the children confront each other amongst the rocks were shot at the other end of the island, on **Castle Rock** near **Aguadilla.** The dramatic night scenes in which the boys dance around a fire in a state of ecstasy were shot on the beach at Aguadilla.

8

ENGLAND

LITERARY LANDSCAPES   By Claudine Weber-Hof

To all who know and love England, it is the land's exquisite landscapes that most powerfully reflect the deep emotional connection to the island nation. Most moviegoers associate England with gardens that brim with well-tended flower beds and broad, sweeping vistas dotted with peacefully grazing sheep – as in the paintings of John Constable. Masterpieces of British literature are often set against bucolic backdrops. Filmmakers, understandably smitten with such timeless stories, adapt these novels to the silver screen with a great keenness for authenticity.

Britain's great houses play a key role in film. Dyrham Park features in *The Remains of the Day* with Anthony Hopkins as the butler James Stevens.

Variations in the landscape prove immensely important in this regard, their breadth a veritable catalog of atmospheric settings. Softly undulating hills, rugged cliffs, lonesome pony-trodden moors, and snowcapped peaks have helped transport great books from the printed page to larger-than-life visual experiences. Not only the cinematic versions of Jane Austen's well-loved novels, but also Emily Brontë's *Wuthering Heights* and Thomas Hardy's *Far From the Madding Crowd* live from landscape locations that transform them into cinematic journeys.

The canvas upon which filmmakers may paint their portraits of heroes and heroines is broad, a land that stretches from the Lake District and Yorkshire in the north to the snow-brushed mountains of Wales in the west, Kent on the English Channel, and Dorset, Devon, and Cornwall on the south coast. Of course, it pays to be prepared for all kinds of weather when on the movie location trail. Filmmakers struggle to make the most of the sun's intermittent appearances since in England, according to the CIA World Factbook, "more than one half of the days are overcast." The frequency of inclement weather is attributed to the location of the British Isles in a special climate zone where major fronts of warm air from the tropics meet cold air from the North Pole.

Luckily there is drama to be found in bad weather; precipitation is not always considered an ill-timed thing. Some of the most inspiring scenes in film have occurred during downpours. Key events in *Pride & Prejudice* (2005) starring Keira Knightley

Top landscape film locations

1. Alnwick Castle: **Harry Potter** films
2. Sycamore Gap, Hadrian's Wall:
   Robin Hood: Prince of Thieves
3. Malham Cove, Yorkshire Dales: **Wuthering Heights**
4. Nantmor, Ogwen Valley, and Cwm Bychan:
   The Inn of the Sixth Happiness
5. Llanrhaeadr-ym-Mochnant: **The Englishman Who
   Went Up a Hill…**
6. Burghley House, near Stamford: **The Da Vinci Code**
7. Symonds Yat bend, River Wye: **Shadowlands**
8. Peppard Cottage, Henley-on-Thames: **Howards End**
9. "Temple of Apollo," Stourhead Park:
   Pride & Prejudice
10. Maiden Castle earthworks: **Far from the
    Madding Crowd**
11. Efford House, Flete Estate, Erme River estuary:
    Sense and Sensibility
12. Prussia Cove: **Ladies in Lavender**

The cast of *Howards End* posing on the lawn of Peppard Cottage in Henley-on-Thames (left). Kate Winslet in Ang Lee's *Sense and Sensibility* (above).

as well as Ang Lee's *Sense and Sensibility* (1995) with Emma Thompson and Kate Winslet required characters to brave the rain – a metaphor, in most cases, for hardship or heartbreak.

Great Houses and Parks

Britain's homegrown gardening tradition adds a pretty level of sophistication to the island nation's reputation for attractive landscapes. Not all that appears to be the inimitable hand of nature is: In Britain, sculpting scenery into paradisiacal vignettes is a treasured pastime and art form, an obsession whose roots are found in a long love affair with horticultural activity. Gifted artist-gardeners such as Gertrude Jekyll, admired for her garden design at the turn of the twentieth century, inherited the tradition of "painting with landscapes" already established by giants of park design like Capability Brown. The eighteenth-century landscape architect to such estates as Blenheim Palace is famous for establishing a more "naturalistic" looking park, known today as the paradigmatic English country garden.

Meandering paths, placid, perfectly placed lakes, incidental architectural follies such as miniature classical temples or neo-gothic towers – these aspects of playful landscape "set design" embellish the parks of Britain's great houses, many of which are maintained by the National Trust. Several of these manses and their breathtaking grounds have appeared in recent films.

A bluebell wood, one of Britain's most exquisite types of landscape and a haunting memory from Leonard's dream-like walk in *Howards End*.

The State Room and exteriors of Burghley House near Stamford, Lincolnshire, appear as Castel Gandolfo in *The Da Vinci Code* (2006) starring Tom Hanks and Audrey Tautou. The great house also appears as Rosings in *Pride & Prejudice*.

Dyrham Park near Bath provided the exteriors in *The Remains of the Day* (1993), **Syon House** and **Wrotham Park** close to London stood in for *Gosford Park* (2001), and **Burghley House** near **Stamford,** Lincolnshire, featured with its stunning interiors as Castel Gandolfo in *The Da Vinci Code* (2006).

Ismail Merchant and James Ivory also employed typically English country houses and their gardens for lovely settings, memorably shooting *Howards End* (1992) at **Peppard Cottage** in Henley-on-Thames, Oxfordshire, and scenes from *A Room with a View* (1985) – the Honeychurch residence of Windy Corner – at a gabled private house called **Foxwold** close to Brasted in Kent. Bastions, universities, and churches in the landscape have proffered film-worthy backdrops as well: **Alnwick Castle** in Northumberland, which also features in *Elizabeth* (1998), is best known as the exterior of the Hogwarts School of Witchcraft and Wizardry from the famous high-speed quidditch scenes in the **Harry Potter** film series. These landmark edifices provide filmmakers with backdrops for drama, but also focal points in typically English landscapes. Such scenery is as ineluctably connected to English identity as hedgerows, rabbit-filled downs, and Wordsworth's immortal daffodils.

Jane Austen's England

Nowhere do the great gardens and sweeping vistas of England feature more beautifully than in the film versions of England's great novels. The works of Jane Austen (1775-1817) are classics of literature universally loved in the English-speaking world, and revered through careful translations that have made the stories popular the world over. No wonder the books have been adapted time and again to the silver screen, with such well-known titles as *Pride and Prejudice* first premiering in theaters in 1940 with Laurence Olivier as the inscrutable bachelor Mr. Darcy. The treasured tales of class friction enjoy a particular resonance with contemporary audiences, thanks in part to two recent productions. Ang Lee's *Sense and Sensibility* (1995) and Joe Wright's *Pride & Prejudice* (2005) wowed filmgoers with well-edited shots of the English countryside and extensive use of great houses and their gardens.

The Sensuous South in *Sense and Sensibility*

Actress Emma Thompson wrote the screenplay for *Sense and Sensibility,* a tale of three marriageable sisters and their

In *Sense and Sensibility,* the Dashwoods must leave their elegant home at Saltram House in Plympton in Devon (above) and search for new lodgings.

Elinor (Emma Thompson) writes to estate agents about a new house. Luckily, a relative invites the family from *Sense and Sensibility* to live in Barton Cottage. The new Dashwood home was filmed in the pretty estuary landscapes of Efford House on the private grounds of Flete Estate near Plymouth.

mother, Mrs. Dashwood (Gemma Jones). Central to the story is the problem of inheritance: Mr. Dashwood has died, and his estate must pass to his son from a first marriage. The Dashwoods are forced to leave their home at Norland Park – in reality **Saltram House,** a white Georgian manse with eighteenth-century interiors by design legend Robert Adam that is located in **Plympton** near **Plymouth** in the southwestern county of **Devon.** The eldest daughter, Elinor (Emma Thompson), writes to agents in search of new lodgings. Luckily a well-meaning relative invites the family to live in Barton Cottage on his estate of Barton Park, filmed at **Efford House** on the private grounds of **Flete Estate** near Plymouth. The modest house becomes the backdrop to the family's trials and tribulations as they attempt to find their place in society. Visitors hoping to see the holiday cottage should contact the estate. Accommodations may be found at the Mildmay Colours Inn in **Holbeton.**

Broad vistas of the sloping, hedge-lined fields behind **Efford House** and the **Erme River** estuary at the cottage's front door paint a pretty picture of country life. Still, the sisters – in particular Elinor, but especially the fetching Marianne (Kate Winslet) – spend much of their time fretting over suitors. Elinor pines quietly for the introspective Edward Ferrars (Hugh Grant) while Marianne dreams of the handsome and irrepressible John Willoughby (Greg Wise). The sisters fall in love with their respective admirers soon after taking up residence at Barton Cottage, only to learn that neither man

Pride & Prejudice's **Elizabeth and Mr. Darcy at the Bennet family home, filmed at Groombridge Place.**

may marry as he wishes. Edward harbors a dark secret, and Willoughby proves himself to be an incorrigible cad. Elinor tries to stay "sensible" and represses her emotions, much unlike her younger sister. Marianne casts caution to the wind, leaving everything up to her tempestuous "sensibilities."

When Willoughby slights Marianne at a fancy dress ball in London, events take a turn for the worse. Shooting these scenes was a complex undertaking that involved 250 extras and 120 technicians working for ten days in the famous gilt rooms of **Wilton House** in Wilton, Wiltshire, just west of Salisbury. The house also featured in *The Madness of King George* (1994) and *Pride & Prejudice* (2005), and is renowned for its Single and Double Cube Rooms. The famous **Queen's House** by Palladian architect Inigo Jones at **Greenwich,** London, part of the Greenwich Maritime Museum, also features in the London scenes, as does the capital city's **Chandos House.** Marianne returns in tears to the residence of her hostess, Mrs. Jennings

(Elizabeth Spriggs), shot in Wiltshire at the brick pile of **Mompesson House**, **The Close,** in **Salisbury**'s city center. Elinor decides that they should return to the country at once, accompanied by Colonel Brandon (Alan Rickman), one of Marianne's admirers from Devon, and their friends the Palmers. En route, they stop at the Palmers' residence, Cleveland, and alight to take tea.

The rural charm of England again takes center stage at **Montacute House** in Montacute village near Yeovil, Somerset, an Elizabethan mansion that stands in for the Palmers' estate. Marianne wanders out onto the fields surrounding the estate in the hopes of seeing Willoughby's house from the top of a nearby hill. When a storm unleashes heavy rains, Colonel Brandon sets out to find her. He carries her bedraggled form over the **Cedar Lawn** behind Montacute House and into the great hall marked with a trio of Renaissance stone arches. The manse, which also featured in **The Libertine** (2004), starring Johnny Depp, becomes Marianne's prison as she succumbs to an "infectious fever." She recovers and returns home to the sunny estuary landscape of Barton Cottage and the promise of a more loyal suitor. Both women finally find happiness, as depicted in the merry wedding scenes at the quaint **Church** of **St. Mary** at **Berry Pomeroy** some 25 miles (40 kilometers) east of Plymouth in Devon.

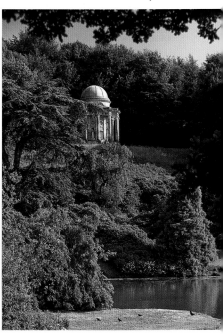

Keira Knightley as Lizzie in *Pride & Prejudice* on rocky Stanage Edge in the Peak District.

(2005). The young filmmaker thrilled moviegoers by winning the immensely popular Keira Knightley for the role of Elizabeth or "Lizzie." Casting Brenda Blethyn as the tittering Mrs. Bennet alongside Donald Sutherland as her down-to-earth husband added humor and charm to the production. The eighteenth-century tale of five sisters – Jane, Elizabeth, Mary, Kitty, and Lydia – begins as many an Austen narrative

Mr. Darcy's imposing estate, Chatsworth House (center). Lizzie braves the rain and her suitor in the "Temple of Apollo" at Stourhead gardens, one of Britain's most famous landscapes.

From Kent to the Peak District: *Pride & Prejudice*

The enthusiasm that greeted *Sense and Sensibility* in the mid-'90s left audiences with an appetite for Jane Austen that director Joe Wright would satisfy a decade later in **Pride & Prejudice**

does: with the challenge and eventual necessity of getting married. The story opens at the Bennet family's house, Longbourn, filmed at **Groombridge Place** near Tunbridge Wells on the border of Kent and East Sussex. Here Lizzie leads a carefree life amid the delightful gardens and endless green fields of her childhood home, a setting that conveys the innocence of youth. Inevitably, her mother brings up the problem of getting married: Like the women of *Sense and Sensibility*, Lizzie and her sisters will be left penniless when their father passes away. The estate will go to a male heir, the Bennet sisters' unsavory cousin Mr. Collins (Tom Hollander).

Nothing would be more convenient than for Mr. Collins to choose one of the Bennet girls to be his bride and live at his parish at Rosings, the imposing estate belonging to his benefactress, Lady Catherine de Bourg (Judi Dench). When Mr. Collins asks for the hand of the eldest daughter, Mrs. Bennet informs him that Jane (Rosamund Pike) is soon to be engaged to Mr. Bingley (Simon Woods), the wealthy bachelor she met at a ball held at his house, Netherfield Park. The great Palladian pile of **Basildon Park** near Reading in Berkshire, 40 miles (65 kilometers) west of London, served as the location for these merry scenes, in particular the Octagon Drawing Room and the west front and loggia. The fête is central to the plot: Lizzie meets Mr. Darcy (Matthew Macfadyen) at the dance, and when he snubs her, it confirms her prejudice that the rich are obnoxiously proud of their social position.

Mr. Collins eventually finds a bride in the practical and plain Charlotte Lucas (Claudie Blakley). Lizzie agrees to visit the newlyweds as they settle into their cottage on the grounds of the Rosings estate. **Burghley House** near **Stamford,** Lincolnshire, some 100 miles (160 kilometers) north of London, stood in for Rosings, whose State Room and exteriors appeared as Castel Gandolfo in *The Da Vinci Code* (2006). Lady Catherine deigns to grant Mr. Collins and his womenfolk an audience in the famous Heaven Room, a scene that again casts Lizzie in a defiant, wilful light.

Landscapes begin to play a prominent role in *Pride & Prejudice* when Mr. Darcy realizes he's in love. Nothing could have shocked Lizzie more than her encounter with Mr. Darcy in an English country garden. Out walking on her own, she escapes a downpour by sheltering in a tiny round temple set in vast parkland. The **"Temple of Apollo"** is a defining architectural feature of England's most famous landscape garden, **Stourhead,** designed by Henry Hoare in the mid-eighteenth century. Mr. Darcy appears out of nowhere and begs Lizzie to marry him. She refuses his proposal, accusing him of having blocked the match between her penniless sister Jane and shy Mr. Bingley.

Having eluded her suitor, Lizzie accepts an invitation from friends to visit the Lake District, renowned as the home of the Romantic poet William Wordsworth. A stop along the way is Pemberley, Mr. Darcy's estate, and Lizzie reluctantly tags along to view the grounds and rooms open to visitors. Imposing **Chatsworth House,** close to the town of **Bakewell,** some 160 miles (260 kilometers) northwest of London, served as Pemberley. The private country house set in **Derbyshire's Peak District National Park** makes a big impression on Lizzie, especially the **grand stair** in the **Painted Hall** and the **Sculpture Gallery** where

she admires a bust of Darcy. Fans of actor Pete Postlethwaite will recall sweeping shots of Derbyshire – **Burbage Rocks** and **Millstone Edge** in particular – in *Among Giants* (1998). The breathtaking Peak District also features in the dream sequence in which Lizzie stands on a rocky outcropping at **Stanage Edge.** Also in Derbyshire, historic **Haddon Hall** stands in for the inn at Lambton where the travelers rest, the same medieval building that featured as Thornfield Hall in Franco Zeffirelli's *Jane Eyre* (1996). The gilt interiors of Mr. Darcy's manse were filmed

Historic Haddon Hall in Derbyshire is Thornfield Hall in Franco Zeffirelli's *Jane Eyre,* with Charlotte Gainsbourg in the title role.

at **Wilton House** in **Wiltshire** near Salisbury. Much to Lizzie's dismay, Mr. Darcy is indeed in residence, but as in many an Austen tale, the chance encounter leads ultimately to the story's happy end.

The Wuthering Heights of Yorkshire

Long before he helped to make Audrey Hepburn a household name in *Roman Holiday* (1953), William Wyler took on one of the greats of English literature: **Wuthering Heights** (1939). The heartrending love story of Emily Brontë's 1847 novel takes on stark visual drama in the black-and-white feature film starring Merle Oberon as Cathy and Laurence Olivier as her moody admirer, Heathcliff. The novel, set in Yorkshire, depends upon topography for the punch in its plot: Cathy and Heathcliff's secret rendezvous point at Penistone Crag, a rocky outcropping on the moors that they nicknamed "the castle," serves as the decisive landscape of passion and tragedy in the film. Wyler went no further than the Conejo Hills in the Thousand Oaks area of the Santa Monica Mountains north of Los Angeles to make the movie, however. Author Graham Greene wasted no time in denouncing the choice of a "Californian-constructed Yorkshire" as singularly unsatisfying.

Ralph Fiennes and Juliette Binoche offer an entirely different dimension to the story in the 1992 production of **Wuthering Heights,** one of the first films to feature Fiennes in a lead role before his breakthrough performances in *Schindler's List* (1993) and *The English Patient* (1996). The torrid affair takes place on the Pennine **moors,** north of the Brontë family's hometown of Haworth in North Yorkshire. The only novel that Emily Brontë wrote before her death in 1848 acquires an almost surreal quality, with Fiennes playing a hunky Heathcliff to Binoche's headstrong Cathy. The brutal tug-of-war over Cathy between Edgar Linton (Simon Shepherd) and Heathcliff, shown toiling for his living at **East Riddleston Hall** in **Keighley,** West Yorkshire,

Merle Oberon as Cathy and Laurence Olivier as Heathcliff in William Wyler's *Wuthering Heights,* filmed in a "Californian-constructed Yorkshire."

is ideally underscored by the film's harsh landscape setting. Cathy and Heathcliff meet at **Aysgarth Falls,** but more hauntingly amidst the rocky stretches of limestone "pavement" of **Malham Cove** near **Grassington** in the **Yorkshire Dales,** a geological wonder of the Ice Age that reflects the utter hopelessness of their romance. **Broughton Hall** at **Skipton,** also in Yorkshire, a private house that often appears in films, stands in as the Linton family residence of Thrushcross Grange. The townsfolk of Grassington are credited with helping erect sets, in particular of the house of Wuthering Heights.

Children's Film Favorites

As universally loved as its "great books" are the numerous classic children's tales set in England. Arthur Ransome's 1930 story *Swallows and Amazons* (1974) was filmed to popular acclaim in the Lake District, where the story is set. Better known internationally, however, is Frances Hodgson Burnett's book

The heartrending love story of Emily Brontë's novel takes on stark visual drama in Ralph Fiennes and Juliette Binoche's 1992 version of *Wuthering Heights.* The love affair between Heathcliff and Cathy was filmed in England's beautiful north, amidst the rocky stretches of limestone "pavement" of Malham Cove in the Yorkshire Dales. This geological wonder of the Ice Age reflects the hopelessness of their romance.

The Secret Garden was filmed in several different English gardens.

The Secret Garden, published in 1911. Supposedly inspired by a walled garden at Great Maytham Hall, Rolvenden, in Kent, the tale of orphan Mary Lennox was first filmed in a studio-bound version in 1949. The charming 1993 reinterpretation braved the outdoors, seeking to recreate the story's fabled garden.

Mary (Kate Maberly) is a child when she loses both of her parents to a tragedy in India. Shipped back to England to become a ward of her uncle, Lord Craven (John Lynch), she discovers a boy locked away in his drafty manor house: her sickly cousin Colin (Heydon Prowse). Mary becomes a crusader for her invalid cousin's health, much to the dismay of Mrs. Medlock (Maggie Smith), the uncompromising housekeeper whose orders are to keep the sick child sheltered and quiet. Against her wishes, Mary sneaks Colin out onto the grounds of the fictitious Mistlethwaite Manor and into a secret walled garden she has discovered. While a garden is often used as a metaphor for Eden or innocence lost, here it serves as a simile for the self. Tending, planting, and caring for the flowers, trees, and shrubs brings both the little patch of earth and the children back to life.

To conjure the estate, its grounds, and the garden, shots were edited together from three main sources. **Luton Hoo** near Luton in **Hertfordshire** hosted the scenes of the children frolicking with animals over lush, green lawns. The eighteenth-century building originally planned by architect Robert Adam is surrounded by extensive parklands that were laid out by Capability Brown in 1767. **Allerton Park** in North Yorkshire, between Harrogate and York, also contributed several scenes. So did the Elizabethan mansion of **Fountains Hall** at **Fountains Abbey** with **Studley Royal Water Garden** in Ripon, North Yorkshire, which stood in for exterior shots of Lord Craven's house. The estate, a UNESCO World Heritage site, features the ruins of a twelfth-century Cistercian abbey on its grounds, as well as a Georgian water garden complete with ornamental cascades and lakes.

Robin Hood's Landscapes of Adventure

A classic beloved of children over the centuries, **Robin Hood: Prince of Thieves** (1991) is popular with adults and kids alike thanks to wickedly comical performances by some of Britain's finest actors. Unlike the original 1938 classic movie – *The Adventures of Robin Hood* (1938), starring Errol Flynn and filmed entirely in California – director Kevin Reynolds's version boasts breathtaking U.K. locations. And despite additions to the storyline for comic relief, the screenplay stays reasonably true to the twelfth-century tale: Robin (Kevin Costner) returns to England from the Crusades with Azeem (Morgan Freeman), a Moor whose life he

Hadrian's Wall and the tree at Sycamore Gap (above) feature in *Robin Hood: Prince of Thieves*, as do the Seven Sisters cliffs.

had saved in Jerusalem. They cross the English Channel and see the bright **chalk cliffs** of the **Seven Sisters** near Eastbourne in Sussex; Robin is home, and hopes to mend fences with his estranged father, Lord Locksley (Brian Blessed).

But bad news awaits: The dastardly sheriff of Nottingham (Alan Rickman) has murdered his father and seized the family lands. **Old Wardour Castle** in Wiltshire stands in for Locksley Castle. His next stop is Northumberland's **Hulne Priory** at Alnwick, the abode of love interest Maid Marian (Mary Elizabeth Mastrantonio), cousin to the absent King Richard "The Lionheart." The age-old tale of Robin Hood and his merry men who rob the rich to help the poor shifts into high gear with fight scenes that underscore the windswept beauty of England's north.

The battle between Robin and the sheriff's cronies at **Hadrian's Wall** in Northumberland, filmed at **Sycamore Gap** near **mile castle 39** – named for the distinctive tree standing between two hills – pits Robin against the sheriff's evil cousin, Guy of Gisborne (Michael Wincott). The action takes place on part of the 84-mile (135-kilometer) Hadrian's Wall Path National Trail that connects the coasts of Britain, a route from Wallsend in the east to Bowness-on-Solway in the west. The route follows the ancient Roman fortification that once stretched 74 miles (119 kilometers) across the country's narrow waist. Emperor Hadrian ordered the wall built to demarcate the northern border of his imperial holdings. It would be extended 100 years later under Severus's reign. While it survives only in fragmentary form, the wall is still considered one of the great remaining monuments of Roman Britain.

The adventures continue as Robin faces off against John Little (Nick Brimble) at **Aysgarth Falls** on the River Ure in **Yorkshire Dales National Park,** his first encounter with the band of vagabonds he will lead against Nottingham's forces. After besting his large, congenial opponent and dubbing him "Little John,"

Robin and the outlaws agree to join forces and erect a camp not in Sherwood Forest, as fans of the tale might hope, but in a combination of locations that includes **Burnham Beeches** (close to London's Shepperton Studios), Yorkshire Dales National Park, and the **New Forest** in Hampshire. Much of the action takes place in a Nottingham erected at Shepperton, but exterior shots of the walled city were provided by Carcassonne, France.

On the Movie Trail of Thomas Hardy

The novelist and poet best known for his tales published in the 1890s, especially *Tess of the D'Urbervilles* and *Jude the Obscure,* was born in the southern county of Dorset, which borders Devon on the east. He set his stories in the countryside, narrating the lives and times of farm folk whose hopes and dreams unfurl in a radiant, thriving landscape. No writer captures the beauty of the south quite like Hardy, whose powers of observation embroider his chapters like a tapestry.

Perhaps no better example of Hardy's country-set dramas exists in cinema than *Far from the Madding Crowd* (1967), directed by John Schlesinger and starring a buxom young Julie Christie as Bathsheba Everdene. Her main admirer, Farmer Oak (Alan Bates), is too poor to wed. He loses everything when his sheepdog drives his flock over the chalk cliffs to the sea below. These scenes were filmed in the valley of **Scratchy Bottom** in Lulworth, Dorset, part of a coastline that is a UNESCO World Heritage site and that most visitors know for the famous Durdle Door natural cliff arch. For Oak, these dramatic vistas represent a plunge into poverty and ruin.

Demoted from farmer to laborer, Oak grudgingly takes a job on the farm that Bathsheba has unexpectedly inherited. The landscapes of Dorset feature in lending epic proportions to the tangled courtships Oak witnesses as local men try to win Bathsheba's heart: the swashbuckling displays of the handsome and

A young Julie Christie stars as Bathsheba Everdene in *Far from the Madding Crowd*. Troy uses his sword exercises to win her on the slopes of Maiden Castle.

Cornwall as a seaside cliché: Novels such as Daphne du Maurier's *Jamaica Inn* and *Rebecca* conveyed the peril of its rugged moors and coastlines. And yet to many, Cornwall is a sort of Floridian paradise by the water's edge. Movies and television shows use its romantic landscapes to fuel this impression.

cruel Sergeant Troy (Terence Stamp) and the pathetic efforts of stodgy Farmer Boldwood (Peter Finch), whose stately residence is represented by the private **Friar Waddon House, Weymouth,** close to the Dorset coast. Bathsheba's home, where she first connives to send poor Boldwood a valentine, is much further inland at **Bloxworth House, Bere Regis,** Dorset. The sword exercise scenes where Sergeant Troy takes Bathsheba's breath away are made unforgettable by their location, filmed on the green and gold slopes of **Maiden Castle,** an ancient set of earthworks just outside of Dorchester. Given the majestic setting, it is little wonder that Bathsheba loses her heart.

The young farm mistress first discovers how bad Troy really is when she hears of the fate of his betrothed. The deeply wronged Fanny (Prunella Ransome) perishes in a poorhouse and is buried in the churchyard, tear-jerking scenes that take place below one of the eleven gargoyles of St. Nicholas Church, filmed at **Sydling St. Nicholas,** a few miles north of Dorchester. Locations in Wiltshire include **Devizes,** which stood in for the town of Casterbridge, and **Gold Hill** in Shaftesbury, where Fanny walks alone to her fate. The **Tithe Barn,** on **New Barn Road** in historic **Abbotsbury,** Dorset, is the setting of the wedding party that goes terribly awry, signaling the capriciousness of Bathsheba's first marriage.

Director Roman Polanski saw to it that Hardy's *Tess* (1979), starring Nastassja Kinski in the title role, was as sensuously depicted on the big screen as it was in the novel. But all the landscapes here – including the key scenes at Stonehenge – were filmed in France. Another tragic female figure of literature, *The French Lieutenant's Woman* (1981) of John Fowles's classic novel, made her mark on the Dorset coast, however. Meryl Streep bewitches Jeremy Irons by walking the **Lyme Regis** seawall amidst the crashing surf in a hooded cape, a role that won her a Best Actress Oscar nomination. The iconic final scenes, far more calm and serene, were filmed at Lake Windermere in the Lake District.

Cornwall: A Cinematographer's Seaside Delight

Increasingly over the years, and to the chagrin of longtime residents, Cornwall has grown in popularity as a place for out-of-towners to purchase holiday homes, or to spend a week by the sea. A drive down the southern coast past St. Austell takes you close to the **Eden Project** biosphere, a futuristic backdrop to James Bond's (Pierce Brosnan) adventures in *Die Another Day* (2002). The route continues on to **Falmouth,** where Bela Lugosi starred in *The Mystery of the Marie Celeste* (1935) after

Ladies in Lavender is an ode to Cornwall's seaside majesty. Maggie Smith and Judi Dench play the elderly sisters Janet and Ursula Widdington. One morning they find a mysterious foreign youth washed up on the beach below their cottage at Prussia Cove, a famous smuggler's haven.

he was immortalized as the bloodthirsty count in *Dracula* (1931). The area also provided seascapes for **Treasure Island** (1950), featuring **Falmouth Harbour** and **Carrick Roads** – which combine to form the third largest natural harbor in the world – as well as the **River Fal, Helford River,** and **Gull Rock.**

Cornwall's topography grows more dramatic the farther southwest you go, but even the Lizard peninsula and pirate-haven Penzance reveal a thoroughgoing gentrification of once modest agricultural and fishing communities, changes funded, in great part, by tourist outlays. Just before rounding Land's End, the English mainland's westernmost point, lovers of landscape drama stop to take a gander at **St. Michael's Mount,** the Benedictine priory and fortress reminiscent of its namesake off the coast of Normandy. The fortified retreat that stands on an island at high tide is featured in funny-man Rowan Atkinson's spoof **Johnny English** (2003).

Lovers of landscape drama must visit St. Michael's Mount, a fortified retreat that appears in funny-man Rowan Atkinson's spoof *Johnny English*.

The north coast, long beloved of artists, is now the home to well-known museums and galleries, such as the Tate Museum in the former fishing village of St. Ives. The comedy **Saving Grace** (2000) about a widow who manages to keep her home by cultivating marijuana showcased North Cornwall's gardening savoir vivre and fishing village charm, with the gorgeous coastlines and rolling greens of **Port Isaac, Bosinney, Boscastle,** and **Trebarwith** sharing the spotlight.

Despite the inevitable tide of progress in Cornwall, the world beyond Britain still views Cornwall as a seaside cliché. Novels such as Daphne du Maurier's *Jamaica Inn* and *Rebecca* – the latter, starring Laurence Olivier and Joan Fontaine, was filmed in 1939 by Alfred Hitchcock entirely in California – conveyed the peril of the rugged moors and coastlines. And yet to many, Cornwall is quite simply a sort of Floridian paradise by the water's edge. Fuelling this impression are the television adaptations of numerous novels by Cornish-born author Rosamunde Pilcher, rich in romantic landscapes. The airing of these films on Germany's public ZDF channel unleashed a storm of vaca-

The green and gold landscapes of the Powys region in Wales (above) feature prominently in the Hugh Grant film *The Englishman Who Went Up a Hill But Came Down a Mountain.* Filming locations include the village of Llanrhaeadr-ym-Mochnant and the nearby mountain of Gyrn Moelfre.

tion-hungry Continentals on Cornwall, an effect that garnered both the author and the series editor the 2002 British Tourism Award. Pilcher was also dubbed an Officer of the Order of the British Empire that same year.

The considerable charms of the far southwest continue to bewitch filmmakers, with actor Charles Dance's screenwriting and directorial debut **Ladies in Lavender** (2004), an ode to Cornwall's seaside majesty. Judi Dench and Maggie Smith play the elderly sisters Ursula and Janet Widdington, who find a mysterious foreign youth washed up on a rocky beach near their house. The year is 1936, and the half-drowned Andrea (Daniel Brühl) turns out to be a Polish concert violinist – a discovery made by the enchanting Russian visitor Olga (Natascha McElhone). The house where much of the story unfolds is a cliff-top cottage at **Prussia Cove,** a famous smuggler's haven. Scenes were shot at **Cadgwith** – a fishing village with a pretty blue cove – and **Helston,** where the sisters order clothes for their houseguest, as well as on the **Lizard Peninsula** and in **St. Ives. Waddesdon Estate** near

Oxford provided several salons, with numerous other interiors shot at **Harrow Boarding School** in London.

Wales in Film: From Ingrid Bergman to James Bond

Cymru to its inhabitants and Wales to the rest of the world, the western peninsula of Britain between the Irish Sea and the Bristol Channel is a paradise for nature-loving holidaymakers. The nation's landscape is stunningly defined by the Cambrian Mountains, and its famous peaks include Snowdon (3,560 feet/1,085 meters), Plynlimon (2,468 feet/752 meters), and Cadair Idris (2,970 feet/905 meters). The English counties that border Wales to the east – Cheshire, Shropshire, Herefordshire, and Gloucestershire – still retain a distinct Welsh flavor, despite the district lines agreed upon when the two nations joined in 1536. Wales, while still culturally distinct, belongs to Britain.

To Ingrid Bergman, Wales belonged to Northern China. In the film ***The Inn of the Sixth Happiness*** (1958), the Swedish-

Is it a hill or a mountain? Hugh Grant as cartographer Reginald Anson intends to scale the slopes of Gyrn Moelfre to find out the truth – with a little help from the inventive villagers and a local beauty named Betty (Tara Fitzgerald).

The story is based upon a tale once told to the writer-director Christopher Monger about his birthplace, the town of Taff's Well, or Ffynnon Taf, and Garth Mountain, both close to the capital of Cardiff. Since these locations in southern Wales would no longer do for filming purposes – they were far too modern-looking – the town of **Llanrhaeadr-ym-Mochnant** and the nearby green slopes of **Gyrn Moelfre** were chosen to help conjure Taff's Well during the first quarter of the twentieth century. The movie's success attracted no end of walkers who flocked to Garth Mountain. Visitors are relieved to learn that the Ordnance Survey records Garth as measuring in at 1,007 feet (307 meters), thus making it, quite officially, a mountain.

Slopes of another sort in Wales turned out to be a saving grace for David Lean's classic **Lawrence of Arabia** (1962). The movie starred Peter O'Toole in the title role, along with Alec Guinness, Anthony Quinn, and Omar Sharif, and boasted a laundry list of exotic film locations – especially the red ridges of Wadi Rum, Jordan, and the sand-surrounded settlement of Aït Benhaddou in Morocco. The dunes at **Merthyr Mawr Warren** near **Bridgend,** in South Wales, also served to augment the movie's desert scenes. Those who recall **The Lion in Winter** (1968) with Katharine Hepburn, Peter O'Toole, Anthony Hopkins, and Timothy Dalton in his first film role may wish to head west to visit **Pembroke Castle** and **Marloes Sands** in Pembrokeshire, where Welsh shores once again played a pretty background to a classic Hollywood film.

Not all films shot in Wales enjoyed great critical success: Jerry Zucker's telling of the Arthurian legend in **First Knight** (1995), starring Sean Connery as King Arthur, Richard Gere as Lancelot, and Julia Ormond as the irresistible Guinevere, is one.

To film Jerry Zucker's telling of the Arthurian legend in *First Knight,* a power station at Snowdonia National Park's Trawsfynydd Lake near Ffestiniog was transformed into the towering ramparts of Camelot.

born actress plays Gladys Aylward, a woman who traveled to China as a missionary in the late 1920s during the Sino-Japanese war. **Nantmor** and **Ogwen Valley** and valleys around Beddgelert in Gwynedd, North Wales, provided the rugged landscape of the Middle Kingdom, perhaps most memorably filmed on a hill behind Nantmor called **Cwm Bychan.** Here, set designers erected the frontage for the walled Chinese city of Yang Cheng along a ridge, one of several elaborate sets created in Wales as well as at Ealing Studios in London. The film also starred Robert Donat as the Mandarin of Yang Cheng, the last role he played before his death the following year.

A real Welsh town and a nearby peak featured in the Hugh Grant hit **The Englishman Who Went Up a Hill But Came Down a Mountain** (1995). The northern Welsh village of **Llanrhaeadr-ym-Mochnant** west of Owestry in the Powys region served as the fictitious town of Ffynnon Garw that Grant's character, Reginald Anson, and his portly boss, George Garrad (Ian McNeice), visit in 1917. The mountain the cartographers aim to survey, also called Ffynnon Garw, is the pride of the town. To the disgust of the locals, Garrad and Anson ascertain that it is a few feet shy of 1,000 feet in height, making it a mere "hill." The villagers scheme to increase its height by some sixteen feet using methods most unconventional, and, above all, top secret.

The English county of Herefordshire on the border with Wales delivered the bittersweet final sequences in Richard Attenborough's *Shadowlands*. The director stands before the "Golden Valley," a bend in the River Wye.

While not universally adored, the technological magic that production designer John Box commanded for the film's "look" is legendary. He and his crew transformed a power station in North Wales at **Snowdonia National Park**'s **Trawsfynydd Lake** near Ffestiniog into the towering ramparts of Camelot. Scenes were also shot in the landscape near the town of **Blaenau Ffestiniog**, with subterranean scenes courtesy of **Llanfair Slate Mine**, Harlech, Gwynedd. Roman Polanski's **Macbeth** (1971) was also filmed near Harlech, as well as at Morfa Bychan and Ffestiniog. Snowdonia hosted Ron Howard's fantastical **Willow** (1988), the story of an apprentice magician, at **Llanberis**, where several scenes of the tale's Nockmaar Castle were filmed. Given Snowdonia's dramatic peaks and lakes, it is no surprise that Sean Connery paid a visit as James Bond in **From Russia with Love** (1963).

While not quite Wales, the English county of Herefordshire on its border delivered the bittersweet final sequence of scenes of Richard Attenborough's **Shadowlands** (1993). The C.S. Lewis biopic starring Anthony Hopkins as the famed author and Debra Winger as his wife is generally short on landscapes, as most

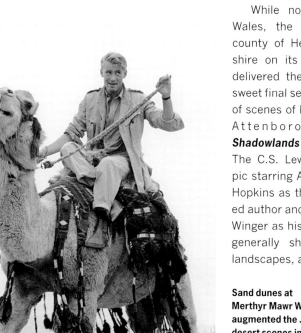

Sand dunes at Merthyr Mawr Warren augmented the Jordanian desert scenes in David Lean's classic film *Lawrence of Arabia*.

Anthony Hopkins and Debra Winger in the C.S. Lewis biopic *Shadowlands*.

of the movie was filmed at Oxford. But its dramatic close uses the countryside of this region as a metaphor for the fleeting happiness of love found late in life. The couple set off on a final journey together to a place called Golden Valley, spending the night at **Pengethley Manor Hotel** close to Ross-on-Wye before driving through a bucolic paradise filmed at the picturesque **Symonds Yat** bend in the **River Wye**.

9

SCOTLAND

HIGHLAND DRAMA — By Claudine Weber-Hof

Scotland's movie appeal can be summed up in two words: the Highlands. The mist-veiled, mountainous landscapes and isles coveted by Norse invaders and English overlords for millennia have cast spells on directors as diverse as Alfred Hitchcock with *The 39 Steps* (1935), Terry Gilliam and Terry Jones with *Monty Python and The Holy Grail* (1975), and Mel Gibson with *Braveheart* (1995). No matter the genre – thriller, comedy, or historic epic – the upper reaches of the United Kingdom's most steadfastly independent but geographically contiguous nation exert an enduring attraction for directors who crave dramatic landscapes for their productions.

Bounded by the Atlantic Ocean to the north and west and the city of Stirling, the "gateway to the Highlands," in the south, this region is known first and foremost as a hiker's paradise. Its mountains, lakes, or *lochs,* valleys or *glens,* and vast heathered moors are traversed annually by more than 50,000 visitors who come to walk the famed West Highland Way between Milngavie near Glasgow and Fort

Fans of the Harry Potter books and the films that followed come to watch the West Highland Railway train – better known as Hogwarts Express – take the curve over the Glenfinnan Viaduct.

William in the Highlands. From golfer's nirvana Loch Lomond in the south over the Highland Boundary Fault and up into the fabled homelands of clans such as the MacLeans and the Campbells, the 94-mile (152-kilometer) journey is a voyage of discovery similar to the one that moviegoers make when viewing Scotland's Highland expanses on the silver screen. The breathtaking transition from the sweeping grasslands of the central moors to the wilder slopes of the highest peaks or *munros* is as dramatic as it is memorable.

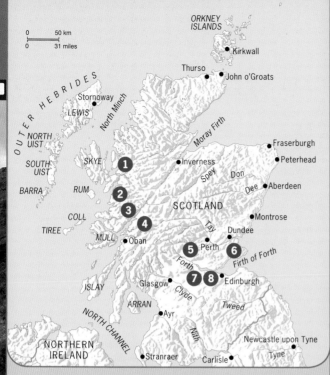

Top landscape film locations

1. Eilean Donan: **Highlander**
2. Silver Sands, Camusdarach, Morar: **Local Hero**
3. Glennfinnan Viaduct: **Harry Potter** series
4. Glen Coe: **Braveheart**
5. Castle Doune: **Monty Python and the Holy Grail**
6. West Sands, St. Andrews: **Chariots of Fire**
7. Blackness Castle: **Hamlet, Macbeth**
8. Firth of Forth: **The 39 Steps**

The Hogwarts trio in 2001: Rupert Grint as Ron Weasley, Daniel Radcliffe as Harry Potter, and Emma Watson as Hermione Granger.
Harry Potter and the Order of the Phoenix (2007) features locations in the Scottish Highlands such as Fort William, Glen Coe, and Glen Etive.

What happens when you miss the only train to Hogwarts? Ron Weasley and Harry Potter try to control their flying car in *Harry Potter and the Chamber of Secrets* (2002). The choice of a 1962 Ford Anglia was inspired by a car that author J.K. Rowling rode around in with her best friend from school.

Filmmakers and audiences alike find the imagery of Scotland's countryside exhilarating. Castles stand on lone islands in foggy fjords, thatched crofters' farms nestle into green glens amidst majestic peaks, and silver lakes reflect broad skies and snowy slopes. Despite interminable bouts with inclement weather, the Highland cliché takes on a new magnetism when employed by filmmakers as settings or backdrops. Wild-eyed warriors wearing kilts and brandishing daggers storm across otherwise tranquil meadows in *Braveheart* and *Highlander*. The cult film *Monty Python and the Holy Grail* sees famous comedians laying siege to castles dressed as knights and clapping coconut halves together. Some thirty years after the film made its debut, this scene still inspires tourists from as far away as Japan to make a beeline to Castle Doune from the airport with coconut halves in hand. Just as many visitors arrive in hopes of seeing the West Highland Railway train take a famous curve over the **Glenfinnan Viaduct,** transporting young **Harry Potter** to boarding school on the Hogwarts Express in several of the films about the boy magician. In the 2007 film *Harry Potter and the Order of the Phoenix,* the Scottish Highlands frame several scenes, with locations such as **Fort William, Glen Coe, Glen Etive,** and **Clachaig Gully.** The hut where Hagrid (Robbie Coltrane) lives is situated just under the peaks of Buachaille Etive Mòr, one of the U.K.'s most beautiful mountains. With this much cinematic appeal, it's no wonder Scotland prides itself as "the land of beauty," rain showers and all.

In *Braveheart*, William Wallace (Mel Gibson) returns to the Highlands to discover that the local English lord has been taking advantage of the Scots. He assembles the clans, and they charge off to battle past Buachaille Etive Mòr (above) and its shining lake in Glen Coe.

Exploring the Highlands with *Braveheart*

The filmic tale of William Wallace's thirteenth-century struggle against the English for Scottish independence is best remembered by fans for blue face paint and fierce warriors racing across the Scottish moors. And while much of the filming took place in Ireland – thanks to tax incentives and the low cost of extras hired on for extensive battle scenes – the mist-shrouded peaks and breathtaking vales of the **West Highlands** also played a central role. The Scottish tourist board may be among the last to forget, what with the upsurge of visitors to the William Wallace monument near Stirling and to the verdant film locations featured in this blockbuster film. Mel Gibson's sophomore directorial effort would take five golden statuettes at the 1996 Oscars – including Best Picture, Best Director, and Best Cinematographer – a sweep that gave him the confidence to soldier on to much more controversial moviemaking, such as 2004's *The Passion of the Christ*.

Mountain panoramas furnish *Braveheart* with its hardy, savage character. While not particularly steep, the two towering natural monuments of the West Highlands region – Ben Nevis (4,406 feet or 1,343 meters) and Buachaille Etive Mòr (3,343 feet or 1,019 meters) – are tall peaks for the United Kingdom. The former, which translates from Gaelic into "Stormy Mountain," is the highest in the British Isles, and is located close to the tourist hub of Fort William. The latter, the "Great Herdsman of Etive," is renowned as the most photographed. The initial scenes in *Braveheart* employ the majesty of **Ben Nevis** and the green valley of **Glen Nevis** as the site of the medieval village where little William (James Robinson) grows up. Here, on the banks of the rushing River Nevis, he witnesses both the brutality of the English lords and the bucolic sweetness of his native

culture. When his father is slain battling the soldiers of King Edward I "Longshanks" (Patrick McGoohan), his uncle Argyle (Brian Cox) arrives to take him away and educate him.

Years later, William returns to the villages in the shadow of Ben Nevis a grown man (Mel Gibson) only to find the local English lord taking advantage of the Scots. He assembles the clans and they charge off into the countryside past the snowy pyramid of **Buachaille Etive Mòr** and its shining lake in **Glen Coe,** a 30-mile (50-kilometer) drive southeast of Ben Nevis. Filmed in the valley of Glen Nevis, William and his compatriots kill the lord and burn the garrison at Lanark, just as Wallace's men did in May 1297. **Loch Leven** and its mountain backdrop make a brief appearance after William's rendezvous with the French Princess Isabelle (Sophie Marceau). Whether William will prevail and free Scotland from the dastardly English – a hope reflected in his inspiringly choreographed hike over the **Mamores Mountains** – depends on his ability to keep the clans together, and the wiles of his lovely new ally.

Mel Gibson makes for a fearsome Scottish hero in *Braveheart*, especially with his face painted up for the fierce fighting against the English overlords.

Highlander: North to Eilean Donan and the Isle of Skye

Another film to capitalize on the warrior tradition of Scotland's north is *Highlander* (1986) directed by Ozzie talent Russell Mulcahy, known also for his high-energy rock videos for artists such as Elton John and Duran Duran. Sean Connery stars as the hoary old warrior Ramirez while muscle-bound Frenchman Christopher Lambert is Connor "The Highlander" MacLeod. Although the plot is no showstopper, the film's ebullient sci-fi elements make for an amusing story set against the jagged skylines of the **Highlands.**

The film commences with Ramirez's teaching Connor the ancient art of swordplay and educating him about his immortality: Connor has no choice but to follow his unusual fate and battle his evil and long-lived counterparts or perish in the process. Possibly the most striking and recognizable landscape of the film is the island castle called Glenfinnan under attack by medieval warriors. In reality, this is the much-photographed island castle of **Eilean Donan** on **Loch Duich** in **Dornie** near **Kyle of Lochalsh,** some 60 miles (100 kilometers) north of the Glen Nevis and Glen Coe area of *Braveheart* fame. While the isle has

And while it smacks of something out of *Rocky* (1976), the two men engage in a foot-race on a beach – here the sands are along **Refuge Bay, Cuartaig** close to **Morar.** Some of the filming also took place at Loch Shiel at Glenfinnan.

Muscle-bound Christopher Lambert is Connor "The Highlander" MacLeod in a film that reflects Scotland's warrior tradition. Of the landscapes that appear in *Highlander*, the lake castle of Eilean Donan (below) is one of the most striking.

been used as a defensive position for more than 800 years, the fortifications extant today are the picturesque product of a twenty-year restoration effort that ended in 1932.

More wielding of swords takes place when the clans join in battle at **Glen Coe,** a location that would also pop up in *Highlander III* (1994), along with Glen Nevis and the Ardnamurchan Peninsula. Ramirez demonstrates his finest moves to his student as they engage in one-on-one combat at the **Cioch Rock** in the Cuillin Hills on the Isle of Skye, a place hikers have since nicknamed "The Gathering" for this memorable scene from the film. Also known as the "Cloudy Isle," Skye is a climbers' playground in Scotland's untamed west, a long island accessible by a toll bridge some 75 miles (120 kilometers) from Fort William.

The storming of Glenfinnan was filmed at Eilean Donan on Loch Duich in Dornie. The castle has been a defensive position for more than 800 years.

Monty Python: Stirling and the Lakes

A decade before Lambert donned his kilt and two decades preceding Mel Gibson's own debut in a skirt, six comedians known for utter silliness invaded Scotland's countryside on an impossible mission. With **Monty Python and the Holy Grail** (1975), the troupe known for its television series with the BBC made the jump to feature-length films with a tale of the knights of the Round Table and their mythic quest. Terry Gilliam and Terry Jones directed the film, but still managed to join Michael Palin, Eric Idle, John Cleese, and Graham Chapman in multiple acting roles. The lack of funding took its toll on the merry band, as did the weather in the Scottish Highlands. Working only for the promise of returns at the box office, the group braved soggy conditions in cold metal costumes to produce a critically acclaimed film that is now a cult classic. Even today, more than thirty years later, college kids gleefully quote the film's numerous oddball lines, everything from "It's just a flesh wound" to "What? A swallow carrying a coconut?"

The film opens with King Arthur (Graham Chapman) riding up to a castle on an imaginary horse, his attendant clapping the empty halves of coconuts together to emulate the sound of hooves. The four-teenth-century **Doune Castle** just north-west of Stirling in the central highlands served many scenes in the film's bewildering storyline. The production designer added fake battlements to the fortress so that the snotty French guard (John Cleese) could toss animals and all matter of debris over the wall without damaging the historic masonry of the castle. The sentry's warning to "go away, or I shall taunt you a second time" was memorably answered with a bizarre and poorly planned Trojan rabbit. The same stronghold stood in as Swamp Castle where Lancelot (John Cleese) runs wild through a wedding party, and for the perilous Castle Anthrax, where the white-clad Zoot (Carol Cleveland) tempts Sir Galahad "The Chaste" with a

The snotty French guards peek out of the gates of Doune Castle in *Monty Python and the Holy Grail.*

King Arthur on his imaginary horse. His men use coconut halves to emulate the sound of hooves.

bevy of bathing beauties. Adjacent to these rooms is a great hall whose window niches were used for the musical Camelot scenes with the "Knights of the Round Table" song.

Perhaps the most memorable scenes were Python's adventures amidst the hills of the Highlands. Cast and crew clambered up muddy slopes near **Killin** in Perthshire, 40 miles (60 kilometers) northwest of Stirling, on the southern side of **Loch Tay** to film the Cave of Caerbannog sequences. The holy hand grenade is lobbed into what is, in fact, a defunct copper mine. The steeps of the **West Highlands** at **Glen Coe,** another 43 miles (70 kilometers) to the north-west, served as the site of the Bridge of Death over the Gorge of Eternal Peril, in particular the ravine near the **Meeting of the Three Waters.** On the heels of these scenes, Arthur and Sir Bedevere (Terry Jones) walk off into the broad sweeping landscapes of the Glen Coe region, descending a slope with mountain peaks to their backs and the silver surface of **Loch Bà** and **Rannoch Moor** stretching before them. With their journey drawing to an end, Arthur and Bedevere board the dragon boat to **Castle Aaargh,** the privately owned fifteenth-century **Castle Stalker** on Loch Linnhe near **Port Appin,** only to be repelled by the crafty French — and, strangely enough, the local police. Notable, too, are a pair of locations close to Stirling: The armies massing to attack Castle Aaargh were far off at **Sherriffmuir,** and the ruined **Arnhall Castle** served as the site of the Famous Historian's demise.

From Hitchcock to *Chariots of Fire*

Before he abandoned the United Kingdom to make movie history in the Hollywood hills, Alfred Hitchcock directed the black-and-white thriller *The 39 Steps* (1935) in the U.K.,

The West Highlands offer the most idyllic setting in *Local Hero,* especially Silver Sands beach at Camusdarach in Morar, with its lovely views to the Inner Hebridean islands of Rum and Eigg (above). Bill Forsyth's tale shows how nature's beauty can bring even the most calculating capitalists to their knees.

filming part of it on location in Scotland. The pre-World War II spy story starts out with a murder in London, a crime that forces the good-natured Richard Hannay (Robert Donat) to flee to the Scottish Highlands in search of answers. He boards a northbound train, the famous Flying Scotsman, only to make a daring exit with the police in pursuit on the **Forth Bridge.** The steel structure over the Firth of Forth was completed in 1890 and is still considered a marvel of Victorian engineering. The chase continues along the **Falls of Dochart** by **Killin,** 40 miles (60 kilometers) northwest of Stirling, where Hannay seeks refuge with a farmer before continuing on his journey.

Water is a recurring theme in films that use Scottish landscapes, predictably so in **Loch Ness** (1995), a monster-search flick directed by John Henderson and starring Ted Danson. At the edge of this famous lake stand the ruins of the thirteenth-century **Castle Urquhart,** the very same structure reputed to have inspired novelist Bram Stoker when he wrote *Dracula* (1897). The best-known location in the popular comedy **Local Hero** (1983) starring Burt Lancaster and Peter Riegert is the

village of **Pennan** – or Ferness in the film, with its bright red telephone box and the Pennan Inn – a settlement 43 miles (70 kilometers) from Aberdeen on the east coast of Scotland. But it is the West Highlands that prove the most idyllic and memorable setting, in particular the **Silver Sands** beach 185 miles (300 kilometers) west of Pennan at **Camusdarach** in **Morar** with its magical views to the Inner Hebridean islands of **Rum** and **Eigg.** Director-writer Bill Forsyth's cross-cultural tale of Scottish fishermen about to strike it rich with American oil-men shows how nature's beauty can bring even the most calculating capitalists to their knees.

Hugh Hudson's directorial triumph **Chariots of Fire** (1981), an Oscar-winning tale of the 1924 Summer Olympics, makes excellent use of sandy stretches, too, with its iconic Vangelis-accompanied opening scenes of athletes sprinting along the shore filmed at the **West Sands** beach by the famed golf club of **St. Andrews.** One of the golf club's buildings by the **18th hole** stood in for the exterior of the Carlton Hotel, where the athletes stay. The scenes of the traditional games and its races take us back to the Highlands, this time **Sma' Glen** in **Perthshire,** some 25 miles (40 kilometers) north of Stirling.

A handful of Scottish castles make noteworthy appearances in major productions. **Hamlet** (1990), directed by Franco Zeffirelli and starring Mel Gibson and Glenn Close, puts **Blackness Castle** in **Falkirk** and **Dunnottar Castle** near **Stonehaven, Grampian** to good use in Shakespeare's tragic tale. **Macbeth** (1997) directed by Jeremy Freeston, features Blackness Castle again, and **Dunfermline Abbey** near **Kinross. Duart Castle** makes a pretty impression in **Entrapment** (1999) directed by Jon Amiel and starring Sean Connery and Catherine Zeta-Jones.

The best-known location in the comedy *Local Hero* with Burt Lancaster and Peter Riegert is the village of Pennan, or Ferness in the film, with its bright red telephone box and the Pennan Inn.

THE EMERALD ISLE IN FILM By Claudine Weber-Hof

The Republic of Ireland's twenty-six counties have long represented a kind of promised land to movie directors. Its popularity is due on the one hand to a rich history of Irish emigration to the United States, and on the other to the island nation's legendary beauty. For these two reasons, American filmmakers tend to fetishize Ireland's landscapes, from the dramatic cliff-edged coastlines of every tourist brochure to remote, hardscrabble farmsteads. If any part of the country is more popular with filmmakers than others, it is Ireland's west, where heavy rains encourage the grass to grow the brilliant shade of green for which the "Emerald Isle" is so celebrated.

While far more famous for his Westerns, John Ford would win his fourth Oscar as Best Director with his family drama

The Quiet Man (1952). The film took the director born John Feeney – known also by his Irish name, Sean Aloysius O'Fearna – back to the land of his forefathers, a fact that finds echo in the screenplay. John Wayne plays Sean Thornton, an Irishman who is fed up with life in America and decides to return home. **Cong** and landscapes close to **Ashford Castle** in County Mayo stood in for the fictitious village of Innisfree, where Thornton falls for the feisty Mary Kate Danaher (Maureen O'Hara). He feuds with her brother, "Red" Will (Victor McLaglen), over property and his sister's hand, culminating in an epic fight scene. The depiction of rural Ireland is as charming as the film is entertaining. Some scenes were shot in **Oughterard** in County Galway, with the dramatic horse race filmed on **Tully Strand** to the northwest.

Jim Sheridan of *My Left Foot* (1989) fame presents a very different side of Irish country life in his masterfully directed film *The Field* (1990). Shot in western County Galway, the tiny village of **Leenane** in the mountainous region of **Connemara** stands in for fictional Carraigthomond, and features quaint locations such as Gaynor's Pub, the Green Dance Hall, and the Stone Cottage on Clifden Road. The story, set in the 1930s, centers on farmer Bull McCabe (Richard Harris) and the acreage his family has tilled for generations. When the landowner announces her intention to auction the property off, McCabe dares anyone to challenge his claim. The wealthy "Yank" (Tom Berenger) tops

Ryan's Daughter (right) won an Oscar for cinematography, thanks to gorgeous shots of the Dingle Peninsula. It appears in numerous films.

Top landscape film locations

1. County Donegal: **The Secret of Roan Inish**
2. Leenane and the Connemara region: **The Field**
3. Cong and Ashford Castle: **The Quiet Man**
4. Dingle Peninsula: **Ryan's Daughter, Far and Away**
5. Curracloe Beach: **Saving Private Ryan**

Richard Harris is the feisty farmer Bull McCabe (far left) in *The Field*, shot in the Connemara region. Tom Cruise plans to leave Ireland for a fresh start in America in *Far and Away* (center). The magical landscapes of Donegal at Ireland's northwestern tip come to life in *The Secret of Roan Inish* (above).

McCabe's bid and outlines a plan to build a road over the plot. The dispute between the McCabe clan, who seem at one with the very soil, and the American recently returned to his ancestral village spirals out of control. The conflict is reflected in the harsh beauty of Connemara's melancholy peaks and riverswept valleys. The church, the rector's house, and famous falls at **Aasleigh** in County Mayo also make appearances in the film.

The famous, rugged coastlines of County Clare star in **Ryan's Daughter** (1970), a love story that unfolds at the outset of the 1916 Irish rebellion. The movie was honored with two Oscars, one of which went to the gorgeous cinematography of the **Dingle Peninsula** in County Kerry. Audiences had come to expect breathtaking scenery from David Lean, the director of *Lawrence of Arabia* (1962) and *Doctor Zhivago* (1965). *Ryan's Daughter* is nothing if not an ode to the charms of Ireland. Sets for fictional Kirrary were built on **Maoilinn na Ceathrun** hill near Carhoo, with some scenes shot at **Inch Strand** near Dingle and **Coumeenoole Strand,** Dunquin, the site of the schoolhouse. The **Bridges of Ross** feature in the storm scenes, the **Cliffs of Moher** in the opening sequences, and more filming took place on **Barrow Strand** near the county town of Tralee. Dingle also featured in the filming of Ron Howard's emigrant drama **Far and Away** (1992) starring Tom Cruise and Nicole Kidman, a movie that put **Killruddery House & Gardens,** Bray, in County Wicklow and **Ma'am Cross** in County Galway in the spotlight as well.

Movies such as **Tristan + Isolde** (2006) and **The Wind That Shakes the Barley** (2006) are two films that have kept Irish landscapes on the silver screen in recent years, showcasing the dramatic beaches of Ireland's west coast and the green slopes of **Timoleague** in County Cork, respectively. **King Arthur** (2004), starring Keira Knightley as Guinevere and Clive Owen as the betrayed monarch, featured **Ballymore Eustace** in County Kildare as Hadrian's Wall and fortifications, with further scenes filmed in County Wicklow. The breathtaking islands and wildlife of **Donegal** at Ireland's northwestern tip hosted **The Secret of Roan Inish** (1994), an astonishingly beautiful film. The opening D-Day scenes from **Saving Private Ryan** (1998) provide a violent contrast, filmed not on Omaha Beach in Normandy but on **Curracloe Beach** in County Wexford, on the country's southeastern coast. Although everything else about it is Irish, *Waking Ned* (1998) was in fact filmed entirely on the U.K.'s Isle of Man, with Cregneash standing in for the village of Tullymore.

FRANCE

BETWEEN SEDUCTION AND NOSTALGIA

By Kate Cochran

Comprising twenty-one continental *régions*, some of which remain true to ancient provincial boundaries, France's varied landscapes offer much to filmmakers, from the seduction of the Riviera to the nostalgia of Normandy. The distinctly regional flavors embodied in the French landscape relate to geography – the Côte d'Azur's sensuous coastlines, the aromatic allure of Provence, Brittany's rugged Atlantic cliffs, the extensive forests of Aquitaine – as well as to history, as seen in the medieval strongholds of the Dordogne and the wartime monuments of Normandy.

Côte d'Azur: Playground of the Riviera

It's tough to beat the turquoise waters, picturesque cliffs, sunny beaches, and temperate climate of the Côte d'Azur for landscapes that translate well to celluloid. Once the exclusive playground of the idle rich, some resort towns have managed to retain an elite cachet. **Beaulieu-sur-Mer** is one. Just outside Pont-Saint-Jean and a few miles from Nice, the town is renamed "Beaumont-sur-Mer" for Frank Oz's *Dirty Rotten Scoundrels* (1988), and serves as Lawrence Jamieson's (Michael Caine) hunting ground for gullible wealthy women.

Lawrence seeks out his targets in the chic **Grand-Hotel du Cap-Ferrat,** where the marble pillars mimic those of his own fantastic villa on the coast of **Cap d'Antibes.** The meticulously landscaped grounds overlook the calm waters of the Mediterranean, and the Italianate architecture provides the perfect venue for playing his favorite role: that of a displaced prince in need of funding for his coup. When Freddy (Steve Martin) and Janet (Glenne Headly) move into Lawrence's villa, the trio perfects the picture of well-placed con artists taking advantage of the Riviera's "natural resources."

St. Tropez: Birth of a Sexpot

No wonder a major suntan oil – Bain de Soleil – invokes St. Tropez when hawking its wares. The very name of this seaside resort town conjures visions of everlasting sunny days, golden beaches, private yachts, and the "beautiful people." St. Tropez was largely unknown until Brigitte Bardot's starmaking turn in Roger Vadim's *... And God Created Woman* (1956), after which bikinis burst onto the fashion scene. In the film, St. Tropez is still a humble fishing port. Juliette's (Bardot) modest house in **La Ponche,** the sea wall and steps on **Môle Jean Réveille,** where she sunbathes, and the quaint waterfront contrast with Eric's (Curd Jürgens) world of yachts and calculating plots: He plans to manipulate sexy Juliette into destroying two brothers so he can convert their shipyard into a casino. While famous for discovering Bardot's many charms, the film beautifully captures the unspoiled simplicity of 1950s St. Tropez.

The many charms of the French Riviera: Brigitte Bardot in a bikini on the beach at Cannes (far left), the broad sweep of the Nice coastline, which she helped to popularize, and the once quiet town of St. Tropez, where she starred in *... And God Created Woman*.

Top landscape film locations

1. D-Day beaches, Normandy: **The Longest Day, Saving Private Ryan**
2. Brittany coast, Département du Finistère: **A Very Long Engagement**
3. Flavigny-sur-Ozerain: **Chocolat**
4. Vercors Range, Rhône-Alpes: **The Girl from Paris**
5. Gordes and La Canorgue vineyard, Bonnieux: **A Good Year**
6. Carcassonne: **Robin Hood: Prince of Thieves**
7. St. Tropez beaches: **... And God Created Woman**
8. Monte Carlo coast, Cannes beaches: **To Catch a Thief**

Alfred Hitchcock confers with Cary Grant and Grace Kelly during the filming of *To Catch a Thief* on the beach of the Carlton Hotel in Cannes.

Seduction in Cannes

Directors as varied as Brian De Palma, Lawrence Kasdan, and Alfred Hitchcock have paid tribute to the Côte d'Azur's beauty by setting some of their most fascinating films here. More often than not, Cannes sets the stage for acts of seduction, as in De Palma's sexy thriller **Femme Fatale** (2002), starring a deceitful Rebecca Romijn. The seaside city is also the place for romance in Kasdan's **French Kiss** (1995). At the impossibly luxurious **Carlton Inter-Continental Hotel,** with its private beach lined with tall palm trees and dotted with striped umbrellas, Kate (Meg Ryan) and Luc (Kevin Kline) seduce others, only to discover their passion for each other.

Hitchcock's **To Catch a Thief** (1955) is the classic example of this region's perennial pull, a film that also employs the Carlton Hotel in **Cannes.** *Nouvelle riche* but *toujours belle* Francie Stevens (Grace Kelly) resides at the Carlton, sunbathes on its private strand, and uses a diamond necklace to seduce cat burglar John Robie (Cary Grant) during an orgasmic fireworks display. After Robie is arrested in the vibrant flower market on the **Cours Saleya** in **Nice,** Francie takes him on a terrifying chase on the **Grande Corniche** above **Monte Carlo,** careening along the treacherous narrow mountain road overlooking the sea. In a final businesslike marriage proposal, Francie informs Robie that she – and her mother – will be moving into his Mediterranean villa below the **Baou de St. Jeannet,** a few miles from Nice in the **Alpes-Maritimes** region. Like all of Hitchcock's famous icy blondes, Francie tempers her sexuality with coolness, her composure all the more striking against the sensual backdrop of the Côte d'Azur.

Provence and the Rhône-Alpes

The varied landscape of the sea, rivers, and mountains of Provence make it an ideal location for directors and their characters to realize their dreams, whether professional, romantic, or artistic. The dream of becoming King of England inspires the three power-hungry sons of Henry II (Peter O'Toole) and Eleanor of Aquitaine (Katharine Hepburn) to practice their Machiavellian moves in the Oscar-winning ***The Lion in Winter*** (1968). However, even at their best they cannot match the clever calculations of their parents; Henry and Eleanor spar in the 1183 Christmas court filmed at the suitably medieval **Montmajour Abbey** outside **Arles** in **Fontvieille.** By the end of the film, when Henry sees Eleanor off in **Tarascon** on the **Rhône River,** it becomes even more apparent that their mutual admiration is best realized in these acerbic battles for the throne.

Southern France in all of its tourist-brochure glory comes to life when Ridley Scott teams up with Russell Crowe in the vineyard idylls of the **Côtes du Luberon** region of Provence to

channel Peter Mayle's pretty escapist travelogue in ***A Good Year*** (2006). The author – who wrote the novel *A Year in Provence* – offers rural tranquility as a panacea to modern living: London bond trader Max Skinner (Crowe) inherits French property from an uncle and embarks on a search for meaning in his money-obsessed life. Located in Bonnieux between Avignon and Aix-en-Provence, the vineyard of **La Canorgue** and its dreamy gardens are central to the story as the house and lands he inherits. So is **Château Les Eydins,** which stood in as the home of the winemaker Duflot (Didier Bourdon). Excursions to area towns paint a quaint picture of country life, and include **Gordes** – the location of Café Renaissance, known as Fanny's Café in the film – **Avignon, Cucuron,**

In ***The Girl from Paris,*** Sandrine is a Parisienne who moves to the bucolic Rhône-Alpes region to escape the city.

Ménerbes, and **Lacoste.** Some scenes mimic the pratfalls of comedian Jacques Tati in ***Les Vacances de Monsieur Hulot*** (1953), a classic of French film memorably played out at the **Hôtel de la Plage** in **Saint-Marc-sur-Mer** at the mouth of the Loire.

The Provençal countryside again takes center stage as ***The Girl from Paris*** (2001), thirty-year-old Parisienne Sandrine (Mathilde Seigner), quits her job after spotting a travel poster encouraging city dwellers to "Move to the **Rhône-Alpes** region ... a breath of fresh air!" The ad promises greenery tucked into the strata of craggy hills, expansive meadows, and trickling waterfalls: Sandrine cannot resist. She buys a farm outside **Vercors** in the Rhône-Alpes of Upper Provence; the Vercors hills were once a mountain stronghold, lying between the town of **Grenoble,** the **Drac** valley, and the Rhône plain. This range of limestone hills covered by thick forests offers spectacular views of the distant **Alps,** beautifully showcased when Sandrine first takes her goats out to graze. Director Christian Carion gives the celestial landscape its due, whether portraying a mid-winter blizzard or spring's pastoral rebirth as the source Sandrine's salvation.

The Côtes du Luberon region of Provence stars alongside Russell Crowe in *A Good Year*. He rides his motorcycle in La Canorgue vineyard, falls in love in the hillside town of Gordes, and stops to make a call near Lacoste.

"Move to the Rhône-Alpes region ... a breath of fresh air!" Will Sandrine find what she's looking for when she quits her job and moves to the country? Director Christian Carion thought so when he chose the Vercors Range in Upper Provence as the setting for *The Girl from Paris*. Craggy and forested, the mountains provide the heroine with a landscape of salvation that is especially dramatic during winter blizzards and spring's pastoral rebirth.

The town of Arles is another focal point in Provence, where extensive Roman ruins provide a manmade counterpoint to the region's **Alpilles** mountains and lavender fields – seen memorably, if only briefly, in Tom Tykwer's **Perfume: The Story of a Murderer** (2006). Avant-garde director Jean Cocteau famously filmed **Orpheus** (1950) amid the medieval remains of **Les Baux de Provence** near Arles. The town and its countryside also feature in **Lust for Life** (1956), Vincente Minnelli's adaptation of Irving Stone's biography of Vincent van Gogh. The movie was filmed on location, and Minnelli uses clever cinematography to recreate some of Van Gogh's most famous paintings.

In one scene, Van Gogh (Kirk Douglas) and Paul Gauguin (Anthony Quinn) sit at a sidewalk café beneath a star-studded sky as in *Café Terrace at Night*. The café, since renamed **Café van Gogh,** is just off the Rue du Forum. Van Gogh's famous **Yellow House** – his "studio of the South" – at No. 2 Place Lamartine, the **Hôpital l'Espace,** and the **Alyscamps** in Arles feature, too, as does the wheat field in nearby **Auvers-sur-Oise** where the painter committed suicide. Minnelli constructs the final

scene in honor of the artist's last painting, the suitably melancholy *Wheatfield with Crows*. The contrast between the buff yellow of the field and the rich blue of the sky captures the dreamy palette of Provence itself.

Dordogne to the Pyrenees

The large west-central province of Aquitaine contains the regions of the Dordogne, Gironde, Landes, Lot-et-Garonne, and Pyrénées-Atlantiques. While there is some variation in landscape here, the region balances the Pyrenees' mountainous sublimity with Atlantic shores and inland forests. Those

The famous lavender fields of Provence appear in Tom Tykwer's *Perfume: The Story of a Murderer* (2006). Ben Whishaw is Jean-Baptiste Grenouille, a gifted young man driven by his acute sense of smell to kill pretty women.

then as the sun rises. Once the travelers arrive in Bordeaux, the scenic parks – verdant oases of embracing shade trees and wide paths that are enclosed by wrought-iron fences – provide a setting for multiple collaborations among the characters, mimicking the era's political machinations. Near the end of the film, Frédéric (Grégori De-

Kevin Costner is *Robin Hood: Prince of Thieves*. Carcassonne, one of the few remaining walled cities in France, stands in for the castle of Nottingham in the film. The fortified town is the backdrop to many of the movie's action scenes.

forests – the most extensive in France – provide a sense of seclusion, as evidenced in Jean Renoir's sex comedy ***Picnic on the Grass*** (1959), in which stuffy politician Étienne Alexis (Paul Meurisse) finds himself in the midst of a pastoral bacchanal in the **Les Collettes** forest in **Auvergne.** As Alexis finds an escape in the arms of Nénette (Catherine Rouvel), so, too, do other filmmakers use this landscape as sanctuary. While some view Aquitaine as a refuge from danger – as in James Bond's adventure in the Pyrenees in ***Tomorrow Never Dies*** (1997) – others discover in this region an escape into the past, capitalizing on its many surviving medieval villages and châteaux.

La Gironde: *Bon Voyage* to the City

A winegrowing region of world renown, Gironde also offers filmmakers vast spaces that include Europe's largest forest, a landscape is well-utilized in the World War II-era tragicomedy **Bon Voyage** (2003). Set mostly in June 1940, *Bon Voyage* follows the converging storylines of seven Parisians who flee to **Bordeaux's Hotel Splendid** just before the Germans occupy the city. From train windows, the serene countryside of rolling green hills and the Gironde's waving trees zip by, first in near blackness and

rangère) and Professeur Kopolski (Jean-Marc Stehlé) leave the shore at the resort town of **Arcachon** to escape to Britain by boat. Additional scenes recounting the birth of the puppet **Vichy** regime ensure that, although the film ends in 1942, viewers have no question as to France's impending fate.

Remnants of a Feudal Past in the Dordogne

The Dordogne Valley, or **Périgord,** is home to many of the most beautiful and historic villages in France, a region that is increasingly popular with filmmakers. The town of **Carcassonne,** one of the few remaining walled cities in France, has played host to several films, including **Robin Hood: Prince of Thieves** (1991) and **The Bride** (1985). In *Robin Hood*, starring the excellent Alan Rickman and the accent-challenged Kevin Costner, the fortified city stands in for Nottingham's castle. In the hokey Sting-Jennifer Beals horror melodrama *The Bride*, Carcassonne indicates the exterior of Frankenstein's ominous abode, although the interiors were shot at the **Château de Cordes,** a fifteenth-century castle southwest of **Clermont-Ferrand.** *The Bride* also filmed in **Sarlat-la-Canéda,** a town built around a ninth-century Benedictine abbey, a location Ridley Scott used in **The Duellists** (1977).

In nearby rural **Thonac,** the Renaissance castles of **Château de Fénélon, Château de Hautefort,** and **Château de Losse** provide the setting for Drew Barrymore's update of Cinderella, ***Ever***

Renaissance castles in Thonac, including Château de Hautefort, provided the royal setting for *Ever After,* Drew Barrymore's version of the Cinderella fairy tale.

Roux (Johnny Depp) and Vianne (Juliette Binoche) succumb to the aphrodisiac effects of *Chocolat* in rural Burgundy. Hoping to find a home for herself and her daughter, Vianne sets up shop in the uptight French village of Lansquenet. In reality, this is the little medieval town of Flavigny-sur-Ozerain.

upset the oppressive status quo, especially during the Catholic season of fasting, Lent. The majority of the exteriors of Lansquenet were shot in **Flavigny-sur-Ozerain** in **Burgundy**, a medieval town known, ironically enough, for its aniseed candy. The town's gray stone buildings and packed dirt roads beautifully represent the opening voiceover assertion that Lansquenet was a "little village in the French countryside that believed in *tranquillité* – tranquility." Reynaud's office in the grand Hôtel de Ville, the exterior of Vianne's

After (1998). Both Sarlat and Thonac are located in **Périgord Noir**, or "Black Perigord," so called for its abundance of oak forests blanketing the landscape.

The film that takes finest advantage of the Dordogne's various charms is Lasse Hallström's *Chocolat* (2000). Based on Joanne Harris's novel of the same name, the movie depicts the liberating effects of chocolate – and its bohemian purveyor, Vianne (Juliette Binoche) – on an uptight French village in the 1950s. Although the town of Lansquenet is fictitious, many of the ravishing location shots were filmed in the **Dordogne valley**. The winding, windswept road that Vianne and her daughter climb in the first scene is the **Caminal del Panieraire** in the feudal village of **Beynac**. In the background, **Château de Beynac** rises to overlook the valley dotted with hills and crowned with castles, including those of **Marqueyssac, Castelnaud,** and **Fayrac**. The beauty of the locations employed in the film suggests the rapture of enjoyment and life's pleasures, a convincing contrast to the sour denizens of Lansquenet.

Vianne opens a *chocolaterie* in Lansquenet by capitalizing on her mother's Mayan recipes, and in doing so casts a gentle spell on the town. She rescues kleptomaniac Josephine (Lena Olin) from her abusive husband, reunites landlady Armande (Judi Dench) with her young grandson, and infuriates the mayor Comte Paul de Reynaud (Alfred Molina) for daring to

Vianne tries to cheer up her unhappy landlady, Armande (Judi Dench), in her chocolate shop on the main square of Flavigny-sur-Ozerain.

charming shop, and the Romanesque town church are all authentic Flavigny, although the statue of Reynaud's ancestor in the central square was added for the shooting. The river where the band of vagabonds led by the handsome Roux (Johnny Depp) live on boats was added to the foot of Flavigny's hill by the magic of film editing.

The beaches of Normandy were once the scene of the Allied invasion that began on D-Day, June 6, 1944. The decisive landing sites appear in the 1962 war film *The Longest Day.*

The Atlantic Coast

France's Atlantic Coast offers its fair share of history as grist for the filmmaking mill as well as breathtaking ocean vistas. While the calm, sandy beaches of Normandy are equally powerful as a wistful lovers' venue or a memorial to the Allied invasion of World War II, Brittany's rockier character lends itself to sometimes cruel historical drama and bitter memories of World War I. Whether Normandy or Brittany, movies filmed in these two provinces share a strong sense of nostalgia coupled with dramatic landscapes.

Longest Day (1962); the film holds the distinction of being one of the few to stage a reenactment of D-Day on the very beaches where the invasion occurred. The film includes few broad vistas of the beaches, employing instead shots of dunes, nearby villages, and primitive roads shrouded in rain and haze to convey the confusion of war. Steven Spielberg's **Saving Private Ryan** (1998) uses as the setting for its opening and closing scenes the **World War II Normandy American Cemetery and Memorial** in **Colleville-sur-Mer.** Located on a cliff overlooking **Omaha Beach** and the **English Channel,** the sea of white crosses includes the grave markers of those who died in the search for the American paratrooper Private Ryan (Matt Damon). Ryan's visit to the grave of Captain John Miller (Tom Hanks) includes long shots of the cemetery and its breathtaking perch over the sea.

Not all in Normandy is connected to war and loss. Several towns in the region were developed into tourist resorts, such as the well-heeled seaside resort of **Deauville,** the setting of Claude Lelouch's **A Man and a Woman** (1966). Launched in the

Remembrance in Normandy

Part rich farmland, part beachy coast, Normandy is perhaps best known as the site of the famous Allied invasion that began when British and American soldiers stormed ashore in the early hours of D-Day, June 6, 1944. The decisive beaches of **Gold, Juno, Omaha, Sword,** and **Utah** are well represented in **The**

In *The Vikings,* Morgana's castle is the fourteenth-century Fort la Latte on the Breton coast between St. Brieuc and St. Malo.

Director Jean-Pierre Jeunet takes advantage of Brittany's unspoiled coast to tell the story of Mathilde (Audrey Tautou) in *A Very Long Engagement*.

1860s by the Duc de Morny, cousin of Napoleon III, Deauville was envisioned as a picturesque retreat for wealthy Parisians. Its attractions include wide avenues and impressive villas, like the one converted into a school for the children of the film's main characters, racecar driver Jean-Louis (Jean-Louis Duroc) and script girl Anne (Anouk Aimée). The film follows the budding romance between these two widowed single parents on weekends when they drive from Paris to Deauville to visit their respective children. The scenes in Deauville mainly take place on or near the beach: The opening shot of five-year-old Antoine chauffeuring Jean-Louis along the sands on Avenue Lucien Barrière showcases the long pier, gentle waves, and diffuse light that characterize all of the beach scenes in this film. The misty landscape conveys a sense of nostalgia as the main characters yearn for each other even as they are haunted by the memory of their departed spouses.

Memory on Brittany's Rocky Shore

Prized by filmmakers for its raw coastline of rocky crags and crashing waves, Brittany is often used as a stand-in for other locations. In **The Vikings** (1958), Morgana's castle is the fourteenth-century **Fort la Latte** on the north Breton coast between **St. Brieuc** and **St. Malo.** La Latte is a Romanesque fortress situated on a rock peak jutting into the sea, and the film makes the most of the castle's enclosed stone walls and drawbridge. To make **Tess** (1979), Roman Polanski conjured the fictional county of Wessex from Thomas Hardy's novel *Tess of the D'Urbervilles* on the northern coast of Brittany. The town of **Morlaix** stands in for Marlott and Tantridge, places that provide the increasingly confined and bleak settings that mark Tess's ruin.

Other movies, like Jean-Pierre Jeunet's **A Very Long Engagement** (2004), take advantage of Brittany's many unspoiled locations to stage historical events. Shot almost entirely in the **Département du Finistère** – called the Department of the End of the World for its location in the extreme west of France – the film tells the story of Mathilde (Audrey Tautou), a Breton girl

Because of its location in France's far west, this region of Brittany is called the Département du Finistère – the Department of the End of the World.

who awaits her lover Manech's (Gaspard Ulliel) return from World War I. Her stone farmhouse is on the coast, flanked by boulders and rolling hills covered with ferns. Flashbacks reveal her memories of playing with Manech atop a gray-and-white lighthouse, scenes filmed on a lot using special effects.

The town where young Manech pursues Mathilde and the abandoned farmhouse where they consummate their affair were filmed on location in and around **Locronon** and **Plogonnec** north of **Quimper.** Mathilde's search for Manech after the war also takes her to Paris and **Rennes** – where she meets a Polish widow played by Jodie Foster – as well as to the vast field of wildflowers that was once the dreaded **Somme** army trench "Bingo Crépuscule." Scenes recreated on military terrain near **Poitiers** show the countryside transformed by war, bleak fields of mud covered with barbed wire and pocked with craters. Still, Brittany is the star of this lush film, the multiple aerial shots depicting the rugged splendor of its coastal vistas.

THE SPAGHETTI WESTERN By Katrin Utzinger

Its forests are lush and verdant, its deserts as dry as dust. Long, sandy beaches stretch along the Mediterranean coast and steep cliffs plunge into the Atlantic. It is the variety of landscapes in Spain that has attracted such acclaimed directors as David Lean and Sergio Leone to film here. The province of Almería in eastern Andalusia and sections of central Spain have provided landscapes that have been used enthusiastically as backdrops in numerous movies.

Almería is surrounded by a landscape of barren, undulating hills that are eminently suited to providing movie settings that represent desert and steppe regions. The province began its film career in *Lawrence of Arabia* (1962). Many of the scenes in David Lean's epic about the British officer T.E. Lawrence (Peter O'Toole) were shot in the deserts of Jordan, a choice that presented hard work for the film team. Spain, of course, was far more accessible and proved a welcome alternative. A replica of the Jordanian seaport of Aqaba was constructed on the coast at **Algorocibo** near **Carboneras** in Almería. The ambush of the famous Hejaz railway, which connects Damascus with Medina over a distance of 800 miles (1,300 kilometers), was staged a little farther south in the sand dunes just off the coast at **San José** on the **Cabo de Gata** peninsula. David Lean returned here for his next project, *Doctor Zhivago* (1965), filming in the deserts around Almería, but also in the hills near **Guadix.** The latter, which is situated in the province of Grenada, was used to stage scenes in snow-covered Russia – with artificial snow.

Sergio Leone discovered the region in 1964. In his Western *A Fistful of Dollars* (1964), starring Clint Eastwood as a quiet stranger caught between two rival families, the desert of Almería successfully stood in for the border area between Mexico and the U.S. **Cortijo El Sotillo** represented the gloomy little town of San Miguel. Leone returned to Almería for other spaghetti Westerns, too: The bandits in *For a Few Dollars More* (1965) fought their duels close to **Tabernas,** just outside the city of Almería. You can still visit a miniature Hollywood there today, and travel back in time to the era of the Wild West. The third and final part of Leone's so-called "dollar trilogy," *The Good, the Bad and the Ugly* (1966), was shot in this coastal region and in the province of **Almería** itself. Leone intended to film his last Western, the revenge epic *Once Upon a Time in the West* (1969), in Arizona, but the landscapes there disappointed him. He and his film team returned to Spain. The famous opening scene, showing three men waiting for a train, was filmed in the stony desert around Almería.

Colmenar Viejo, the gate to the **Guadarrama Mountains,** is a little town situated where the plains close to Madrid merge with a craggy landscape. Sergio Leone had already filmed one scene from *For a Few Dollars More* here. His rival Sergio Corbucci shot **Django** (1966) at this location, too: The landscape through which Django (Franco Nero) drags his coffin is dismal and wild. Once again, to audiences, Spain became the American West. In Stanley Kubrick's *Spartacus* (1960), Colmenar

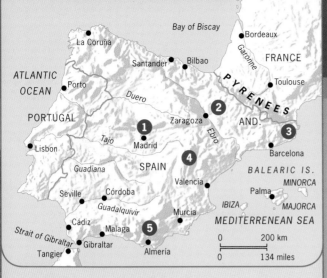

Top landscape film locations

1. Colmenar Viejo and the Guadarrama Mountains:
   Django, Spartacus, Chimes at Midnight
2. Loarre Castle near Huesca: **Kingdom of Heaven**
3. Figueras: **Perfume: The Story of a Murderer**
4. Fortress of Belmonte near Cuenca: **El Cid**
5. Desert near Almería: **Lawrence of Arabia,
   A Fistful of Dollars, The Good, the Bad and
   the Ugly**

Sergio Leone's "dollar trilogy" with Clint Eastwood (left) established the deserts of Almería as a substitute location for the American Southwest. *The Good, the Bad and the Ugly* (above) was shot in this coastal region.

Viejo embodies the Roman empire of antiquity, while in Orson Welles's *Chimes at Midnight* (1965) it stands in for England.

Spain was finally allowed to play itself in *El Cid* (1961). In this three-hour epic, Charlton Heston plays the Spanish hero Rodrigo Díaz de Vivar – El Cid – who drove the Moors from eleventh-century Spain. The hero's exile was filmed in the **Guadarrama Mountains,** but most of the movie was shot in and around the fortress of **Belmonte.** The castle is located in the town of the same name, surrounded by fields and the broad plains of Castile. The three-sided structure presents the spectator with three very different views. Director Anthony Mann took advantage of this and used the castle as several fortresses.

Directors have continued to favor the Iberian peninsula in the twenty-first century, too, using it as a substitute for other countries such as France in Ridley Scott's crusader flick *King-dom of Heaven* (2005). **Loarre Castle** lies in the shadow of the **Pyrenees** in the north of Spain – an almost perfectly preserved fortress from the eleventh century that Scott chose as the location for crusader Godfrey of Ibelin's (Liam Neeson) family seat. From its position on the southern Pyrenean slopes, it overlooks the vast, thinly populated regions of **Aragon.** Much of Tom Tyk-wer's film version of Patrick Süskind's novel *Perfume: The Story of a Murderer* (2006) was filmed in Spain, although the story itself takes place in eighteenth-century France. The Parisian scenes were filmed in **Barcelona,** with several of the beautiful landscapes shot near **Figueras** in the province of Girona.

GERMANY

FAIRY-TALE CASTLES & MAGIC MOUNTAINS By Larissa Vassilian

Whether it's the North Sea and Baltic Sea coastlines, the rolling slopes of central Germany, the romantic river valleys of the Danube and the Rhine, or the snowcapped Alps, Germany's varied landscapes have long inspired poets and painters – but surprisingly few filmmakers. Germany's cities beat its landscapes hands down in their popularity as movie locations, although Bavaria is an exception. Thanks to its dramatic mountains and castles, the beautiful south remains a favorite among directors wishing to make a memorable impression on the big screen. At the other extreme, some young filmmakers have demonstrated a fascination with German landscapes of a less attractive kind. The bare industrial and urban milieus seen in Fatih Akin's study of immigrant lives *Solino* (2002) or the barren provincialism of Mecklenburg-Western Pomerania in Detlev Buck's East German road movie *No More Mr. Nice Guy* (1993) exemplify the trend.

The German Road Movie

Road movies provide the best insights into the diversity of Germany's landscapes. A number of German directors have tried their hand at this genre: Wim Wenders started the trend with a trilogy: **Alice in the Cities** (1974), **Wrong Move** (1975), and **King of**

the Road (1976). In the last of these three movies, Wenders sent his protagonists on a long trip from **Lüneburg** to **Passau** along the border between East and West Germany. Wenders spent eleven weeks on the shoot, picking locations spontaneously as he went along. After reunification, director Detlev Buck used the road movie genre to examine the radical changes that were taking place. In his warmhearted satire **No More Mr. Nice Guy** (1993), Joachim Król and Horst Krause play mismatched brothers on their way east to collect an inheritance. Buck's heroes undertake an odyssey through **Mecklenburg-Western Pomerania** en route to their grandmother's villa. In the tragicomic movie

The moated castle of Mespelbrunn in Spessart serves as a romantic backdrop in *The Spessart Inn* starring Liselotte Pulver and Carlos Thompson.

From the pomp of Castle Neuschwanstein in *Ludwig* (1972) to the landscapes of Mecklenburg-Western Pomerania in *No More Mr. Nice Guy* (1993).

Top landscape film locations

1. Mecklenburg-Western Pomerania: **No More Mr. Nice Guy**
2. Eberbach Monastery in Eltville am Rhein: **The Name of the Rose**
3. Spessart and Mespelbrunn Castle: **The Spessart Inn**
4. Castle Neuschwanstein and surroundings: **Ludwig, Chitty Chitty Bang Bang**
5. Lake Starnberg: **Ludwig**
6. Wendelstein: **Wer früher stirbt, ist länger tot**
7. Berchtesgaden: **Winter Sleepers**
8. Rottal-Inn: **Herbstmilch**

Knockin' on Heaven's Door (1997), Jan Josef Liefers and Til Schweiger play two terminally ill cancer patients who break out of the hospital and live it up – before it's too late. They steal a car and make for Holland and the sea via Thuringia, Hesse, and North Rhine-Westphalia. Their adventure-filled journey takes them onto the autobahn near **Leipzig,** through **Jena,** and on to the small Rhenish towns of **Erkelenz** and **Hückelhoven,** the latter director Thomas Jahn's hometown.

Historic Backdrops: Palaces, Castles, and Monasteries

Big brown eyes, a slick bob, and a cheeky tongue: That's how we remember Liza Minnelli in her showpiece role as the singing, dancing, man-crazy nightclub singer Sally Bowles in *Cabaret* (1972). The self-confident young dancer finds herself torn between two admirers during the closing years of the Weimar Republic. The movie, which garnered eight Oscars, was shot mainly in Berlin but would not have been complete without the scenes shot at **Castle Eutin** near Lübeck. Surrounded by tall trees, the former residence of the Bishop of Lübeck is situated on the shore of Lake Eutin amid a plateau of lakes known as Schleswig-Holstein's mini-Switzerland.

The makers of the popular comedy *The Spessart Inn* (1958) found a similarly picturesque site when they chose the moated castle of **Mespelbrunn** between Frankfurt am Main and Würzburg as the film's setting. Today, numerous little footpaths lead visitors through the forested **Spessart** hills to the vine-covered

Name of the Rose (1986). In the movie version of Umberto Eco's novel, directed by Jean-Jacques Annaud, Sean Connery plays the Franciscan monk William of Baskerville, sent out in 1327 to investigate a gruesome series of murders in a monastery. Exteriors were shot at a specially constructed monastery on a hillside not far from Rome, but the most important interiors were filmed in the great monastery and grounds of **Eberbach Monastery** in **Eltville am Rhein** in the state of Hesse. Nature still seems untouched and unwelcoming here, and the monastery, an impressive example of medieval monastic architecture, looks as remote and lonely as it was in its heyday some 700 years ago.

castle that was home to Countess Franziska von Sandau (Liselotte Pulver) in the movie. Sadly, the legendary inn where the countess is set upon by robbers no longer exists: It was torn down in 1959 to make way for the Rohrbrunn motorway service station.

Landmark buildings also played a role in the blockbuster film **The**

Director John Sturges filmed *The Great Escape* with Steve McQueen in Upper Bavaria.

The interior shots for *The Name of the Rose* were filmed at Eberbach Monastery (bottom left).

Straight Out of a Fairy Tale: Bavaria

The castles and palaces built by King Ludwig II of Bavaria – one of which allegedly inspired the Disney castle – never fail to attract swarms of tourists and filmmakers. American, British, and Italian film teams flock here like bees to honey. In ***The Great Escape*** (1963), Steve McQueen, Richard Attenborough, and James Garner play officers in the Allied air forces plotting their escape from a German POW camp toward the end of the war. The drama, based on a true story, was filmed on a hill called the **Perlacher Mugl,** a popular day-trip destination from Munich, as well as in and around the historic town of **Füssen** in Allgäu.

Prettily situated at the foot of the Alps, Füssen is one of Bavaria's most popular film locations. The exuberant musical comedy ***Chitty Chitty Bang Bang*** (1968), the tale of a magical flying car with Dick Van Dyke in the main role as the eccentric professor, was filmed in and around the historic settlement. The book on which the movie is based was written by none other than James Bond author Ian Fleming. He wrote the children's story about an unusual racecar that could not only drive, but also swim and fly, for his son. And what better a setting to fly over than extensive forests and the fairy-tale **Castle Neuschwan-**

Many contemporary films feature the beautiful foothills of the Bavarian Alps.

stein near Füssen, or the romantic little town of **Rothenburg ob der Tauber**? The latter also featured as a location in *Kaspar Hauser* in 1993. The magic Chitty Chitty Bang Bang car has remained so popular in Great Britain that it goes on tour every year, basking in the adulation of its fans at local fairs.

Even the great Luchino Visconti, a stickler for original locations, made the pilgrimage to Bavaria. While filming **Ludwig** (1972) around **Lake Starnberg** and **Lake Chiemsee** in the Bavarian foothills of the Alps, Visconti and his crew endured freezing February and March temperatures in their quest to ensure the authenticity of the tale of the crazy German king. Ludwig's (Helmut Berger) final hours were transferred at the last minute from Berg on Lake Starnberg to the opposite lakeside at **Possenhofen.** The royal castles of **Neuschwanstein, Hohenschwangau, Herrenchiemsee,** and **Linderhof** also served as locations. Following *The Damned* (1969) and *Death in Venice* (1971), this movie marks the conclusion of Visconti's German trilogy. The Bavarian **Chiemgau** region with its picturesque lakes and Alpine landscape was rediscovered as a film location decades later in **Hierankl** (2003). This mother-daughter drama represents a specifically German-language film genre that uses local landscapes as symbols for local values: the *Heimatfilm*. The movie title refers to the lonely mountain farm at the center of the film to which a young woman from Berlin suddenly finds herself exiled.

One director in particular has proved a special fan of Bavaria: A native of Lower Bavaria, Joseph Vilsmaier learned about the Anna Wimschneider story by chance when his grandfather was mentioned in her memoirs. The autobiographical account, which Wimschneider had written for her grandchildren, became an international bestseller, and the film, entitled **Herbstmilch** (1989) ("Autumn Milk"), brought 2.5 million viewers to the cinemas to see his new variation on the *Heimatfilm*. In the very first scene, young Anna (played by Vilsmaier's wife, Dana Vávrová) cycles through the idyllic landscape near **Rottal-Inn,** past harvested fields, over meadows, and through the woods. The hardscrabble agrarian culture of Vilsmaier's home territory became an integral part of the picture – the hard work involved in tilling the fields with an ox-drawn plow, the heavy winter

snow on the roof of the old farmstead. Vilsmaier stuck with the genre and filmed the postwar drama *Rama Dama* two years later before embarking on *Stalingrad* (1993) and the international hit *Comedian Harmonists* (1997).

The Bavarian surprise hit **Wer früher stirbt, ist länger tot** ("Die Earlier, and You're Dead Longer") (2006), directed by Marcus H. Rosenmüller, offers yet another take on the *Heimatfilm* genre. Black humor and use of the Bavarian dialect throughout are underscored by the stunning landscapes of Upper Bavaria. The plot follows the adventures of a village boy, the young scallywag Sebastian, and his attempts to achieve immortality. His greatest fear, helped along by his strict Catholic upbringing, is to be stuck in Purgatory, a horror hilariously presented in dream sequences. Sebastian's adventures involve a trip to a radio presenter's studio located on the summit of a high mountain, the **Wendelstein,** as well as an accident involving his friend's grandmother, who hurtles down a hill in **Waakirchen** in her hospital bed. Last but not least, he sets up a romantic encounter between his teacher and his widowed father on a small lake, the little **Hackensee** in Kleinhartpenning. The cemetery and the Kandler Inn, the center of much of the movie's action, are situated in the small village of **Oberbiberg.** Some of the scenes were also shot in **Bayrischzell** at the foot of the Wendelstein.

Joseph Vilsmaier's *Herbstmilch* was filmed at the book's locations in Lower Bavaria.

Critics praised Tom Tykwer's **Winter Sleepers** (1997) as a "film about landscapes and emotions." Although it is less well known than Tykwer's great successes *Run Lola Run* (1998), *Heaven* (2002), and *Perfume: The Story of a Murderer* (2006), its use of specific localities as part of the action is far more intense. In *Winter Sleepers,* two couples go in for some serious self-exploration during a winter spent in a remote house in the **Berchtesgaden** area. In the book on which the movie is based, the action takes place in a house by the sea. Tykwer thought that the snowy, glacial landscapes above **Lake König** were a better reflection of the protagonists' emotional state: At first glance, the icy mountains look like a smooth monolith. It's only when you take a closer look that the dangerous cracks and crevices become apparent.

FROM SISSI TO THE SOUND OF MUSIC

By Larissa Vassilian

Austria is not called the Alpine Republic for nothing: Two thirds of its terrain is mountainous. Looking at the movies that have been filmed here, in fact, one could be forgiven for thinking that the country consists only of mountains. Snow-covered peaks, alpine pastures, and colorful meadows – such is Austria's cinematic image. Only recently have directors begun to show audiences a different Austria, a no-frills, more authentic country. But on the big screen, the Alps continue to dominate the picture.

Once upon a time, the real Baron von Trapp, a widower, hired a governess to look after his seven children. Fresh from the convent, she taught them how to sing and make the world a better place. Hollywood added kitsch by the bucketful when it brought this essentially true story into movie theaters. **The Sound of Music** (1965), starring Julie Andrews as the gentle Maria and Christopher Plummer as Von Trapp, would win five Oscars and break records at the box office. Even today the movie plays an important role in shaping Austria's image. Popular tours take visitors to the original locations in and around **Salzburg** where the feel-good movie was filmed. **Fuschl Castle** on **Lake Fuschl** features in an early aerial shot, and is also where the famous mountain panoramas were filmed. Maria's nunnery is the **Nonnberg Benedictine Convent** in Salzburg, while the Baron's villa is **Leopoldskron Palace.** The famous **Sound of Music Pavil-**

ion where Liesl von Trapp sings "I Am 16 Going on 17" is situated today on the grounds of Hellbrunn Palace, but used to be in the park at Leopoldskron Palace. Maria and the children sing "Do-Re-Mi" in the **Mirabell Castle** gardens while the Baron croons "Edelweiss" at the **Felsenreitschule,** a summer riding school. Maria and the cheered aristocrat celebrate their wedding in a ceremony shot on the **Mondsee** lake, a perennial favorite with honeymooners.

Seventeen-year-old actress Romy Schneider immortalized the legendary Empress Elizabeth of Austria on celluloid when she took on the role in **Sissi** (1955). The monarch's Bavarian home was reconstructed on **Lake Fuschl** close to Salzburg. The small lake stands in for Lake Starnberg near Munich, with **Fuschl Castle** serving as a credible replacement for Possenhofen Castle, where the empress was born. After the success of the first *Sissi*, two further films followed: **Sissi – Die junge Kaiserin** (1956) ("Sissi – the Young Empress") and **Sissi – Schicksalsjahre einer Kaiserin** (1957) ("Sissi – An Empress Follows her Destiny"). In the second movie, Sissi and the young Emperor Franz Joseph spend their honeymoon on **Hafelekar Mountain,** with its stupendous views over the Karwendel ridge stretching down to Innsbruck. Further scenes were shot at the elegant Schönbrunn Palace in Vienna, in **Bad Ischl** in Upper Austria, and on the Danube close to **Dürnstein.**

Top landscape film locations

1. Garnera Valley: **Schlafes Bruder**
2. Hafelekar Mountain: **Sissi – Die junge Kaiserin**
3. Lake Fuschl and Fuschl Castle: **The Sound of Music, Sissi**
4. Mondsee lake: **The Sound of Music**
5. Wachau Valley: **Vier Mädels aus der Wachau, Der Hofrat Geiger**

Austria's movie magic: The hills are alive for Julie Andrews as Maria before a mountain panorama in *The Sound of Music*. Romy Schneider is the Empress "Sissi" on the Danube near Dürnstein. Schloss Fuschl (far left) served as a location in both films.

In the aftermath of World War II, moviegoers yearned for films that showed them an ideal world. *Heimatfilme*, a film genre that uses local landscapes to personify and celebrate local values, provided them with a few hours of distraction in natural surroundings unscathed by war. The plots tended to be trivial but emphasized family, friendship, love, and tradition. The charming landscape of the Danube's **Wachau Valley** became famous for its *Heimatfilme*, including *Vier Mädels aus der Wachau* (1957) ("Four Girls from Wachau") and *Hofrat Geiger* (1947) ("Court Councilor Geiger"), with Hans Moser and Paul Hörbiger in the main roles. Shooting took place in the Hotel Mariandl in **Spitz** on the Danube. The remake of the classic *Geierwally* (2005) ("Wally, the Mountain Lass") with Christine Neubauer presents a modern take on the genre and was shot principally in the Upper Austrian region of **Hinterstoder** near Kirchdorf an der Krems.

Director Luchino Visconti shattered the Aus-

The many charms of the Danube's Wachau Valley.

trian landscape idyll of mountains, deep blue lakes, and picturesque churches in his film **The Damned** (1969). Scenes of target practice amid banners bearing the Nazi regime's swastika were filmed at **Lake Attersee** near Salzburg. The country's image fares little better in the cult road movie **India** (1993), in which two men, played by Josef Hader and Alfred Dorfer, argue their way across flat expanses of **Lower Austria** past desolate fields and lonely oil drills. In the drama **Schlafes Bruder** (1995) ("Sleep's Brother"), Bavarian director Joseph Vilsmaier sets the tragic tale of an unusual musical genius in the Austrian Alps – in the **Montafon** region, in **Gaschurn,** and in the area around Arlberg and Silvretta in the remote **Garnera Valley.** The deeply fissured mountain world, where streams and waterfalls trickle over flowering slopes, appears utterly untouched by man. The crew moved derelict barns and farm equipment in from the vicinity for the shoot, and dismantled them – as well as the village built specially for the movie – once filming was completed.

SWITZERLAND

HOME OF THE MOUNTAINEERING FILM

By Larissa Vassilian

While associated with only a handful of films, Switzerland's locations have served admirably as a catalog of backdrops for directors the world over. The nation's spectacular Alpine scenery, lush meadows, and crystal clear mountain lakes have appeared in a few memorable international productions, as well as in important domestic films. Some of the best-known movies made in this trilingual country are mountain-climbing dramas and film versions of *Heidi* – as well as a selection of Bollywood's effusive musicals and thrillers.

Mountains have captured people's imaginations since time immemorial, and they appeared on the silver screen fairly early on. Paradoxically, Swiss mountain tourism and filmmakers' interest in the region were first fired by tragedy. In 1865, an Englishman by the name of Edward Whymper and his rival, Jean-Antoine Carrel, competed for the honor of being the first to ascend the 14,690-foot (4,478-meter) **Matterhorn** in the Wallis region. The Englishman won, but four lives were lost during the record-breaking expedition.

Luis Trenker played the tragic role of the mountaineer Carrel in the 1928 silent film *Fight for the Matterhorn,* and again in 1938 in *The Mountain Calls*. A British version of the same story, *The Challenge* (1938), was filmed at the Matterhorn, too, with Trenker playing Carrel in both. Movie pioneer Arnold Fanck's hugely successful movies were shot under extremely dangerous conditions at locations in the **Wallis** region near **Zermatt** and the **Matterhorn**. Leni Riefenstahl, who later earned notoriety as Hitler's favorite filmmaker, often appeared in the lead female role in mountain movies. In the famous silent film *The White Hell of Pitz Palu* (1929), she plays a climber's wife who perishes during a daring expedition.

More than 130 years ago, Johanna Spyri wrote the tale of Heidi, an orphan sent to live with her grandfather in the mountains. Nearly two dozen movie versions of the novel have been made, but the first of these to be shot in Switzerland was Luigi Comencini's *Heidi* (1952) set in idyllic **Albula Valley** in **Graubünden**.

The Mountain Calls (1938) with Luis Trenker brings the first ascent of the Matterhorn to life.

Top landscape film locations

1. Matterhorn: **The White Hell of Pitz Palu**, **The Mountain Calls**
2. Schilthorn: **On Her Majesty's Secret Service**
3. Bernese Oberland: **Star Wars: Episode III – Revenge of the Sith**, numerous Bollywood films
4. Furka Pass: **Goldfinger**
5. Verzasca Reservoir dam: **GoldenEye**
6. Albula Valley, Graubünden: **Heidi**

Graubünden hosted several *Heidi* films. Framed by the mountains of the Bernese Oberland, the restaurant at the peak of the Schilthorn (left) hosted scenes from the James Bond film *On Her Majesty's Secret Service*.

Fans can visit the film's locations on foot, starting at the grandfather's mountain home in **Bergün**, a route that continues on to **Latsch** and **Falein**. Swiss filmmaker Markus Imboden provided a modern take on the story by transforming Heidi into a contemporary teenager. His **Heidi** (2001) was filmed in the **Lower Engadin** area of the Graubünden region's northeast, locations that are now signposted for tourists. The tour stretches from **Vastur**, a 5,400-foot (1,650-meter) mountain with a spectacular view, to the heights of **Zeznina**, where Heidi's grandfather lived, as well as to the tiny hillside village of **Sent**.

Even Hollywood was unable to withstand the allure of Switzerland's mountain vistas. George Lucas shot episodes of the Jedi saga **Star Wars: Episode III – Revenge of the Sith** (2005) in the **Bernese Oberland** region, with the landscapes around **Lake Bachalp, Kleine Scheidegg,** and the **Susten Pass** standing in for the planet of Alderaan. James Bond has made frequent forays into Switzerland, too: In **Goldfinger** (1964), 007 (Sean Connery) drives his Aston Martin over the **Furka Pass** at an altitude of 8,080 feet (2,436 meters). Bond girl Tilly Masterson (Tania Mallet) attempts to kill Goldfinger (Gert Fröbe) near **Andermatt,** not far from the Gotthard Pass. In **On Her Majesty's Secret Service** (1969), Bond's archenemy Blofeld (Telly Savalas) sets up his laboratory on

top of the 9,740-foot (2,970-meter) **Schilthorn.** In the movie, the mountain was called **Piz Gloria** – now the name of the revolving restaurant that offers a stupendous 360-degree view of the Bernese Oberland. In **GoldenEye** (1995), a daredevil Bond (Pierce Brosnan) jumps down the face of a dam that, according to the screenplay, is part of a Russian chemical weapons factory. In reality, it is the **Verzasca Reservoir dam** in the canton of **Ticino.** At 720 feet (220 meters), the dam is now renowned as the highest bungee jump in the world.

The Indian film industry has developed a penchant for the Swiss Alps. Director Yash Chopra filmed his lengthy musicals in Kashmir until 1984, when political unrest prevented further shooting in the region. He looked elsewhere for backdrops, and discovered the **Bernese Oberland** as a replacement. In the wake of successes such as **Dilwale Dulhania Le Jayenge** ("The Brave Heart Will Take the Bride," 1995) he has been awarded honorary citizenship for bringing the movie business to the area.

Bollywood productions are made on a budget of between $2 and $6 million, and some fifteen to twenty Bollywood films are made in Switzerland annually. Thanks to Bollywood's moviemaking, there has been a dramatic increase in the number of Indian couples honeymooning in Switzerland – yet another boost to local commerce.

A LOVE AFFAIR WITH LOCATIONS

By Claudine Weber-Hof

As a land brimming with beautiful film locations, Italy promises much and delivers. Pledges of sun and *la dolce vita* – wine, good food, a slower pace of life – draw tourists from central and northern Europe like moths to a flame. Americans and especially the Brits come looking for the kind of romance that Diane Lane finds in the 2003 film adaptation of Frances Mayes's novel *Under the Tuscan Sun*. And for directors hoping to find bright, beautiful locations, Italy's geographic diversity ensures a range of landscapes that is nothing if not many-splendored.

Order up a sun-drenched vineyard, a breezy balcony over the Mediterranean, or snow-covered mountains – Italy has it all. Films made here almost market themselves on the strength of picturesque places alone, with locations such as the vertical peaks of the Dolomites, the picture-postcard prettiness of Lake Como, playground of Milan's elite, and Tuscany, many a director's dream. Coastlines and islands like Ischia and Procida in the Bay of Naples, the dramatic Amalfi Coast, the volcanic Aeolian Islands, and Sicily allow cinematographers to bring the land's dramatic cliffs, quaint fishing villages, and turquoise coves to the silver screen.

No précis can do justice to all of Italy in the movies, but its presence is undeniably colossal. Screen divas Sophia Loren and Gina Lollobrigida always knew their homeland as a great

frame for filming, as did the nation's great directors, among them Vittorio De Sica, Bernardo Bertolucci, Roberto Rossellini, Luchino Visconti, and, of course, Federico Fellini with longtime actor-friend Marcello Mastroianni. With the charm and humor of its people, the beauty of the language and the wonderful light spilling over unforgettable vistas, *la bella Italia* is a filmmaker's and an audience's big-screen dream come true.

Tuscany: Everybody's Darling

Tuscany has long enjoyed an exalted place in the cultural imagination of filmmakers worldwide. Envisioned as quiet, bucolic,

Top landscape film locations

1. Lake Como: **Casino Royale, Ocean's Twelve**
2. Dolomites, Val di Fassa: **Cliffhanger**
3. Fiesole: **A Room with a View**
4. Villa Vignamaggio: **Much Ado About Nothing**
5. Sant'Anna in Camprena: **The English Patient**
6. Montepulciano: **Heaven**
7. Val d'Orcia: **Under the Tuscan Sun**
8. Ischia: **The Talented Mr. Ripley**
9. Amalfi Coast, Ravello: **A Good Woman, Beat the Devil**
10. Salina: **The Postman**
11. Panarea: **L'Avventura**
12. Stromboli: **Stromboli**
13. Lago Piana d'Albanesi: **The Leopard**
14. Forza d'Agrò: **The Godfather I & II**

Tuscany is always popular with filmmakers. Envisioned as quiet and sun-soaked, landscapes like Val d'Orcia (left) in *Under the Tuscan Sun* capture our imaginations as tranquil retreats far from the modern world.

and perennially sun-soaked, it reigns in our collective imagination as a secret garden hidden away from the modern world. Director Audrey Wells discovers Tuscany's regenerative power in her 2003 screen adaptation of the popular novel **Under the Tuscan Sun.** Departing somewhat from the original storyline, Wells sends the depressed divorcée and writer Frances (Diane Lane) on a bus trip through Tuscany. Early landscape sequences showing a hamlet in the distance were filmed in the **Val d'Orcia,** or **Orcia Valley,** just outside of **Pienza,** one of the region's Renaissance architectural gems.

Frances's tour passes the Renaissance church of **Madonna di San Biagio** just outside the walls of **Montepulciano,** and then stops for a taste of the good life amid the market stalls of **Cortona.** The small city, birthplace of Pietro da Cortona, a master of Baroque painting and architecture, immediately enchants her. She spies a real estate ad for a villa named "Bramasole," and before she knows it, she has purchased the ramshackle house and committed herself to an extensive renovation – a metaphor, of course, for piecing her life back together.

The house shown in the film is in fact a private residence, **Villa Laura** on **Via delle Contesse** near Cortona. Wells told the *Financial Times* that she was looking for "a believable house of modest scale," which is exactly what this residence located

In *Under the Tuscan Sun*, divorcée Frances (Diane Lane) takes a bus trip through Tuscany and decides to stay. The movie makes the most of landscapes near Pienza (left) and the gardens of Farneta Abbey (right).

within walking distance of the town provides – all ensconced in the dreamlike vistas of Tuscany.

Frances makes friends and finds her place in the bustling life of the town, centered on Cortona's **Piazza Signorelli.** She realizes that she has truly found a new home in Tuscany when she accepts a Christmas gift from the real estate agent Signor Martini (Vincent Riotta) as carolers sing on a snowy **Piazza della Repubblica.** All the while work on her house progresses, thanks to the hilarious troupe of Polish builders and her own sense of humor and determination. A chance meeting in Rome brings her together with the handsome Marcello (Raoul Bova). Their affair in the cliff-hanging seaside town of **Positano** on the **Amalfi Coast** is memorable for the sense of release Frances experiences at meeting her first post-divorce admirer, but also for the sheer beauty of this lovely region just south of Naples.

When her pregnant friend Patti (Sandra Oh) shows up from the States, Frances neglects the romance and finds herself the "patron saint" of two neighborhood teenagers whose love affair plays out back in Tuscany on the **Piazza Grande** in **Montepulciano,** a location central to the film *A Midsummer Night's Dream* (1999) starring Kevin Kline and Michelle Pfeiffer. An exterior shot of the church of **Madonna di San Biagio** in Montepulciano is employed here as the film cuts to the wedding ceremony. Happiness finds Frances in the scenes of the wedding at the film's close, shot in the lush gardens at **Farneta Abbey,** located just off the road between **Camucia** and **Foiano.**

Beauty Spots in Romantic Dramas

Just outside **Pienza** lies the quiet abbey of **Sant'Anna in Camprena,** a location that served Anthony Minghella's masterful film *The English Patient* (1996) as a taste of Tuscan landscape heaven, a welcome, bucolic refuge from the horrors of World War II. It is in this abbey surrounded by shade-giving pines that Hana (Juliette Binoche) attempts to nurse a mysterious burn victim (Ralph Fiennes) back to health. The charming scenes of Hana

Kenneth Branagh plays Benedick to Emma Thompson's Beatrice in the screen adaptation of Shakespeare's *Much Ado About Nothing.* The movie was filmed in the gardens and fields of Villa Vignamaggio.

being hoisted up in a rope seat to admire the fifteenth-century frescoes by Piero della Francesca were shot in the **Basilica di San Francesco** in **Arezzo,** some 50 miles (80 kilometers) southeast of the great Renaissance city of Florence.

One of the most striking movies to explore the beauty of the Tuscan landscape is the lesser-known film ***Heaven*** (2002). Tom Tykwer, director of surprise hit *Run Lola Run* (1999) and *Perfume: The Story of a Murderer* (2006), casts Cate Blanchett as Philippa, a schoolteacher who takes the law into her own hands, and Giovanni Ribisi as Filippo, a young police officer who comes to her aid. Philippa is arrested after she bombs an office

Just outside Pienza lies the quiet abbey of Sant'Anna in Camprena, a location that served in *The English Patient* as a welcome refuge from the carnage of World War II. In this Tuscan abbey, Hana (Juliette Binoche) attempts to nurse a mysterious burn victim (Ralph Fiennes) back to health.

building in Turin, and Filippo helps her to escape. Together they flee to the golden hills of Tuscany that stretch to the horizon and fill their minds with the futile hope of a future together. When they reach **Montepulciano,** Philippa spots a friend of hers at a wedding on the main piazza who arranges a place for them to spend the night. After a brief meeting with Filippo's father (Remo Girone) at the church of **Madonna di San Biagio,** they settle in at a rustic country house. The sequences that follow are stunning and almost surreal, with the couple walking the golden hills punctuated by lonely trees like Adam and Eve in a dream-like Garden of Eden.

Loss of Innocence: Hill Towns and Villas between Florence and Siena

Innocence and its loss are the central themes in a Tuscan-shot film that features the beautiful young actress Liv Tyler. **Stealing Beauty** (1996) by legendary Italian director Bernardo Bertolucci is a movie with all the right trappings: a house party at sixteenth-century **Villa Bianchi Bandinelli** at **Via Geggiano 1** in **Pianella** just northeast of Siena, cypress trees in the moonlight, olive groves, vineyards, good wine, and a nubile starlet on the verge of womanhood, best known these days as the elfin beauty Arwen from the *Lord of the Rings* trilogy (2001-2003).

The New York Times observed that the film was imbued with "the intellectual heft of a cotton puff," and audiences seemed to agree. Bertolucci's first film in his homeland after fifteen years of self-imposed exile flopped at the box office, despite casting Jeremy Irons in a lead role. Nevertheless, it is worth a peek if only to admire Liv Tyler's looks against a backdrop of charming locations. Several scenes were shot in exclusive little hamlets near Siena, including **Castelnuovo Berardenga, Villa Spender** at **San Sano, San Regolo,** and **Gaiole in Chianti.** Narrow, winding roads lead from Siena to these tiny hilltop refuges dotted with old manor houses and kitchens that wear their Michelin stars with a lightness typical of carefree Italian living.

A ravishing landscape, a barley field near Fiesole where George sweeps Lucy into his arms, frames a memorable scene in *A Room with a View.*

The good life can be enjoyed closer to the Tuscan capital as well. Kenneth Branagh's romantic comedy **Much Ado About Nothing** (1993) was set not as Shakespeare would have liked it, in Sicilian Messina, but on a Tuscan hilltop a hearty stone's throw from Florence. The gardens and fountains of **Villa Vignamaggio** offer a delightful playground for the Bard's cavorting lovers, a veritable Eden in miniature and a perfect foil to Don John's dastardly plots. The manor house at **Via Petriolo 5** just south of Greve in Chianti and 20 miles (30 kilometers) south of Florence is the hilly, wine-country setting that captured the "hot-tempered Italianate qualities" of the 400-year-old play. Today the noble house is a hotel offering wine tastings and country tours, as well as a popular stop for film aficionados.

Another romantic frolic that inhabits an important position in recent film history, **A Room with a View,** also employs Tuscany's charms to great effect. James Ivory and Ismail Merchant adapted E.M. Forster's 1908 novel to the silver screen with enough sensory overload and strong performances for an Academy Award. The directing and producing duo's 1985 film

One of the most striking movies to explore the beauty of the Tuscan landscape is *Heaven.* Key scenes take place at the hillside church of Madonna di San Biagio in Montepulciano (below). The surreal sequences show Filippo (Giovanni Ribisi) and Philippa (Cate Blanchett) walking over endless golden hills.

Capri appears as the backdrop to Joan Fontaine and Joseph Cotten's *September Affair* (right). The islands in the Bay of Naples – Ischia, Procida, and Capri with its famed Faraglioni rocks (above) – have appealed to filmmakers since the days following World War II.

captured the sense of adventure and naughtiness abroad under the guise of an educational English holiday, with Lucy Honeychurch's (Helena Bonham Carter) most important lessons set before pretty churches. Florence played an important role in the film – especially the legendary view from the **Hotel degli Orafi** at the end of the film – but it was a ravishing landscape, the barley field near **Fiesole** where George sweeps Lucy into his arms, that makes for the most memorable scene.

Bay of Naples: Ischia and Procida

A trio of islands in the Bay of Naples – Ischia and her little sister Procida, as well as the sun-kissed playground of Capri with its famed Faraglioni rocks – has sung its siren song to filmmakers since the days following World War II. When on the mainland, visitors' attention is focused squarely on the volcano of Mount Vesuvius and the ruins at Pompeii and Herculaneum. Board a ferry from Naples or Pozzuoli, the hardscrabble hometown of Sophia Loren, and the urban din of Naples slips away. The light is infused with the evanescent rainbows of the ocean's spray, and the scent of lemon trees heavy with the fruit that flavors the region's sweet Limoncello liqueur perfumes the breeze. The

slopes of the hilly isles emerge above the boat's bow like a promise fulfilled.

The dramatic isle of **Capri** makes a memorable appearance as the backdrop to Joan Fontaine and Joseph Cotten's ***September Affair*** (1950), as well as in ***It Started in Naples*** (1960) starring Clark Gable and Sophia Loren. But it is the other two main isles in the Bay of Naples that really shine on the silver screen. Ischia is the largest of the three, and the location that French director René Clément chose to showcase the first Mr. Ripley film, **Plein soleil** (*Purple Noon*, 1960).

According to Andrew Wilson, who wrote *Beautiful Shadow: A Life of Patricia Highsmith,* the idea for the 1955 thriller *The Talented Mr. Ripley* occurred to the author when she watched a young man strolling on the beach at Positano on the nearby Amalfi Coast. The screen adaptation was shot on the isle of **Ischia,** whose handsome cliffs and secret coves could be outshone only by the sheer physical beauty of actor Alain Delon, cast as wily Tom Ripley. The little fishing village of **Sant'Angelo,** with its steep cobbled streets and curiously formed peninsula, plays fictional Mongibello in this movie, the fishing village hideaway where Tom Ripley is sent by a wealthy shipping magnate to retrieve his son.

Better known these days is director Anthony Minghella's **The Talented Mr. Ripley** (1999), an ode to the city of Rome that takes a detour to Naples but begins memorably in Ischia and Procida. Mixing martinis and sailing the Bay of Naples fill Tom's (Matt Damon) first hours with the Greenleaf heir Dickie (Jude Law) in Mongibello, filmed on the pretty isle of Ischia. **Ischia Ponte** and its dramatic **Castello Aragonese** form a striking backdrop to Tom's arrival on the island. He plots an "accidental" meeting with Dickie and his girlfriend Marge (Gwyneth Paltrow) at Ischia's **Bagno Antonio beach,** its umbrellas dotting sands just off of the promenade of Ischia Porto that offer a view of the castle.

One island, two Ripleys: Matt Damon grows into his role as *The Talented Mr. Ripley* when he arrives at Ischia Ponte with the dramatic Castello Aragonese (above), and looks for his prey on Bagno Antonio beach (left). In the first Mr. Ripley film, *Plein soleil* from 1960, Alain Delon plays the mysterious pretender lurking in the village of Sant'Angelo (below).

The action moves seamlessly to the neighboring isle of **Procida** and its port of **Marina Grande** and the fishing village of **Marina Corricella.** The town's distinctive streets, squares, and churches figure heavily in conjuring Mongibello, but are also known from another famous film. Marina Corricella hosted the dockside

Marina Corricella on Procida hosted scenes from *The Postman*, with Philippe Noiret as the poet Pablo Neruda and Massimo Troisi as his friend Mario.

scenes at the Vino e Cucina bar in **The Postman** (*Il Postino*, 1994) starring Philippe Noiret as exiled Chilean poet Pablo Neruda and the delightful Massimo Troisi as his friendly post-man, Mario. The church dome of **La Chiesa della Madonna delle Grazie** features in scenes in which Mario makes recordings toward the end of the film, as does Procida's cliffy beach of **Pozzo Vecchio.**

Producer Tom Sternberg noted that in *The Talented Mr. Ripley,* the Italian location was part of the film's "romantic style." Co-producer William Horberg agreed, adding that "the landscape is an important part of the story. The canvas in the film is the Italy of the late 1950s – its music, the high style of the Via Veneto in Rome, the clothes, the cars, the motor scoot-ers, the atmosphere of rich Americans abroad, even the great movies of the period by Fellini, Antonioni, and Visconti." Film buffs may recall that Billy Wilder was of the same opinion: Similar reasons convinced the comic director to send Jack Lemmon as Wendell Armbruster, Jr. to Ischia in **Avanti!** (1972). The harried businessman follows in his father's footsteps and unexpectedly meets the love of his life, Pamela Piggott (Juliet Mills), on the island's sunny shores.

"The View" from the Amalfi Coast

From Naples the drive south to the adjacent Sorrento Peninsula and the stunning Amalfi Coast on its south face is short but eventful. With the sprawling metropolis in the rearview mirror, a steep, two-lane road ascends the forested hills until the fabled town of Ravello appears. The hamlet has long been famous for residents such as the composer Richard Wagner and writer Gore Vidal, but above all for its astonishing panoramic views out into the endless blue of the Mediterranean a thousand feet below.

From Ravello, visitors descend via a winding road to numer-ous fishing villages. Clutches of cubic houses in gleaming white or pastel tones cling precariously from the steep, lemon-trel-lised slopes of the Lattari Mountains, the range that lends the entire peninsula its rugged aspect. Alternating between sunny Elysium in summer and the tempestuous high seas of winter storms, the Amalfi Coast is a landscape of drama dotted with Saracen towers and infused with an oriental air. No wonder film-makers find it easy to envision their leading ladies and dashing male stars draped across this stunning UNESCO World Heri-tage-listed coastline bathed in a golden light.

The location certainly matched director Mike Barker's ver-sion of Oscar Wilde's breakthrough play "Lady Windermere's Fan." While **A Good Woman** (2004) was pooh-poohed by the famous *New York Times* film critic Stephen Holden as a "misbe-

Humphrey Bogart and Gina Lollobrigida in *Beat the Devil:* adventure and comedy set against "the view" from Ravello on the Amalfi Coast.

gotten Hollywood-minded screen adaptation," its spectacular Amalfi Coast locations infuse the movie with an undeniable visual charm. Helen Hunt plays the experienced seductress Stella Erlynne to Scarlett Johansson's loyal young newlywed Meg Windermere in a suspenseful tug-of-war over men and money.

to strike it rich in Africa enjoys cult status now, but the film's bizarre characters baffled audiences when it made its debut. Humphrey Bogart, Jennifer Jones, and Gina Lollobrigida star in the spoof that features several of Ravello's highlights – the **Piazza Duomo, Villa Rufolo,** and **Villa Cimbrone** – as locations.

The café scenes in the film's early sequences were shot on the **Piazza del Duomo** in **Amalfi,** one of a consortium of powerful medieval "maritime republics" along with Pisa, Venice, and Genoa. Numerous long shots of this Arab-influenced seaside town embellish the film. The town of **Atrani** just above Amalfi makes an appearance when Meg goes for a walk and a flirt with the distracting Lord Darlington (Stephen Campbell Moore). The pink house where Stella winks at the man who calls her "bella signora" is across from **La Risacca Bar** in Atrani, and the opera house she visits with her admirer, the angelic Tuppy (Tom Wilkinson), is a small church in the same town.

The storied **Villa Rufolo** in **Ravello** is the star of the club scenes. Aristocrats nod off in the dining room and occasionally drive golf balls into the great blue yonder, the all-important view of the sea that lends this exclusive stretch of coastline its rarefied cachet. Ravello's **Hotel Palumbo** hosts a touching scene between Stella and Tuppy, and the town's pretty main square appears in several scenes. The camera work, with its generous use of the Amalfi Coast's dramatic position far above the sea, helps to bring the tensions mounting between the characters into sharp focus.

The German-speaking world may recognize **Ravello** and its famous villas as the ersatz locations for Madeira and Corfu where Romy Schneider plays an ailing empress in the **Sissi** trilogy's third film (1957). Ravello had spent a glorious day in the cinematic sun a few years earlier when John Huston filmed the first segment of **Beat the Devil** (1953) on this coast. The story of crooks hanging out in an Italian port before sailing off

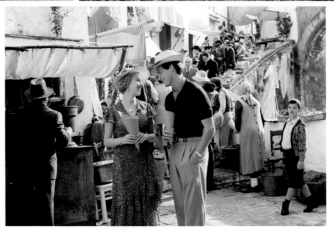

The towns of Amalfi (top left) and Ravello, with its famous vista from Villa Rufolo (top right), present a pretty stage for a summer flirt in *A Good Woman.* Newlywed Meg Windermere (Scarlett Johansson) and the distracting Lord Darlington (Stephen Campbell Moore) go for a stroll in Atrani (above).

Scenes shot at the popular Hotel Palumbo did not make the final cut, but the auberge featured prominently as a social hub during filming. The cast and crew of Roberto Rossellini's **Viaggio in Italia** (*Journey to Italy,* 1953), which was filming in the nearby town of **Maiori,** visited the *Beat the Devil* troop at the Palumbo and turned it and Ravello's Piazza Duomo into their playground. Bogart and writer Truman Capote – flown in to write scenes for the film – also frequented the swank Hotel Caruso, whose view Gore Vidal has immortalized as "the most beautiful in the world." A plaque in the gardens adjacent to the Palazzo Sasso hotel in Ravello commemorates the filming.

The Gorgeous North – The Mighty Peaks of the Dolomites

Eighteenth-century French geologist Déodat de Dolomieu would have scoffed at the idea that the range that bears his name could ever be mistaken for the Rocky Mountains. And yet it is Sylvester Stallone's rock-climbing flick *Cliffhanger* (1993) that paints the most extensive portrait of the Dolomites in modern action movies. The film's kidnapping plot was forced to vie for viewers' attention with the dramatic crags on the Italian-Austrian border, a natural wonderland for skiers and hikers. For cinematographers, it is an ideal topographical expression of danger.

Jean-Jacques Annaud's heartwarming nature film *The Bear* (1988) was shot not in the Canadian Rockies, but in the Dolomites. It was here, too, that Arnold Fanck filmed his ground-breaking silent flick *Mountain of Destiny* (1924), starring climb-

ing idol Luis Trenker. The picture helped to launch mountaineering movies as a genre, and inspired Leni Riefenstahl, best known for her notorious Nazi propaganda film *Triumph of the Will* (1935), to devote her life to filmmaking.

Visually fascinating and daringly precarious, the pale massifs of the Dolomites attracted the attention of *Cliffhanger* director Renny Harlin as a stand-in location. The filmmaker chose them as the stage for his stunt-rich action flick when the U.S. environmental authorities prohibited him from filming in the Colorado Rockies. The cameras concentrated on the landscapes of **Passo Pordoi,** the breathtaking Val di Fassa or **Fassa Valley, Sella Pass,** and **Val Gardena. Passo di Falzarego** with its **Cinque Torri,** or "Five Towers," credited as having inspired J.R.R. Tolkien when he wrote *The Lord of the Rings,* also played

Sylvester Stallone's rock-climbing thriller *Cliffhanger* paints the most extensive portrait of the Dolomites in modern action movies with peaks like those visible from the Sella Pass (above). Arnold Fanck's groundbreaking silent film *Mountain of Destiny* starring climbing idol Luis Trenker was shot in this region, as were scenes from Jean-Jacques Annaud's nature film *The Bear.*

a part. All are close to the renowned climbers' base at **Canazei** and the famed Catinaccio or "Rose Garden" peaks with the exception of Passo di Falzarego, a mountain pass that witnessed fierce fighting between Austrian and Italian Alpine units during World War I. These battles were waged along the *vie ferrate* trails, rock-hewn paths equipped with iron rungs, pegs, and ladders that hikers and climbers still use today.

The Great War visited the capital of the Dolomite region, too, but the tiny ski town of **Cortina D'Ampezzo** has all but forgotten it. Nestled at the bottom of a peak-ringed valley, the home of the 1956 Winter Olympics attracts a well-heeled crowd from Milan and Venice. The dramatic landscapes radiating out from Cortina are a symphony of majestic snowcapped peaks. A slope-side highlight is the sprawling Victorian **Miramonti Majestic Grand**

Hotel, a five-star residence just outside the old town where James Bond (Roger Moore) lodged in *For Your Eyes Only* (1981). Bond meets the bubbly blond ice-skater Bibi Dahl (Lynn-Holly Johnson) and her dastardly trainer Aristotle Kristatos (Julian Glover) at the **Olympic Ice Stadium** at Via dello Stadio 1. Memorable scenes showing the snowy slopes include daredevil ski chases past the **Olympic Bob Track "Eugenio Monti"** at **Ronco** and the concrete **Olympic Ski Jump "Italia"** in the **Zuel** area, not far from the Miramonte. Comedies have found reason to visit Cortina as well, among them the original *Pink Panther* (1963) and the sequel to *Bridget Jones's Diary* (2001), *Bridget Jones: The Edge of Reason* (2004).

The ski town of Cortina D'Ampezzo and the landmarks of the 1956 Winter Olympics appear in the Bond film *For Your Eyes Only* with Roger Moore.

Villa Erba in Cernobbio exudes an air of privilege, making it an ideal setting for *The Luzhin Defence* (left) and *Ocean's Twelve* (right).

Luck and Love on Lake Como

Nestled into the foothills on the south side of the Alps lies Lake Como, favored by filmmakers as both a location and a holiday retreat. In most cineastes' minds, it is legendary director Luchino Visconti who is most associated with the area. The late nineteenth-century **Villa Erba** in **Cernobbio** was his childhood home and where the veteran filmmaker would reside in later years. The stuccoed and gilt salons and gracious gardens have always attracted movie crews to the grand house.

The Visconti villa is now a conference center that promotes itself as a film location, a role it captured in **Ocean's Twelve** (2004). George Clooney and Julia Roberts tease wealthy thief François Toulour (Vincent Cassel) while sitting on a lakeview terrace by the house, chosen to stand in as the crook's sumptuous digs. Production designer Philip Messina was pleased with the location, and praised the villa's pretty position as "an amazing and beautiful little spot with several rock formations in the water and a great seascape." He and the crew were barred from filming inside the house, so he had to improvise. "We built a small wing onto the building, as well as an entire terrace onto the front of the house, which cosmetically refurbished it." The effect is one of privilege and luxury, one that fit as beautifully to the atmosphere of *Ocean's Twelve* as it did to the excellent drama **The Luzhin Defence** (2000). The movie, based on Vladimir Nabokov's novel, employed Villa Erba's exterior and gardens to represent the hotel central to the story of chess player Sascha Luzhin (John Turturro) and his saucy society love interest, Natalia (Emily Watson).

Another fine house and lakeside panorama often seen on the silver screen is **Villa Balbianello** near **Lenno**, a town across the water from Bellagio, one of the lake's main municipalities.

Built for Cardinal Angelo Maria Durini at the close of the eighteenth century, the residence is now in the hands of the Fondo per l'Ambiente Italiano (FAI), Italy's national trust. While the mansion brims with artefacts that recall its last owner, explorer Guido Monzino, it is the villa's paradisiacal gardens that attract filmmakers. Embellished with panoramic terraces and a picturesque, triple-arched loggia that marks the promontory's highest point, the house and its blossoming surroundings extend like a fairy barge into the lake.

This otherworldly landscape hosted the elaborately costumed Princess Amidala (Natalie Portman) and Anakin Skywalker (Hayden Christensen) on their visit to the leisure planet of Naboo in **Star Wars: Episode II – Attack of the Clones** (2002). Scenes from **A Month by the Lake** (1995) starring Vanessa

Julia Roberts and George Clooney sip bubbly and tease a wealthy thief from a lakeview terrace built onto Villa Erba for the filming of *Ocean's Twelve*.

"Blond Bond" Daniel Craig puts in an appearance at Villa Balbianello, a fine house on Lake Como with a magical lakeside panorama often seen on the silver screen. Fans of *Casino Royale* can visit during opening hours to trace Craig's footsteps from his first role as secret agent James Bond.

Villa Balbianello provides a lush landscape for Princess Amidala (Natalie Portman) and Anakin Skywalker's (Hayden Christensen) trip to the planet of Naboo in *Star Wars: Episode II – Attack of the Clones*. Scenes from *A Month by the Lake* with Vanessa Redgrave were also filmed here.

Redgrave were filmed here, too, as were the sequences from *Casino Royale* (2006) directed by Martin Campbell of *Golden-Eye* (1995) fame. Fans of British heartthrob Daniel Craig can visit Villa Balbianello to trace his footsteps from his first role as secret agent James Bond, followed by a short excursion to Mr. White's (Jesper Christensen) **Villa La Gaeta** near **San Siro** where the film's final scenes were shot.

Sicily's Movie Mafia

Possibly the most famous movie to be associated with Italy's south is **The Godfather** (1972), the first film in the legendary trilogy directed by Francis Ford Coppola. Based on the novel by Mario Puzo, the tale of the New York City-based Corleone clan centers on the transfer of power from aging organized crime chief Don Vito Corleone (Marlon Brando) to his youngest son, Michael (Al Pacino). Locations in and around Manhattan abound, but among the most touching scenes are those featuring Michael in exile: He hides out amidst the breathtaking vistas of his family's native Sicily after executing the men responsible for shooting his father.

The initial scenes of Michael's time with the "real" Sicilians were filmed against the terraced **foothills of Mount Etna** on Sicily's northeast coast. The initial sequence, in which

past olive trees and rough scrub en route to Corleone, they are in fact approaching the fortified Norman town of **Forza d Agrò.** Topped with castle ruins, Forza is instantly recognizable in the film by the distinctive sixteenth-century **Chiesa Madre,** a church whose façade attests to a clumsy remodeling in Baroque times. Fans will spot this church

Michael hikes through fields with his bodyguards Calo and Fabrizio, uses the sweeping melody of the *Godfather* theme to underscore the drama of a countryside rendered spectacular by eons of volcanic activity. The sense of foreboding that weighs upon Michael in light of his crimes could hardly have found a better expression in landscape.

The Mafia family in Mario Puzo's novel was supposed to have hailed from Corleone. But the town south of the Sicilian capital of Palermo was too modern-looking in the early 1970s to match the film's setting in the years after World War II. Instead, Coppola chose to shoot in a more bucolic part of the island. He scouted the mountainous region just south of the "toe" of the Italian boot, the immensely popular **Ionian Coast** between Messina and Taormina. When Michael and his bodyguards ramble

throughout the trilogy, especially in the first flashback sequences of **The Godfather II** (1974), when the boy Vito Andolini, later Corleone (Oreste Baldini), flees his hometown to sail to America.

In the first *Godfather* film, Michael and his sidekicks emerge from an orchard and encounter wide-eyed beauty

In *The Godfather,* Michael (Al Pacino) meets his first wife, Apollonia (Simonetta Stefanelli), in Sicily. They live in the Castello degli Schiavi (above) until tragedy strikes. Michael then returns to New York and his father, Don Vito Corleone (Marlon Brando).

Apollonia (Simonetta Stefanelli), the daughter of a barkeep in Corleone. They ask about the girl at **Bar Vitelli,** a watering hole that still exists today in **Sávoca,** a tiny medieval town 8 miles (13 kilometers) north of Forza popular for its picturesque hilltop position. Michael requests an introduction, and after a brief courtship the two wed in the **Chiesa di San Nicolò** in Sávoca. Members of the wedding party walk in procession through the dusty streets, mopping their brows with handkerchiefs against the sweltering temperatures as the sparse flora wilt and the earth cracks on the sunbaked hills.

Tragedy strikes the young couple in the driveway before the eighteenth-century **Castello degli Schiavi** close to **Fiumefreddo di Sicilia,** just south of Taormina. This same house with its eccentric corner turrets appears in all three films of the trilogy, including the flashbacks in *The Godfather II,* when Vito Corleone (Robert De Niro) returns home to avenge his mother, and the family meeting in Sicily in Part III. The final film of the series is notable, too, for its use of locations in **Palermo,** such as the restored **opera house,** which appears in the shocking finale. Even more impressive is the role played by the director's gorgeous young daughter, now regaled as one of Hollywood's favorite directors. Sofia Coppola plays Mary Corleone, the silken-haired Mafia princess who falls for her handsome cousin "Vinnie" Mancini-Corleone (Andy Garcia).

The Godfather reigns over Sicily's array of big-picture movie locations, but other famous films have flirted with this region as well. Woody Allen filmed the chorus scenes from **Mighty Aphrodite** (1995) at the ancient Greek amphitheater in **Taormina,** a structure dating to the second century B.C. with an enviable view of Mt. Etna. A famous summer arts festival takes place here every year; the theater has even hosted Italy's version of the Oscars. The city's **San Domenico Palace,** whose cloisters were transformed into a hotel in 1896, has appeared as a location in several successful Italian films, including Michelangelo Antonioni's classic **L'Avventura** (1960).

Drama with Visconti and Tornatore

Sicily meets the sea north of Catania in a rocky stretch known as the Riviera dei Ciclopi, or Cyclops's Coast. It was here that director Luchino Visconti filmed his post-war masterpiece **La Terra Trema** (*The Ground Trembles,* 1948) with the help of the hardy denizens of **Aci Trezza.** He hired townspeople as extras, crediting them as "Pescatori Siciliani," or Sicilian fishermen. The film based on Giovanni Verga's novel *I Malavoglia* would win Visconti a coveted nomination for the Golden Lion at the Venice film festival.

The story of poor Sicilian fishermen pitted against the powerful companies that buy their catch reflects Visconti's Marxist views while demonstrating a documentary style typical of Italian neorealism, the genre he is credited with founding. The ordinary citizens of Aci Trezza, speaking in their heavy regional dialect, attempt to break the stranglehold the wholesalers have

Scenes of Michael's courtship and wedding were filmed not in Corleone, but in Sávoca. Highlights include the Bar Vitelli and the Church of San Nicolò.

Visconti filmed *La Terra Trema* (*The Ground Trembles*) with the help of the fishermen of Aci Trezza. The Rocks of Cyclops (left) feature in the film.

on their livelihood, rising up in protest against the backdrop of the **Faraglioni dei Ciclopi.** The **Rocks of Cyclops** are mentioned in *The Odyssey* as the boulders Polyphemus lobbed at Ulysses after the hero blinded him with a burning stake. The sweeping cinematography of this film made a star out of the little harbor town. Additional scenes were also shot in **Aci Castello,** a seaside town to the south whose Norman castle offers excellent views of the Rocks of Cyclops and isle of Lachea.

Italian director Giuseppe Tornatore invites movie lovers to travel farther south in his native Sicily to **Siracusa,** or Syracuse, an ancient city known for its dictators – called "tyrants" – and for the battles between the Greeks and Carthaginians waged there. It is the city's sun-bleached waterfront with the mighty **Castello Maniace** in the background that frames the tragic tale of **Malèna** (2000), a woman whose husband has gone to war and left her to fend for herself. Model-actress Monica Bellucci plays the title role of a local beauty universally adored by men, but above all by the teenager Renato (Giuseppe Sulfaro). The tale turns dark when news arrives that Malèna's husband has died on the front. Open season is declared on the city's most lusted-after woman, a drastic development set against the backdrop of the ubiquitous blue sea. Some 20 miles (35 kilometers) south of Siracusa, **Noto,** rebuilt as a Baroque gem after an earthquake in 1693, also stood in for several city scenes.

Fans of Tornatore will recall an earlier visit the director made via the movies to his hometown of **Bagheria** in *Cinema Paradiso* (1988), whose famous **Palazzo Palagonia** makes an appearance in Michelangelo Antonioni's classic *L'Avventura* (1960). *Cinema Paradiso,* winner of the Oscar for Best Foreign Language Film, takes a long look at life centered on the **Piazza Grande** in the hamlet of **Palazzo Adriano,** 53 miles (85 kilometers) south of Palermo. Here, a boy named Totò (Salvatore Cascio) befriends the projectionist Alfredo (Philippe Noiret) at the local movie house. In reality there's no cinema here: The movie house where the young man dreams of becoming a filmmaker was a carefully constructed set.

On the Trail of the Leopard

"One of the films I live by" is how Martin Scorsese described **Il Gattopardo** (*The Leopard,* 1963), a dramatic tour de force that won the Golden Palm at Cannes and set a milestone in film history. Luchino Visconti shot the epic film in Palermo and amid the golden hills that roll inland from the island's northern coast. Starring Burt Lancaster, Alain Delon, and Claudia Cardinale, the screenplay is based upon Giuseppe Tomasi di Lampedusa's posthumous 1958 novel of the same name. The story of Prince Fabrizio Salina reflects the turmoil that the author's monarchist forefathers would have experienced when the revolutionary leader Garibaldi arrived in Sicily in 1860 to depose Francis II and establish a united Italy. The subsequent decline of the ruling class and the ascent of the Risorgimento define the film's plot and frame the vivid opening scenes.

Little Totò and the projectionist Alfredo in the hamlet of Palazzo Adriano in *Cinema Paradiso.*

The sun-bleached waterfront of Siracusa and the mighty Castello Maniace frame the tragic tale of *Malèna,* starring model-actress Monica Bellucci.

The film commences with the announcement that Garibaldi has landed in Sicily, a development that the aristocratic Salina (Burt Lancaster) greets with disgust. He storms out onto the terrace of his villa and demands a carriage to Palermo, sequences that were shot at the **Villa Boscogrande** on **Via Tommaso Natale 91, Palermo,** now a hotel whose neoclassical lines are framed by high, sunbaked hills. Salina, his wife, and the family priest set off for the clan's palace in Donnafugata – a real town in southeast Sicily, but not used in filming.

En route, they traverse an unforgiving landscape until the dry ridges give way to a surprising vista. The bright blue waters of **Lago Piana d'Albanesi** some 15 miles (25 kilometers) south of Palermo come into view, a lake framed by a mountainous backdrop. The carriage is soon ordered to halt: The rebels refuse to let Salina drive on. Luckily help arrives. Salina's nephew Tancredi, played by Alain Delon, flexes his authority as an officer in the resistance and secures their safe passage. The metaphor of monarchic privilege is mirrored in the events that unfold, but also in the way the landscapes are used: Only the free – that is, the wealthy upper class, regardless of their political affiliation – can enjoy this degree of mobility.

The subsequent picnic and hunting scenes are a celebration of the undulating landscape of Sicily's **Conca d'Oro** or **Golden Conch region** and the areas inland from it. The family eventually arrives at its city palace on the main square of Donnafugata, in reality the town of **Ciminna,** shown several times in the course of the film. The seat of the Salinas is across from the cathedral, **Chiesa Madre,** a church that numbers among the main attractions of this hill town 25 miles (40 kilometers) southeast of Palermo. The family attends mass before retiring to the house.

Burt Lancaster is "the Leopard" in *Il Gattopardo.* **The Prince of Salina confronts Garibaldi's revolutionaries when they stop his carriage on a ridge above the bright blue waters of Lago Piana d'Albanesi (below).**

The Prince of Salina realizes that times are changing, and that the aristocracy must adapt or die. He raises no objection when Tancredi declares his wish to "marry down." The daughter of a wealthy landowner, Angelica (Claudia Cardinale), is beautiful, but not nobly born. What she lacks in social grace is made up for by her father's money, and the engagement is celebrated with pomp in the **Palazzo Monteleone** on **Piazza San Domenico** in **Palermo.** Tensions remain despite the strategic alliance of the classes, culminating in the long and elaborate ball scene filmed in the eighteenth-century **Palazzo Valguarnera-Gangi** on **Piazza Croce dei Vespri** in Palermo.

The Aeolians enjoy a reputation of breathtaking beauty. Michelangelo Antonioni filmed parts of *L'Avventura* on several of these volcanic islands.

Archipelago of Mystery and Magic: The Aeolian Islands

Draped across the Tyrrhenian Sea like a necklace of precious gems, the Aeolian Islands enjoy a reputation of breathtaking beauty derived from the archipelago's tumultuous volcanic origins. French novelist Guy de Maupassant extolled the isles off of Sicily as "little pieces of heaven which have fallen into the sea," a sentiment shared by holidaymakers who flock to the small beaches at summer's height. Michelangelo Antonioni filmed parts of his classic **L'Avventura** (1960) on several of the islands, most notably **Panarea, Basiluzzo,** and **Lisca Bianca.**

Situated some 25 miles (40 kilometers) from Milazzo, a city just west of Messina on Sicily's northern coast, smoking Vulcano is the southernmost isle in the Aeolian group. The dominion of King Aeolus from Homer's *Odyssey* is a jet-set hideaway with three mostly calm volcanoes. Adjacent to it is touristy **Lipari,** the largest of the seven inhabited isles and the site of an episode from the Italian movie **Kaos** (1984). More peaceful is Salina, the geographic center of the archipelago and a bucolic retreat revered by fans of **The Postman** (1994). To its west lie remote Filicudi and Alicudi, where movie stars moor yachts in secluded coves below their villas. East of Salina is pretty little

Panarea, the smallest of the isles and the most aristocratic of the group. It is the last stepping-stone leading to the pyramidal enigma of Stromboli, whose rising clouds of gases hint at its schizophrenic status as volcano and island.

This last isle will always be synonymous with Ingrid Bergman and Roberto Rossellini and the scandal-fraught making of **Stromboli** (1950). During filming, Bergman left her husband for the Italian director, a decision that incited a wave of moral outrage in the United States. Senator Edwin C. Johnson denounced the movie, claiming that bad boy Rossellini "has deceived the American people with an idiotic story of a volcano and a pregnant woman. We must protect ourselves against such scourges." The Swedish-born actress, who had become a star with her Hollywood breakthrough movie *Intermezzo: A Love Story* (1939) and box-office hits *Casablanca* (1942) and *Gaslight* (1944), suddenly found herself blacklisted by the major Hollywood studios.

To make matters worse, *Stromboli* was a flop: The story of Karin (Ingrid Bergman), a war refugee who weds a local island fisherman (Mario Vitale) to escape a displaced persons' camp, hardly reflects the director's – or his female lead's – talents. The grumbling volcano obligingly provided a threatening meta-

Ingrid Bergman, Roberto Rossellini, and their scandal-fraught film will always be synonymous with the island of Stromboli.

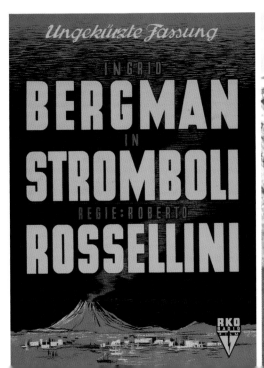

Ungekürzte Fassung

INGRID
BERGMAN
IN
STROMBOLI
REGIE: ROBERTO
ROSSELLINI

RKO

phor for a loveless marriage and a hopeless future on an island overshadowed by constant danger. Visitors who know the story never fail to visit the little red house where Bergman and Rossellini lived in **San Vincenzo,** close to the Chiesa di San Vincenzo church and the Locanda del Barbablu. Their love nest is now a pilgrimage site, its significance marked with a plaque.

The volcanic cone of Stromboli also lends the film **Ginostra** (2002) a bass note of drama. Harvey Keitel plays Matt Benson, an FBI agent tracking a Mafia murderer in the Aeolian isles. The story centers on the boy Ettore (Mattia De Martino), who has witnessed the crimes and must be protected so he can testify

Salina, Stromboli, and Alicudi in the critically acclaimed **Dear Diary** (*Caro Diario*, 1993).

The Sunny Side: Salina and *Il Postino*

Visitors know the quiet isle named after its defunct saltworks for its juicy green capers and golden dessert wine. But lovers of literature and the silver screen will immediately associate its bucolic peaks with **The Postman** (*Il Postino*, 1994). The movie, starring Philippe Noiret as exiled Chilean poet Pablo Neruda and his postman, Mario (Massimo Troisi), was nominated for five Oscars, including Best Picture. The sweet tale of

Peaceful Salina (right) is the geographic center of the Aeolian archipelago and a bucolic retreat revered by fans of *The Postman*. The friendship between two men is played out before the green peak of Monte dei Porri, on the porch of poet Pablo Neruda's little house, and on the narrow, cliffy beach at Pollara.

against the gangsters. Unwisely, Benson brings his wife and child along, a pair of innocents who attempt to provide Ettore with a home during their brief stay.

Jessie (Andie MacDowell) sets up house in a villa on the east coast of the tiny isle of **Panarea.** From the kitchen window and the terrace she can see **Stromboli's** crater spewing smoke and flame, an unsettling sight since her husband is busily hunting criminals in **Ginostra,** a settlement of white houses on Stromboli's west coast. He ventures out onto the lunar landscapes of the volcano's flank: Rivers of molten rock scorch the slopes of the **Sciara del Fuoco** lava canal as mysterious figures like the red-robed nun played by Asia Argento flee into gale force winds. Set designers and camera crew were forced to grapple with drastic and at times treacherous changes in the weather, a reflection of the archipelago's great dependence on nature's clemency. If the film reveals anything about the region, it is that these isles are an unpredictable volcanic wilderness far out to sea, not simply the breezy destinations of tourist brochures as depicted on Nanni Moretti's peripatetic boat ride from Lipari to

friendship and the pursuit of true love ended on a bitter note with Troisi's premature death. The actor devoted the last months of his life to this film, a project that involved numerous islanders: Locals played fishermen delivering their catch at the cliffs below the crater town of **Pollara** with the **Scoglio Faraglione** rocks silhouetted in the background.

Mario rides away from this scene with the peak of **Monte dei Porri** rising in the distance. It is this extinct volcanic peak that is so often seen in shots featuring him on his bicycle or in the background as the poet Pablo Neruda stands on the porch of his little house. The dwelling borrowed for filming is the private house of painter and lyricist Pippo Cafarella in Pollara, an address that still attracts its fair share of film enthusiasts, some of whom rent the cottage from the artist. Nestled amidst blossoming potted plants and olive trees, the terrace becomes the stage upon which Mario and Pablo play out their friendship, a relationship that begins with an exchange of literary lines and ripens with fresh verse on the beauty of the island spontaneously composed on the small, cliffy beach at **Pollara.**

THE LEGEND OF KARL MAY By Claudia Hellmann

The Germans have always had a soft spot for the North American Indians. Their enthusiasm for the Wild West can be attributed in great part to the writer Karl May (1842-1912). The author's travel and adventure stories took young readers to exotic locations such as the Orient and the Wild West. May himself never actually traveled to the American West, but relied on travel accounts written by Friedrich Gerstäcker for his material. May's prodigious imagination created the characters of Winnetou, the noble Apache chief, and his cowboy blood brother Old Shatterhand. In the 1960s, both protagonists found their way onscreen in the persons of French actor Pierre Brice and American Lex Barker, famous for his Tarzan roles.

A total of seventeen movie versions of Karl May's works were filmed between 1962 and 1968 – the most successful cinema series in postwar Germany. The formula was very simple: courageous heroes and dastardly scoundrels,

thrilling adventures in untamed landscapes, and all of it in glorious Technicolor and CinemaScope wide-screen format. The Karl May films may be old-fashioned Western fairy tales, but their success gave other filmmakers a new idea: shooting Westerns in Europe. Indirectly, May's work can be credited for the breakthrough of the spaghetti Western.

For the purposes of filming Karl May's novels, the wild, wild, West was transposed to Eastern Europe. It sounds strange, but it works: The beauty of landscapes in the former Yugoslavia guaranteed a certain authenticity of Western atmosphere in these films, even if the red sandstone of the American Southwest was replaced by the white limestone peaks of the Dalmatian range. Most of the scenes were filmed in a handful of spectacular film locations situated in what has since become Croatia. The **Lakes of Plitvica** are one such locale: The sixteen turquoise-blue lakes, stunningly interconnected by a series of cascades and waterfalls, formed the backdrop for the first film, *Treasure of Silver Lake* (1962). The silver lake is actually **Lake Kaluderovac,** one of the lower lakes, but no matter. The legendary cave where the treasure is hidden is located in a cliff face on the lake shore. Further scenes were shot at the great falls of **Lake Galovac** near the upper lakes and around **Lake Kozjak,** where final scenes show the blood brothers and their companions riding up the mountainside. Scenes in parts one and two of the Winnetou trilogy, such as the pursuit of Winnetou on Bear River, were also shot in the Lakes of Plitvica area.

Top landscape film locations

1. Lakes of Plitvica: **Treasure of Silver Lake**
2. Great gorge in Paklenica National Park: **Treasure of Silver Lake, Frontier Hellcat**
3. Zrmanja Canyon and its high plateau: **Apache Gold, Winnetou: The Desperado Trail**
4. Tulove Grede: **Apache Gold, Winnetou: The Desperado Trail**
5. Krka Waterfalls: **Apache Gold, Winnetou and Shatterhand in the Valley of Death**

Nscho-tschi dies at Tulove Grede (above). Winnetou on the River Zrmanja (center). The blood brothers ride by the peaks near Platak (far left).

The landscapes near the **Krka Waterfalls,** where many scenes were filmed, are just as appealing. These picturesque surroundings were chosen as the spot where Nscho-tschi (Marie Versini) and Old Shatterhand (Lex Barker) sit on the banks of the river in **Apache Gold** (1963); it is also where the evil Santer (Mario Adorf) meets the young Indian Black Eagle in the same film. This, too, was the site of the Apache camp in **Apache's Last Battle** (1964). In **Winnetou and Shatterhand in the Valley of Death** (1968), the blood brothers' canoe trip was filmed here.

In the films, the verdant countryside around the Lakes of Plitvica and the Krka Waterfalls were supplemented by the rugged cliffs in the **Paklenica National Park.** The great gorge or **Velika Paklenica** was the location chosen to represent the Ghost

Winnetou and Old Shatterhand at the picturesque Krka Waterfalls.

Canyon in *Treasure of Silver Lake,* while the smaller canyon that narrows at one end represents the Valley of Death in **Frontier Hellcat** (1964). Another popular shooting location was the dramatic **Zrmanja Canyon** and the high plateau directly above it, situated a few miles farther south near Obrovac, an area that resembles the American West. The Apache pueblo constructed for **Apache Gold** and **Winnetou: The Desperado Trail** (1965) was built on the plateau above the deep blue river. The River Zrmanja itself was the scene of the fight between Old Shatterhand and Chief Intschu-tschuna in *Apache Gold,* and was also where the burning rafts in *Winnetou: The Desperado Trail* were filmed.

The Mali Halan Pass winds its way up from the Zrmanja Canyon in a series of serpentine curves to **Tulove Grede,** a peak with a surprisingly impressive appearance considering its modest height – only 3,600 feet (1,100 meters). The peak is situated in the southeast of the Velebit mountain range, whose white limestone cliff faces have achieved iconic status as Karl May landscapes. Many fans are familiar with the chalky white crags on the summit as the location of Nugget Tsil in **Apache Gold.** Nscho-tschi dies in Old Shatterhand's arms at the foot of this mountain. Later, Santer confronts Apache spears at **Kapljuv Crater.** It is here that the trilogy comes to its conclusion: Winnetou's death was filmed high amid the craggy rock faces of Tulove Grede. In the distance, it's even possible to spot the Zrmanja Canyon. Unfortunately, film fans can't visit Tulove Grede. The area is extremely dangerous because of landmines left over from the recent war in Yugoslavia.

ZORBA THE GREEK MEETS CAPTAIN CORELLI By Maggie Martin

Greece's myriad sun-kissed islands, shimmering azure seas, rocky coastlines and white-sand beaches have set the scene for some of the most memorable movies of our time – as well as some of the not-so-memorable. Besides capturing the stereotypical images of ouzo-fueled wedding parties and deeply tanned Adonises frolicking on the sands, directors who journey to Greece have their pick of some of the most awe-inspiring landscapes in the world. Over the past few decades, the dramatic vistas and fascinating culture of the Greek archipelago have set the stage for Zorba's iconic *Syrtaki* dance, given Hollywood viewers their first eyeful of a busty Sophia Loren in *Boy on a Dolphin* (1957), and established

Greek actresses Irene Papas and Melina Mercouri as household names around the world.

No movie filmed on location in Greece can be faulted for its scenery. The casting may be questionable, as in *Captain Corelli's Mandolin* (2001), the plot can be a bit ridiculous, as in the tale of a beach ménage à trois in *Summer Lovers* (1982), or the story line can be utterly forgettable, as in Jacqueline Bisset's 1987 flop *High Season*. No matter the case, Greece consistently lives up to its reputation as a land of mythic beauty. Directors and visitors flock to the country's 2,000 islands for their never-ending sunshine, exquisite landscapes, and passionate lifestyle.

Kefallonia: An Enchanted Isle

Oscar-winning director John Madden visited nearly all of the Ionian Islands to find the perfect location for **Captain Corelli's Mandolin** (2001), but he ultimately chose to film on **Kefallonia,** the very island that inspired Louis de Bernières to write his widely acclaimed 1994 novel. Dense vegetation, sandy hillsides, and a deep harbor near the northeastern port village of **Sami** frame Madden's adaptation of the author's tale of war, passion, and natural disaster. *New York Times* movie critic Stephen

Captain Corelli's Mandolin **was filmed on Kefallonia, the same island that inspired Louis de Bernières to write his popular novel. Standing on Myrtos Beach, Nicolas Cage and his men prepare to occupy the island.**

Hollywood got its first eyeful of a busty Sophia Loren in *Boy on a Dolphin* (center). No one can get enough of today's reigning beauty, Angelina Jolie, as Lara Croft (below). In *Tomb Raider: The Cradle of Life*, the bikini-clad heroine jet-skis below the dramatic cliffs of Oia (far left and above).

Top landscape film locations

1. Myrtos Beach, Kefallonia: **Captain Corelli's Mandolin**
2. Meteora: **For Your Eyes Only**
3. Mykonos: **Shirley Valentine, The Bourne Identity**
4. Kalotaritissa Bay and Agia Anna, Amorgos: **The Big Blue**
5. Oia, Santorini: **Tomb Raider: The Cradle of Life**
6. Stavros Beach, Crete: **Zorba the Greek**
7. Rhodes: **The Guns of Navarone**

Holden praised the cinematography as a "glorious ode to the sun-baked island on which it was filmed."

The film opens with views of a hillside celebration framed by the turquoise waters of the **Ionian Sea.** The year is 1940, just prior to Kefallonia's Italian occupation in World War II. The pleasant strains of folk tunes echo the village's easygoing atmosphere and provide the backdrop for Pelagia (Penélope Cruz), the daughter of a local doctor (John Hurt), and the dashing fisherman Mandras (Christian Bale) to fall in love. Shortly after their engagement, war breaks out and Mandras must leave to fight with the Greek resistance forces in Albania. Italian troops led by the opera-loving Captain Antonio Corelli (Nicolas Cage) arrive and set up camp on the sandy beach at dramatic **Antisamos Bay,** not far from Sami.

When Corelli sets eyes on Pelagia, it's love at first sight, but it takes time, several mandolin serenades, and the explosion of a dud bomb on **Myrtos Beach** – consistently ranked among the world's most beautiful seashores – before the skeptical young woman acknowledges her feelings for him. The lovers succumb to romance beneath the verdant cypresses near Sami, only to be separated after a Nazi betrayal. Corelli goes home to Italy and years pass before an earthquake destroys Kefallonia, crumbling the ancient copper-colored buildings that wind their way up the terraced slopes of the **Agioi Fanendoi** and **Palaiokastro** hillsides above Sami. Somewhat predictably, Corelli returns to Kefallonia and its gorgeous beaches close to **Agia Efimia village.**

Face off in *The Big Blue:* Scenes from the cult film about free divers by director Luc Besson were filmed on the island of Amorgos.

Escape to the Cyclades

Soaring toward **Santorini** at bird's-eye view, video game enthusiasts hungry for Lara Croft's second cinematized mission zoom in over gleaming white houses, massive cliffs, and sapphire surf. *Tomb Raider: The Cradle of Life* (2003) opens with scenes from a wedding celebration perched precariously on what director Jan de Bont rightly termed "incredibly dramatic" cliffs above the **Aegean Sea.** The crew exercised great care when filming in the village of **Oia,** especially when a cinematic earthquake destroys it and shifts a submerged ancient Greek temple off the coast. Inside the sanctuary, a glowing orb points the way to Pandora's box: In the myth as in the movie, if the box is opened, boundless suffering will be unleashed upon the world. Cue Lara Croft (Angelina Jolie), who jet-skis onto the scene in the world's only little black bikini with a gun holster. She dives into the temple, only to lose the orb to the villainous Jonathan Reiss (Ciarán Hinds). The buxom beauty spends the rest of the movie globetrotting with Scottish mercenary Terry Sheridan (Gerard Butler) on a quest to get it back.

The dramatic scenery of **Santorini** also set an exotic backdrop for Daryl Hannah, Peter Gallagher, and Valérie Quennessen to film parts of *Summer Lovers* (1982). The film sews together scenes shot on several Greek islands, with sequences specific to Santorini, including the steamy ménage à trois in one of the island's many cliff houses. The risqué film inspired swarms of well-heeled visitors to seek out the isle and a romance of their own. **Mykonos** features as an idyllic, brilliant white beach escape for the

Mykonos features as a beach escape in *Shirley Valentine* as well as in *The Bourne Identity*.

original desperate housewife, **Shirley Valentine** (1989), with Pauline Collins in the title role. Matt Damon visits the isle as Jason Bourne in **The Bourne Identity** (2002). Mykonos Town's chic **Little Venice** quarter appears in both movies.

Gorgeous landscape cinematography, dreamy underwater sequences, and a mystifying ending made **The Big Blue** (1988) a hit. French director Luc Besson (*The Professional, The Fifth Element*) captivates audiences with an elegant dramatization of the rivalry and friendship between professional free divers Jacques Mayol and Enzo Maiorca, renamed Enzo Molinari in the film. The movie kicks off in **Amorgos,** a small, untouristed isle in the Cyclades where young Jacques (Jean-Marc Barr) learns the dangers of diving when his father drowns during an underwater accident. Later in life, former childhood rival and Italian braggadocio Enzo (Jean Reno) becomes a world champion free diver and rekindles his friendship with Jacques. At diving events around the Mediterranean, the two men push each other to dive to ever greater – and more dangerous – depths. Scenes from the boys' childhood on Amorgos are filmed in black and white, but their adult lives are shown in full color, the sandy beaches and dazzling waters of **Kalotaritissa Bay** and **Agia Anna** shining on the silver screen. Fans of the movie who travel to Amorgos may be surprised to find that the *Olympia*, the ship from which Enzo makes a daring rescue, is still anchored in the harbor.

Crete: A Touch of Madness

Just south of Mykonos lies the center of ancient Minoan civilization and the rocky birthplace of Zeus, El Greco, and *Zorba the Greek* author Nikos Kazantzakis. As Greece's largest island, it is only appropriate that Crete is home to Greece's larger-

The *Syrtaki* dance on Stavros Beach: Anthony Quinn shuffles his way to film immortality to Mikis Theodorakis's unforgettable melody as *Zorba the Greek*.

than-life character Alexis Zorba, or **Zorba the Greek** (1964). Of seven Oscar nominations, the black-and-white film won three, including Best Cinematography. Greek director Michael Caco-yannis, who received a Golden Globe for Best Foreign Film in 1956 with *Stella* starring Melina Mercouri, chose dramatic backdrops like **Chania,** the **Apokoronas region,** and the **Akrotiri Peninsula** to set the scene for Zorba's dramatic screenplay. Anthony Quinn shuffled and hopped his way to film immor-tality with his improvised *Syrtaki* dance to Mikis Theodorakis's melody on **Stavros Beach,** a ten-minute walk from **Artemis.**

Rhodes and the Dodecanese Islands

Known in ancient times for its Colossus, a Statue-of-Liberty-sized tribute to the sun deity Helios, the island of **Rhodes** is also the dramatic home of a war film classic, **The Guns of Navarone** (1961). Written and produced by Carl Foreman (*The Bridge on the River Kwai*), based on a novel by Alistair MacLean, and directed by J. Lee Thompson, *The Guns of Navarone* was nominated for seven Academy Awards, won Best Special Effects, and still ranks among the American Film Institute's 100 most thrilling films. The fictional World War II drama details a desperate Allied mission to infiltrate a Nazi-held island. Its goal: to destroy two massive pieces of artil-lery whose deadly aim is preventing the safe evacuation of 2,000 Allied soldiers from nearby Kheros Island.

Captain Keith Mallory (Gregory Peck) and Corporal John Anthony Miller (David Niven) lead the troop, while Anthony Quinn is the Greek officer Colonel Andrea Stavros. Irene Pa-pas joins the cast as hardened resistance leader Maria Pappa-dimos, a woman hell-bent on defending her country against the odds. Even Greece's King Paul, Queen Frederika, and their two teenage daughters wanted in on the action during a visit to the set; a close look at the extras in the café scene reveals a royal presence. During filming, the actors connected with Rhodes and its people in different ways. Quinn was so en-amored with the idyllic setting that he purchased a parcel of land that was later christened **Anthony Quinn Bay.**

007 in Corfu and Central Greece

In **For Your Eyes Only** (1981), Roger Moore's fifth Bond film, the secret agent's adventures take him to the azure waters off the island of **Corfu** – and to the spectacular cliff-top monasteries of **Meteora.** In a race against the Russians, Bond and Melina Have-lock (Carole Bouquet) search for the sunken device that controls Britain's nuclear missiles, a gadget believed to have fallen into the hands of bad guy Aristotle Kristatos (Julian Glover). **Kalami Bay** in Corfu provides the backdrop for Melina's parents' murder on a houseboat, while **Villa Sylva** sets the scene for Bond's initial briefing and Gonzales's pool party.

The action accelerates when Melina and Bond embark on a car chase through the olive groves of **Pagi Village** and **Bouas-Danilia Village** in Corfu. Bond dines with the scheming Kristatos at the Eastern Square in the Achillion Palace in **Gastouri,** just outside **Corfu Town.** He makes a dangerous assault on Krista-tos's hideout, the **Agia Triada** or Holy Trinity monastery in **Me-teora,** central Greece, dubbed St. Cyril's in the film. Dangling from the vertiginous rock tower – a geological happenstance that has protected one of the region's six remaining cliff-top monasteries since the 1400s – was terrifying for the acrophobic Moore. But the film crew had more pressing problems: The Greek Orthodox monks deemed the Bond films too violent, and draped the monastery in ugly plastic sheeting in protest. Legal intervention cleared the way to shoot the breath-taking scenes.

James Bond scales the heights of the Agia Triada monastery in Meteora in *For Your Eyes Only*.

MOROCCO

TINSELTOWN IN THE SANDS By Claudia Hellmann

As Africa's northwestern outpost, Morocco supplies travelers and filmmakers alike with an intoxicating foretaste of the continent's many charms. The country known in the Arab world as *Al Maghreb al-Aqsa* – the land of the setting sun – brims with fascinating landscape contrasts:

The Californian deserts served as the original stand-in location for North Africa, as in *The Son of the Sheik* (1926) with heartthrob Rudolph Valentino.

barren desert wastes dotted with boulders and molded by sand dunes, snow-topped peaks and fissured rock, palm-fringed oases punctuated by red clay buildings. The mild climate, sunny weather, and a well-established film industry have created ideal conditions for producing movies of all genres. The land's varied landscapes appear as backdrops to biblical dramas, modern adventure films, and historical epics, and have included films such as *Othello* (1952) and *Gladiator* (2000). Thanks to its natural diversity, Morocco ably stood in for other locations in Africa and even Tibet, as was the case in Martin Scorsese's *Kundun* (1997). As a film location, Morocco is most convincing when it plays itself, as in *The Sheltering Sky* (1990) and the modern hippie drama *Hideous Kinky* (1998).

Beginnings: Morocco in California

Despite an abiding fascination with Morocco, filmmakers took their time actually getting here. Hollywood's vision of a mythical and exotic Orient was what initially sparked enthusiasm for filming in Morocco, as epitomized in **The Son of the Sheik** (1926), starring heartthrob Rudolph Valentino. The desert that gave the film its North African flair was not the Sahara, but was instead situated close to Hollywood itself: The Imperial Sand Dunes on the border with Mexico were sufficiently sandy to conjure up the image of an African desert. This is also

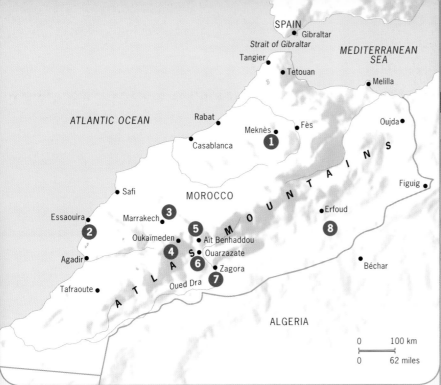

Top landscape film locations

1. Volubilis: **The Last Temptation of Christ**
2. Atlantic coast near Essaouira: **The Tragedy of Othello: The Moor of Venice, Alexander**
3. Menara Gardens near Marrakech: **Hideous Kinky**
4. Toubkal Casbah near Imlil in the Atlas Mountains: **Kundun**
5. Aït Benhaddou: **Lawrence of Arabia, The Jewel of the Nile, Gladiator**
6. Ouarzazate: **The Man Who Would Be King, Kingdom of Heaven**
7. Draa Valley: **The Sheltering Sky, Babel**
8. Merzouga and the dunes of Erg Chebbi: **The Four Feathers**

Movies like *Morocco* (1930) managed to capture the land's exotic character – and yet filming took place just outside of Hollywood.

where Josef von Sternberg's **Morocco** (1930) was shot some years later, a film that managed to combine exotica and erotica and fuel the fire of Hollywood's love for Morocco – even if production remained firmly rooted in California. Following on her famous performance in *The Blue Angel* (1930), Marlene Dietrich plays an androgynous nightclub singer in the film that marked her American debut. Set in a fictitious Moroccan oasis, the movie shows Dietrich at her irresistible best, beguiling a Foreign Legionnaire played by Gary Cooper.

Even the most famous of all Moroccan films, **Casablanca** (1942), has about as much to do with Morocco as the sand dunes of Santa Barbara County have with the real Sahara. The play upon which the film is based was set in the South of France, but the Nazis had occupied the region just as production was getting underway, so the location – in

"Here's lookin' at you, kid": The success of *Casablanca* helped to establish the romantic myth of Morocco.

Morocco's magnetism cannot be denied. In Bernardo Bertolucci's *The Sheltering Sky*, two Americans find this out the hard way as they journey through an oasis town to the fertile Draa Valley, and into the desert beyond.

the screenplay, at least – was moved to the French colony of Morocco. Shooting took place at the Warner Bros. studios in Burbank in the suburbs of Los Angeles, with an almost complete absence of outside shots. Casablanca was portrayed as a vaguely foreign locality, a crossroads for all manner of colorful, questionable characters. The illusion was maintained with the help of exotic costumes and props, some of which had been used in earlier movie productions. Even today, tourists will make their way to Casablanca on the trail of Rick (Humphrey Bogart) and Ilsa (Ingrid Bergman). Rick's Café Américain remains a myth, but the Casablanca Bar in the Hyatt Regency Hotel is a meeting point for film fans searching for traces of the movie. The bar is decorated from top to bottom with photos and posters, and even if the pianist is no replacement for Sam (Dooley Wilson), he manages an adequately routine version of "As Time Goes By."

Port and Kit Moresby (John Malkovich and Debra Winger) don't yet know where their journey leads.

On the Casbah Trail: The Draa Valley

Probably the most beautiful and varied Moroccan landscapes ever seen in the movies are those featured in Bernardo Bertolucci's **The Sheltering Sky** (1990). The novel by Paul Bowles upon which the film is based is set in the late 1940s and centers on a married couple who decide to drop out of American society

The fortified casbah town of Aït Benhaddou has served for decades as a backdrop for large-scale movie productions such as *Lawrence of Arabia, The Jewel of the Nile, The Mummy,* and *Gladiator*.

and search for the meaning of life in the deserts of North Africa. The film begins and ends in the alleys of **Tangier,** the city in which Bowles lived and where Bertolucci set up a scene in a café featuring the author in a cameo role as the tale's narrator. Port Moresby (John Malkovich) and his wife, Kit (Debra Winger), accompanied initially by their friend George Tunner (Campbell Scott) arrive in North Africa in search of new experiences and hopeful of saving their deteriorating marriage. Their journey takes them through Morocco from the northern port of Tangier down to the Draa Valley, on into Algeria and ultimately into deepest Niger. It is Port, first and foremost, who finds himself bewitched by the desert, always on the move and eternally restless, while Kit struggles with loneliness.

The film was shot exclusively at the locations described in the original play, above all on the fringes of the Sahara **between Ouarzazate and Erfoud.** Port and Kit's journey takes them past the Berber market of **Rissani,** a fortified village close to the desert town of Erfoud near the Algerian border. They continue on through the fertile **Draa Valley,** along the "Casbah Trail" from Ouarzazate to Zagora, and to **Ksar Tamnougalt,** a fortified Berber settlement surrounded by palms. In the film, Tamnougalt serves as backdrop for Fort Bou Noura, a Foreign Legion outpost. Port and Kit go cycling close to Zagora. Together they ride through the bleak desert vastness and look out over the immense rock and boulder landscape from a plateau at **Jebel Zagora,** con-

Aït Benhaddou first appeared in the movies in David Lean's 1962 desert epic *Lawrence of Arabia* starring Peter O'Toole and Omar Sharif.

templating the mysteries of the Sahara. When Port catches a fever and dies, Kit, in shock, joins a passing Berber caravan at the oasis of **Finnt** and travels with it southwards through the **Sahara,** as if in a trance.

Bertolucci captured the desert in breathtaking images: dunes as numerous as ocean waves, barren fields of rock, fissured mountains, and wide valleys steeped in searing daylight. Nights are a symphony of ocher, blue, and red in the soft moonlight. These shots were filmed not only in Morocco but also in the Ténéré desert near Agadez in Niger. Kit finally succumbs to the attentions of the Berber Belqassim (Eric Vu-An), who takes her to his maze-like living quarters at the end of the journey and hides her from his other women in a tiny room. The **Casbah of Ouarzazate** served as backdrop for Belqassim's harem. Kit loses touch with herself in the desert, and once Belqassim's ardor cools, she feels just as lonely and fragmented as before. She escapes back to the coast at Tangier, but when her old friend Tunner tries to find her and take her home, she disappears once again to drift through the labyrinth of alleys.

In Alejandro González Iñárritu's drama ***Babel*** (2006), an American couple played by Cate Blanchett and Brad Pitt also travel to Morocco in the hope of solving their marital problems. As their tour bus winds its way through the rocky gorges of the **Draa Valley,** Susan (Blanchett) is hit by a bullet fired by a shepherd boy trying out his father's new rifle. The seriously injured woman finds herself fighting death in a remote Berber village, scenes that were shot in the fortified Berber settlement of **Taguenzalt.** Meanwhile, the media treat the incident as a terrorist attack and the local police initiate a manhunt for the boy and his family with tragic consequences.

Ouarzazate and Aït Benhaddou: Dream Factory Favorites

The landscape around Ouarzazate is doubtless Morocco's most frequently filmed region. A former Foreign Legion garrison lies at the foot of the Atlas Mountains, and the town is surrounded by the magnificent, snow-covered peaks of the High Atlas such as Jbel Saghro and Jbel Sirwa, each exceeding 10,800 feet (3,300 meters) in height. Ouarzazate's location has become a geographic intersection: Here the edge of the Sahara meets both the fertile Draa and Dadès valleys, an area characterized by old-fashioned clay villages and the deep gorges created by the Todra and Dadès rivers. With so much variety to put before the camera, filmmakers shooting in Morocco find it impossible to ignore Ouarzazate.

Lawrence of Arabia (1962) kicked off a trend for filming in this region, with countless movies following in its footsteps. Although David Lean shot most of his epic masterpiece in Spain and Jordan, the casbah town of **Aït Benhaddou,** some 15 miles (25 kilometers) to the west of Ouarzazate, would have its big-screen debut in this film. The settlement is also the most impressive example of the casbah architecture so typical of

Michael Caine and Sean Connery in *The Man Who Would Be King* with Aït Benhaddou in the distance.

While Moroccan clay brick can be rich in ornamentation and zigzag courses, it is also extremely susceptible to weathering. After long periods of rain, whole wall sections can dissolve and collapse. By the time Franco Zeffirelli came to Morocco in the late 1970s to film the six-hour television miniseries **Jesus of Nazareth** (1977), Aït Benhaddou had seen better days. It is to Zeffirelli's credit that he had numerous facades restored for the film. In 1986, UNESCO added the Casbah to the list of World Heritage sites.

Besides providing a scenic backdrop for ambitious art house films, the area around Ouarzazate and Aït Benhaddou also served as location for a number of brilliant adventure movies. John Huston chose the region for his version of Rudyard Kipling's short story **The Man Who Would Be King** (1975). This tongue-in-cheek adventure features Sean Connery and Michael Caine as two British soldiers whose dubious business deals help them make their way through India of the late nineteenth century. When they hear of the distant realm of Kafiristan and its legendary riches, they set off intending to traverse the Himalayas and reign there as kings. Huston used the local Moroccan scenery and thousands of extras to create a wonderfully colorful mountain realm that was vaguely reminiscent of Tibet. Ten years later, Michael Douglas and Kathleen Turner formed another congenial duo in the adventure comedy **The Jewel of the Nile** (1985) in which they attempt to bring down a megaloma-

southern Morocco, the fortresses with their striking corner towers reminiscent of giant sand castles. The Berbers built six of these monumental clay constructions on a hill, and they merge into one vast conglomerate of living quarters and fortifications collectively known as the Casbah. Aït Benhaddou was once an important stop on the caravan route coming out of the Sahara; today it is best known for providing Hollywood's dream factory with exotic images.

In the same year that *Lawrence of Arabia* was filmed in Morocco, an unlikely pair of directors arrived to shoot a gory version of **Sodom and Gomorrah** (1962). The movie that American action filmmaker Robert Aldrich produced is only very loosely based on the biblical text. The Italian filmmaker Pier Paolo Pasolini found his way to Aït Benhaddou as well: He transformed the town into the city of Thebes for **Oedipus Rex** (1967), with clay buildings complementing the surrounding desert into which Oedipus (Franco Citti) flees to escape the prophecy.

Director Ridley Scott had an amphitheater specially built next to the fortress of Aït Benhaddou so that Russell Crowe could be a *Gladiator.*

Director Shekhar Kapur and cameraman Robert Richardson (right) filmed *The Four Feathers* in the broad desert landscapes near Merzouga and in the high dunes of Erg Chebbi. Heath Ledger plays a young British soldier who must fight his way through the endless sea of sand.

niac sheikh. An impressive gate was constructed and inserted into Aït Benhaddou's existing architecture for the scene in which Michael Douglas makes a spectacular emergency landing in a small plane. Today, the airplane may be viewed at the **Atlas Studios** on the outskirts of Ouarzazate – along with a Tibetan monastery from Scorsese's *Kundun* (1997) and Egyptian sets from *Asterix & Obelix: Mission Cleopatra* (2002).

Director Ridley Scott insisted on remodeling Aït Benhaddou in accordance with his vision for **Gladiator** (2000). Disgraced Roman commander Maximus (Russell Crowe) is sold as a slave in a provincial North African town and makes a name for himself as a gladiator in the local arena. The amphitheater needed in these scenes had to be specially built in Aït Benhaddou. Thanks to the efforts of the set builders and their desire to achieve an authentic effect, the newly constructed theater was made to fit perfectly into the architecture of the existing fortifications. The construction unit made a mixture of clay and straw, pressed it into molds, and baked it in the sun, in effect reviving building techniques prevalent some 400 years ago to produce the arena's 30,000 bricks. The unstoppable Ridley Scott would set up camp once again in Ouarzazate to film **Kingdom of Heaven** (2005), framing the medieval tale amongst the mountain ridges, wide plains, and historic clay structures. Aït Benhaddou made an appearance as Golgotha, the hill on which Christ was crucified outside Jerusalem and where the young crusader Balian (Orlando Bloom) movingly buries the crucifix that belonged to his recently deceased wife.

The proximity of the desert and its impressive sand dunes are an added attraction for filmmakers who choose to work in Ouarzazate. The **dunes of Erg Chebbi** near **Merzouga,** piles of sand that achieve heights in excess of 330 feet (100 meters), formed a fantastic backdrop for the makers of **The Four Feathers** (2002). A.E.W. Mason's novel, which had appeared in film form in the 1920s and 1930s, chronicles a British soldier's odyssey through Africa at the end of the nineteenth century. When Harry Faversham (Heath Ledger) resigns his post as his regiment is being sent to Africa to quash a rebel uprising in the Sudan, three of his friends and his fiancée send him four white feathers signaling their belief that he is a coward. Harry resolves to travel to the Sudan and reinstate his honor. Director Shekhar Kapur filmed his updated version of the movie not in the Sudan – as Zoltan Korda did in 1939 – but in Morocco instead. The **dunes near Merzouga** represent the African sea of sand Harry must cross. Once again, **Aït Benhaddou** makes an appearance, this time as the fictitious Sudanese fortification of Abou Clea.

Roman Ruins: Meknes and Volubilis

Martin Scorsese's film version of Nikos Kazantzakis's novel **The Last Temptation of Christ** (1998) set off an unprecedented storm of indignation. The author of *Zorba the Greek* (1964) chose to concentrate on Christ's humanity, portraying Jesus

The picturesque ruins of grain silos near Meknes.

Willem Dafoe as the thorn-crowned Christ on the cross.

The stony desert and a reservoir near Ouarzazate served as backdrops in Martin Scorsese's *The Last Temptation of Christ*. Filming also took place near Volubilis, its famous Roman ruins framed by hills and olive groves.

(Willem Dafoe) as a vulnerable man who was willing to accept his role as Messiah only after a long process of doubt and deliberation. It is on Golgotha itself that Jesus is finally confronted with the tempting possibility of leading a normal family life as husband and father. It took Scorsese five years to get the project up and running, a time during which he was forced to concede that he would not be able to shoot in Israel itself. Morocco proved an adequate replacement location for the Holy Land, not least because it boasts its own authentic Roman ruins.

Scorsese set up camp in Ouarzazate and shot several scenes in the surrounding area. Some were filmed at **El Mansour Eddahbi,** a large reservoir that stretches through the stone desert a few miles to the east of Ouarzazate and a body of water that contrasts beautifully with the barren landscape. The remains of the vast **Villa Imperiale** built for Sultan Moulay Ismail on the outskirts of the royal city of **Meknes** served as location for several of the scenes set in Jerusalem, especially the ruins of the large stable and storage complex of **Heri Souni.** The high grain silos with their massive walls and partially collapsed ceilings appear in the film on several occasions. This is where Scorsese filmed the scenes in the Temple of Jerusalem, the palace of Pontius Pilate (David Bowie), and Jesus's triumphant procession

through the city on Palm Sunday. The thirty-minute segment that caused the most furor with audiences – Jesus's temptation on the cross – was shot in the foothills of the Atlas Mountains and in **Volubilis,** one of the most important Roman ruins in Morocco, situated roughly 20 miles (30 kilometers) from Meknes. The site, revered for its spectacular floor mosaics, well-preserved triumphal arch, and intact columns, is also loved for its stunning landscape setting, framed by hills and olive groves. This is where Jesus listens to Saul preaching on the market square.

The Atlas Mountains

Martin Scorsese would return to Morocco yet again to film **Kundun** (1997). Much to the chagrin of the filmmaker, the ambitious movie project about the Dalai Lama's early years could not be shot in Tibet. The Chinese authorities did everything they could to prevent the film from being shot on location, and they were successful. Scorsese opted to film in **Ouarzazate** – and the flourishing film city that had developed there in the wake of previous productions – instead. With the help of talented craftsmen, he was able to recreate Tibet in the Moroccan desert: Sets were built to bear a remarkable resemblance to the stately Potala Palace, the Dalai Lama's chief residence in Lhasa, and Norbulingka, his summer home nearby. The entrance to the summer palace was constructed on the shore of the great reservoir outside Ouarzazate, where the snow-topped peaks of the Atlas Mountains rising behind the set convey an impression of Himalayan territory.

Julia (Kate Winslet) seeks enlightenment in Marrakech. She hugs her daughter in the courtyard of the Ben Youssef Medrassa in *Hideous Kinky*.

The film begins with scouts being sent out by the current Dalai Lama to find the next spiritual leader of the Tibetan people – in the person of a young boy. The tiny mountain village that was a backdrop in this scene is **Timlougite**, a remote hamlet between Marrakech and Ouarzazate. From here, the crew moved on to **Imlil**, some 40 miles (60 kilome-

ters) outside Marrakech in the Aït Mizane Valley and known as a point of departure for mountain tours to Jbel Toubkal (13,660 feet/ 4,167 meters), Africa's tallest mountain. The **Toubkal Casbah,** transformed for the film into the Tibetan monastery of Dungkhar – the Dalai Lama's initial refuge after he flees a newly occupied Tibet – is situated on a rocky promontory above Imlil. The Casbah was embellished for the shoot with chiseled stonework, carved doors, prayer wheels, and Tibetan towers. Today it serves as a center for field studies and as a hostel for adventurous travelers.

In and Around Marrakech

As in *The Sheltering Sky*, Morocco plays itself in **Hideous Kinky** (1998). Director Gillies MacKinnon filmed wonderfully colorful scenes set in the early 1970s in Morocco, hippie years when Westerners discovered it as an exotic travel destination. Hoping to find a more adventurous life, Julia (Kate Winslet) leaves London and travels to **Marrakech** with her daughters, Lucy and Bea. Initially they are overwhelmed by the world they find there: the teeming acrobats, magicians, and snake charmers on the Djemaa el Fna, the pulsating main square in the city center. Some of the shots were actually filmed in the intricate network of Marrakech's Medina quarter, but for reasons of practicality, the famous square had to be reconstructed within the towering walls of the **Oumnast Casbah,** roughly 12 miles (20 kilometers) outside the city. Hundreds of extras, some of whom usually worked on the Djemaa, helped recreate the plaza's authentic atmosphere of hustle and bustle on the set. Here, Julia and her daughters make the acquaintance of the charismatic artist Bilal (Saïd Taghmaoui), the man who later becomes Julia's lover and a kind of ersatz father for Lucy and Bea.

The authorities denied Martin Scorsese permission to shoot in Tibet, so he chose the peaks of the High Atlas to be the Himalayas in Kundun. The movie tells the life story of the Dalai Lama, from his childhood until he is forced to flee to India. Perched high in the mountains, the Toubkal Casbah became a Tibetan monastery for the film.

Bilal and the little family travel to his remote mountain hometown on a quest to discover the real Morocco. These episodes were shot outside Marrakech and include the scene in the **Menara Gardens** in which Bilal first bids farewell to Julia and the

The Menara Gardens just outside Marrakech

girls. Back in Marrakech, Julia meets a stylish yet dubious European who invites her to stay in his magnificent villa. The filmmakers were granted permission to shoot in the splendid **Palais de la Bahia,** a splendid nineteenth-century residence complete with courtyards and fountains built by the grand vizier to the sultan. Still on the search for spiritual enlightenment, Julia sets out again, this time to see a Sufi in Algeria. The mystic lives in the **Ben Youssef Medrassa,** a sixteenth-century Koran school in the middle of Marrakech that is wonderfully decorated with mosaics and tiles. Instead of providing her with the spiritual enlightenment she seeks, the sage directs Julia's thoughts to everyday life with her daughters. She returns to Marrakech in a sober frame of mind, but even as the young vagabond family is reunited with Bilal, Julia finds herself wondering if this is the life she envisages for her daughters – or whether she should return to London.

Essaouira and the Atlantic Coast

Although there's plenty of it – the Moroccan coastline is more than 1,860 miles (3,000 kilometers) long – the shores of this North African country have only really ever been showcased in one film: Orson Welles's **The Tragedy of Othello: The Moor of Venice** (1952). The movie, a financially ruinous Shakespeare adaptation in which the director also played the title role, was one of the very first foreign big-screen productions made in Morocco. Filming would take three years.

Most of the movie was shot in Venice, but Welles was drawn to Morocco for the outdoor scenes and for those set in Cyprus in the original play. He chose to film near **Essaouira,** still called Mogador in those days, a little bayside town picturesquely situated on a promontory facing the Atlantic Ocean. Seagulls circle over the harbor and long, sandy beaches stretch off into the distance on either side of town. The labyrinthine alleys and souks of the perfectly preserved Medina are the heart of the city, and the splendid **Skala de la Kasbah** its symbol. The magnificent eighteenth-century fortress, complete with battlements and towers, juts into the sea and is lashed by crashing waves. Welles considered it the ideal location for the opening scene in which the Skala's endless exterior wall is shown in a long, drawn-out shot.

In *Hideous Kinky*, Julia (Kate Winslet) hopes to start a new life with her two young daughters in Morocco. But their adopted home presents a host of unexpected challenges.

Filmed here were the scenes in which Othello (Welles) is overwhelmed by jealousy, and in which Iago (Micheál MacLiammóir) is tortured. Welles had just arrived in Essaouira when he learned that his Italian backers were abandoning the project. Financial exigency forced him to improvise: The crew had neither return tickets nor the costumes needed for the first scenes, so Welles decided to relocate the attempted murder of Cassio (Michael Laurence) to a local *hammam* – bathing scenes require little in the way of costly costumes, just towels. Further scenes were shot in the old Portuguese town of **El Jadida,** some 150 miles (250 kilometers) to the north of Essaouira. The town's sixteenth-century vaulted cistern served as backdrop for Iago and Cassio's drinking scene.

In Welles's eyes, **Essaouira**'s Portuguese fortress and its blue-shuttered, whitewashed houses set it apart from other Moroccan towns. The mixture of Arab and Mediterranean

The pretty coastal town of Essaouira attracted numerous hippies in the sixties, as well as musicians such as Jimi Hendrix, Frank Zappa, and Cat Stevens. Orson Welles discovered its charms when he used the Portuguese fortress to film scenes from the 1952 film *The Tragedy of Othello: The Moor of Venice.*

architecture in a picturesque ocean setting contributed considerably to its charms, a fact not lost on the director. Welles is memorialized in town with a small bronze bust in the vicinity of the fish market and the eponymous bar in the slightly dusty Hotel des Iles – a watering hole that Welles liked to frequent. Essaouira recently reemerged into the limelight when Oliver Stone chose it to stand in as a coastal town in Macedonia for the film **Alexander** (2004), starring Colin Farrell. Producer Jon Kilik was delighted with Morocco's diversity: the deserts, broad plains, and snowy mountains around Marrakech on the

Alexander was filmed in Essaouira and near Marrakech.

one hand, and Essaouira's lush vegetation, rock formations, and ocean situation on the other. The Battle of Gaugamela, Alexander's decisive victory over the Persians, was filmed on a large area of rubble and rock outside **Marrakech.** Ridley Scott, who resurrected the Holy Land in Morocco for his **Kingdom of Heaven** (2005), was another director who supplemented desert episodes with scenes shot in and around Essaouira. Also shot here were the arrival of the crusaders and the scene in which

Filming *The Tragedy of Othello* took three years and cost Orson Welles a pretty penny.

Balian (Orlando Bloom) is washed onto shore after being shipwrecked. Set designers added their magic in the form of specially constructed gates and towers built on to the city's old walls and streets to conjure the Old City of Jerusalem.

20

TUNISIA

FILMING IN A DESERT OASIS

By Claudine Weber-Hof

Long ago, in a galaxy far, far away ....." The legendary lines that opened new worlds to millions of fans also apply to the most famous *Star Wars* location, Tunisia. Sci-fi pioneer Aldous Huxley thought the "playground of North Africa" otherworldly, too, when he took notes for his essay "In a Tunisian Oasis" here in the 1920s. No wonder the troglodyte cities of the northern Sahara struck director George Lucas as the perfect backdrop for conjuring up a parallel universe. The sun-kissed country between Algeria and Libya would feature in numerous *Star Wars* sequels and prequels, but never again quite so memorably as in the original 1977 film.

Lucas had just made a name for himself and a small fortune with the 1973 hit *American Graffiti* when he started to hunt for *Star Wars* locations. The rain forests of the Philippines were an early candidate, but the lush, wet environment was deemed too difficult for filming. The director eventually chose Tunisia, a land that would bring its own challenges. Flash floods, sudden sandstorms, and excruciating heat proved nightmarish for actors Kenny Baker and Anthony Daniels, who, as the droids R2-D2 and C-3PO, were encased in tin-can costumes. Still, the dugout dwellings of seminomadic tribes on the caravan trail provided the right atmosphere for Luke Skywalker (Mark Hamill) to intercept a secret message from Princess Leia (Carrie Fisher) and join the rebellion against an evil empire.

Lucas and 130 cast and crew chose Tozeur in central Tunisia as a base and began filming in March 1976. **Tataouine,** a town to the southeast in the **Jebel Dahar hills** whose landscape featured in the crucifixion scenes from Monty Python's **Life of Brian** (1979), provided a name for Luke Skywalker's home planet of Tatooine – along with two of the *ksar* granaries used as slave quarters in **Star Wars: Episode I – The Phantom Menace** (1999). Fans of the Python flick also flock to the **Ribat** monastery in **Monastir,** where most of the filming took place, as well as the **Casbah** in **Sousse,** famous as the location where Brian scrawls anti-Roman graffiti on the city walls.

Among Tunisia's most famous Star Wars locations are the rock-cut caves at **Hôtel Sidi Driss** in **Matmata,** which stood in for Luke's home. Production designer John Barry added in "vaporators" and a high-tech kitchen to transform a modest Berber dwelling into a moisture farm on a distant planet. The painted ceiling in the dining room where Uncle Owen (Phil Brown) and Aunt Beru (Shelagh Fraser) argue over their nephew's future is still there, but the exterior is off to the west near **Nefta:** The famous scene of Luke watching the two suns set takes place on the lunar landscape of a great dry lake called **Chott el-Jerid.** The little domed house behind him is a fiberglass set. The steep, sweeping sands where C-3PO despairs of ever finding transport were filmed at **La Grande Dune,** also near Nefta.

Top landscape film locations

1. La Grande Dune near Nefta: **Star Wars**
2. Sidi Bouhlel ravine: **Star Wars, Raiders of the Lost Ark, The English Patient**
3. Chott el-Jerid salt lake: **Star Wars**
4. Hôtel Sidi Driss, Matmata: **Star Wars**
5. Tataouine: **Life of Brian, Star Wars: Episode I – The Phantom Menace**

In *The English Patient*, the love affair between Count László de Almásy (Ralph Fiennes) and Katharine Clifton (Kristin Scott Thomas) turns tragic after a plane crash in the desert. The scenes in which Almásy carries her to a cave were shot in the Sidi Bouhlel ravine.

Obi-Wan Kenobi's (Alec Guinness) warning that "the Jundland Wastes are not to be traveled lightly" certainly applies to the **Chott el-Jerid salt flats,** but also to what Lucasfilm crew members filming the prequel *The Phantom Menace* would dub "Star Wars Canyon." Close to Tozeur, the **Sidi Bouhlel ravine** where the Tusken raiders attack in the 1977 film, and where Obi-Wan, Luke, and the droids gaze out over spaceport Mos Eisley from the edge of the Dune Sea – dramatically depicted in artist Ralph McQuarrie's production painting – also features in the Indiana Jones film **Raiders of the Lost Ark** (1981) and in the hopelessly romantic movie **The English Patient** (1996).

The breezy isle of **Jerba** to the east of these desert locations provided the outpost of Mos Eisley, where Obi-Wan and Luke search for a ship to Alderaan. The plaza off the main square in the ferry terminal town of **Ajim** serves as the exterior of the music-filled cantina where Obi-Wan meets Han Solo (Harrison Ford), commander of the *Millennium Falcon,* and the Stormtrooper Checkpoint, where the old Jedi exercises the Force. A mosque outside town was used for more shots of Mos Eisley and of Anchorhead station. A nearby barrel-vaulted hut stood in for "Ben" Kenobi's house.

No one was more surprised than director George Lucas when he sat in a burger joint across from Mann's Chinese Theatre in Los Angeles and watched the ticket lines snake around the block. Only thirty-two theaters featured the film when it opened on May 25, 1977, and no one knew then that the monumental success of *Star Wars* marked the birth of the blockbuster – earning a record $54 million in eight months – as well as the age of movie merchandising. For Tunisia, the success of *Star Wars* brought multitudes more to its already popular beaches and new life to the desert splendor of its inland oases.

The Sidi Bouhlel ravine has been in so many *Star Wars* films that it is now called "Star Wars Canyon." Obi-Wan Kenobi (Alec Guinness) and director George Lucas watch as scenes from the original 1977 movie are filmed in the ravine. Locations nearby include Chott el-Jerid and La Grande Dune.

LOVE AND ADVENTURE
IN THE SAVANNAH

By Anja Hauenstein

What is it about Africa that fascinates us so? Is it the kaleidoscope of colors in its varied landscapes, or the immense horizon and the endless sky that seems so much closer to Earth here than elsewhere? Many a traveler has been overcome with humility in the face of such vast beauty. In *Out of Africa*, Meryl Streep reflects this universal fascination with Africa when she quotes from Karen Blixen's 1937 autobiography of the same name: "If I know a song of Africa, of the giraffe and the African new moon lying on her back, of the plows in the fields and the sweaty faces of the coffee pickers, does Africa know a song of me?"

It is this yearning that we associate with Africa, a feeling that inspires the expectation of adventure and of untamed, untrammeled nature: wide savannah landscapes, endless herds of animals, and proud Masai warriors, baobabs, and coffee plantations under the snow-topped peaks of Mount Kilimanjaro or Mount Kenya, the Serengeti or the Masai Mara, Lake Victoria or Lake Baringo. Much of what shapes our image of Africa lies in Kenya or Tanzania.

It is hardly surprising that some of the most impressive landscape movies ever made were shot in East Africa. In 1930, Metro-Goldwyn-Mayer sent a film team to Kenya to shoot *Trader Horn* (1931). It took them six weeks just to get onto the continent, where they battled hostile tribes, wild animals, and persistent illness. Shooting for *Tarzan and the Slave Girl* (1950) began in Africa but had to be abandoned when the rainy season started in Kenya. The film was completed in a Hollywood studio.

Even today, extreme weather, a poor infrastructure, poverty, and the resulting criminality make it difficult for filmmakers to pursue their craft. But for those filmmakers concerned with authentic landscapes, and for those films in which landscape plays a starring role, Kenya and Tanzania are indispensable. They certainly were for Caroline Link, who won the Oscar for Best Foreign Film with *Nowhere in Africa* (2001). "As far as I'm concerned, you can't dress up a Zulu as a Masai or vice versa. These are people who are keen to tell you all about their country, they give the film a special note, that authentically native feeling. None of this is arbitrary. Difficult shoots are no excuse for abandoning this kind of veracity."

Out of Africa: Hollywood's Homage to Kenya

It is precisely this authenticity that made the most famous Africa movie so successful. Thanks to director Sydney Pollack's film **Out of Africa** (1985), many viewers think not only of Meryl Streep and Robert Redford when they imagine Africa, but also of unforgettable Kenyan landscapes. Based on the autobiography by Danish writer Karen Blixen, the film was shot exclusively at

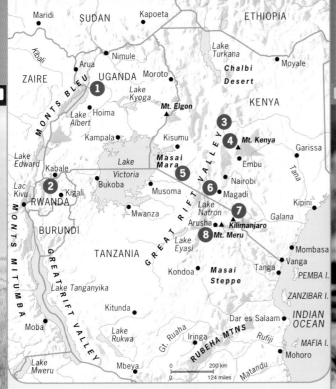

Top landscape film locations

1. Murchison Falls National Park, Uganda: **The African Queen**
2. Virunga volcano ridge, Rwanda: **Gorillas in the Mist**
3. Wamba, Kenya: **The White Masai**
4. Mount Kenya, Kenya: **King Solomon's Mines, Nowhere in Africa, Mogambo**
5. Masai Mara, Kenya: **Out of Africa**
6. Lake Magadi, Kenya: **The Constant Gardener**
7. Amboseli National Park, Kenya: **King Solomon's Mines, The Snows of Kilimanjaro**
8. Arusha National Park and Momella Farm, Tanzania: **Hatari!**

Out of Africa celebrates the beauty of Kenya. The tragic story surrounding Karen Blixen (Meryl Streep) and Denys Finch Hatton (Robert Redford) brims with magnificent landscapes.

the original locations described in the book. The story relates a tragic tale of love between two people as well as the equally doomed relationship between a courageous woman and the foreign land that becomes her home. The film was awarded seven Oscars, including Best Film, Best Director, and Best Music for its original score.

"I had a farm in Africa at the foot of the Ngong Hills." Every moviegoer immediately recognizes the words spoken by Karen Blixen (Meryl Streep) in the opening scene. Blixen wrote her autobiography during a bleak, Danish winter, recalling her time in Africa from 1914 to 1931. The wealthy young woman, who had married her cousin, Baron Bror Blixen (Klaus Maria Brandauer), to escape her family, was attracted by the prospect of moving out to Kenya and helping him to run a farm there. As Bror is more passionate about hunting than about his young wife, the marriage ends up anything but a success. Karen's life changes when she makes the acquaintance of the big-game hunter Denys Finch Hatton (Robert Redford). And yet this love is doomed, too: The freedom-loving Denys will not submit to the bonds of a relationship with a woman any more than he will submit to the wild country in which they both live. He dies when his airplane crashes, and Karen buries him close to where they spent their happiest moments, in the beautiful Ngong Hills. When a fire subsequently destroys the plantation, Karen is forced to return to Denmark.

"I had a farm in Africa at the foot of the Ngong Hills." Filming took place, however, in the Masai Mara.

The movie powerfully reflects the drama of Karen Blixen's life and times. When she arrived in Kenya in 1914, Nairobi was already the seat of government. Nonetheless, it was still a small, provincial town. The film team recreated Nairobi of yesteryear in a meadow near **Langanta,** some 30 miles (50 kilometers) from today's modern metropolis. The Osgood and the Norfolk hotels, a bazaar, a church, and even the railway station at which Karen arrives in Africa after her long journey were all reconstructed here. Karen Blixen's house, a remote farm at the foot of the Ngong Hills in those days, is now a museum in **Karen,** a smart Nairobi suburb that was named after its famous denizen. The house was used in exterior shots only; visitors will note that the rooms inside look much smaller than they appear in the movie. The film crew renovated an old dairy farm close to the museum and filmed all the interiors there, using much of the furniture that had actually belonged to Karen Blixen.

the idea of restricting the animals – especially the trained "lion actors" that had been imported from California for filming – to an island seemed a safer bet.

The scenes in which Karen Blixen travels the length of Kenya in order to bring supplies to her husband and his troops were shot in the **Shaba National Reserve** at the foot of **Mount Kenya.** The reserve had already served as a film location in 1965 for the shoot of **Born Free,** the story of the Adamson family who adopt an orphaned lion cub and teach it how to live in the wild.

Adventure in Wildest Africa

Several movies shot in Africa during the 1950s and 1960s sustained the myth of the continent's reputation for adventure and boundless freedom. Such movies fueled an image of Kenya and Tanzania as countries marked by untamed nature, dramatic safaris, and undaunted big-game hunters.

King Solomon's Mines starring Deborah Kerr and Stewart Granger wowed audiences with its shots of Kenya's national parks of Aberdare and Amboseli (right). The adventure film even won an Oscar for its outstanding cinematography.

Most of the landscape shots were filmed in the **Masai Mara National Reserve,** north of Serengeti National Park. Robert Redford and Meryl Streep lived in the **Kichwa Tembo Camp** during this part of the shoot. **Bateleur Camp** is just a few feet away, at the foot of the hill where the film team shot not only the famous picnic scene that is immortalized on the film poster, but also Denys's funeral. The sequence in which Denys and Karen take off in a plane was also shot in Masai Mara, near the **Oloololo** hills, a short distance from both camps. For the shots involving wild animals, the entire team moved to the small **Crescent Island** in **Lake Naivasha,** taking with them giraffes, zebras, gnus, and gazelles. The change was made for reasons of security after an incident that took place early on in the shooting: A lion got too close to Meryl Streep in a scene in which the animal attacks her husband's camp, a shock that registers clearly on the actress's face in the film. After that,

King Solomon's Mines (1950) generated a wave of Africa enthusiasm with its spectacular animal and landscape shots. Allan Quatermain (Stewart Granger) organizes desert treks for rich Europeans, and is hired on by a wealthy Englishwoman, Elizabeth Curtis (Deborah Kerr), to go on a risky expedition: She wants to go into "unexplored country" to look for her husband. The lost spouse disappeared in an unmapped desert region while searching for the legendary diamonds of King Solomon. During a perilous journey with wild animal attacks and an encounter with cannibals, the wife and the adventurer fall in love. Filming cost $3.5 million, a steep sum in those days. The money went mainly to the logistics of the moviemaking enterprise, such as the transportation of 27 tons of film equipment from Mombasa that required seven trucks to be specially built for the journey. The crew also needed a snowplow to clear the way for shots on the 17,000-foot (5,200-meter) **Mount Kenya.**

Logistics weren't the film crew's only challenge. Filming took place over the course of an incredible five-month, 13,700-mile (22,000-kilometer) safari through Tanzania, Kenya, Uganda, and the Congo. The animal shots were filmed largely in two Kenyan national parks: **Amboseli** and **Aberdare.** Sweltering temperatures were the least of the problems. Almost the entire crew was weakened by sickness. Even the local hires, who worked as extras for 30 cents a day, pushed the boundaries of their physical abilities.

The most dangerous situation occurred when the chief of a Masai tribe lifted the spell that had been cast over ancient tribal dances so that the director could film the warriors performing battle rituals. Some 500 Masai danced, sang, and drummed continuously for two days, ultimately falling into a trance that induced them to think that members of the film crew were enemies and to attack them with spears. Once the warriors had

In *Allan Quatermain and the Lost City of Gold*, Richard Chamberlain tried to repeat Harrison Ford's success as Indiana Jones in *Raiders of the Lost Ark.*

calmed down, the crew tried to make amends by entertaining them with a screening of the film *Perfect Strangers* (1945), also starring Deborah Kerr. Unfortunately, this tactic only led to further uproar. The Masai believed that the crew was trying to use witchcraft to trick them: How could Deborah Kerr be sitting among them when she was also up on the screen?

The difficult location shoot paid off. *King Solomon's Mines* was a hit and won Oscars for Best Cinematography for color and Best Film Editing. And the amount of footage shot for this film was so extensive that the MGM Studios were able to use it in various Africa films for years to come – including the third film version of H. Rider Haggard's novel *Allan Quatermain and the Lost City of Gold*, filmed in 1987 with Richard Chamberlain and Sharon Stone in the main roles.

Ernest Hemingway, himself an Africa enthusiast and big-game hunter, wrote the 1936 novel upon which Henry King based ***The Snows of Kilimanjaro*** (1952). The film begins with

In *The Snows of Kilimanjaro*, writer Harry Street (Gregory Peck) lies ill at the foot of the famous mountain and dreams of his first love, Cynthia (Ava Gardner). Kenyan locations mentioned in the book by Ernest Hemingway also appeared in the film.

Director John Ford went all out to make *Mogambo*. The 1953 film, whose title means "passion" in Swahili, features stars like Grace Kelly, Ava Gardner, and Clark Gable, as well as locations in Kenya, Tanzania, the Congo, and Uganda.

writer Harry Street (Gregory Peck) lying dangerously sick from an infected wound at the foot of Mount Kilimanjaro. In a series of fevered flashbacks, he reminisces about the women who have played a role in his life: his first great love, Cynthia (Ava Gardner), the artist Liz (Hildegard Knef), and his wife, Helen (Susan Hayward). Helen, who helps him through his illness, has accompanied him to Africa on the quest for an answer to the question tormenting him: Does his life have a purpose or has he lost his way? He draws a parallel to the African legend of a wayward leopard whose bones lie frozen in the glacier on Mount Kilimanjaro.

The film was shot mainly in the studio and in the places that pop up in Street's flashbacks, but the Kilimanjaro scenes were filmed on location. To this end, the film team set up a base camp in the **Amboseli National Park** on the border with Tanzania. With an area of some 150 square miles (390 square kilometers), the park is small compared with most natural preserves in Kenya. Nonetheless, it receives the most visitors: The spectacular view of Mount Kilimanjaro, whose snow-capped peaks tower 19,340 feet (5,895 meters) above sea level, is a must for every visitor to East Africa. Once the shoot was over, the small film village was turned over to the Masai, who dubbed it **Ol Tukai** and made it into a camp. The original, rather simple lodgings at Tukai were renovated in 1996 and now constitute a luxurious lodge.

John Ford is famous above all for his classic Westerns, but he is also the man behind the biggest safari adventure in the history of East Africa: the filming of **Mogambo** (1953). Ava Gardner plays the vivacious dancer Eloise Kelly, who bursts into the quiet life of lone wolf Victor Marswell (Clark Gable). Victor and his friend John (Philip Stainton) work as animal catchers together in Africa. Eloise falls for Victor, but he finds himself more attracted to Linda Nordley (Grace Kelly), a young woman who is planning an expedition into Uganda with her husband to film a documentary on gorillas. Both women accompany Victor on the adventurous safari in search of the gorillas, leading to a tumultuous love triangle par excellence.

More than 500 people and 300 tents – including kitchen tents, a movie tent for evening viewings, a party tent with its own billiard table, and a first-aid tent with its own X-ray machine – initially set up camp in November 1952 in **Thika**, a few miles northwest of Nairobi. The crew later relocated almost 1,000 miles (1,600 kilometers) to the **River Kagera** in **Tanzania** where an aircraft landing strip was built to facilitate the delivery of equipment, mail, food, and medication. Filming also took place on Mount Kenya, in Uganda, and in the Congo.

Ford had traveled to Kenya and Tanzania two months before the actors were due to arrive to prepare for the shoot. Simultaneously, a second crew was busy filming mountain gorillas in Uganda. Ava Gardner arrived in Nairobi with her husband, Frank Sinatra, who soon developed acute boredom, with the

The Momella lakes at the foot of Mount Meru: This is where Howard Hawks famously improvised much of the filming of *Hatari!* The high-octane Hawks flew over the area every morning in his propeller plane to order the film crew about by radio, directing them to where the animals were.

result that the couple quarreled all the time. Clark Gable busied himself by flirting with Grace Kelly, who shared his passionate interest in hunting. Shooting did not go smoothly, and several adventures were ad-libbed into the script. One such episode involved a baby elephant that pushed Ava Gardner into the mud. She screamed for help, but John Ford just let the cameras roll. The leopard that finds its way into Eloise's tent one night was not on the payroll – another spontaneous performance that added a certain unplanned appeal to the production.

The spectacular shots of animals in director Howard Hawks's **Hatari!** (1962) have gone down as a highlight in film history. *Hatari* is Swahili for danger, of which there was no shortage during the lively on-location shoot. Hawks never once contemplated using stuntmen for the hunting scenes, and shooting revolved around the real stars of the film: the wildlife. The movie was shot in **Arusha National Park** in Tanzania; the team set up camp in **Momella** at the base of a 14,980-foot (4,566-meter) volcano, **Mount Meru.** Every morning, Hawks climbed into his little propeller plane and directed the film vehicles by radio to where the animals were. Actors had to be ready to depart for the shoot at a moment's notice before driving out at full tilt to the herds that Hawks had spotted. Since normal voice

Signs on the grounds of the Hatari Lodge still point to the time when the popular movie starring John Wayne and Red Buttons was filmed here.

had no screenplay ready when he began filming, just a vague idea about a film on animal catchers in Africa. Nonetheless, Paramount allocated an enormous budget for the movie: $6 million, a sum virtually unheard of in those days.

Just prior to the crew's departure for Africa, it still was not clear whether John Wayne was going to take the part of Mercer. Only when the entire crew was back in Hollywood did Hawks even begin writing the script. The sequences Hawks thought up in California were shot in the studios. The director added in the scenes filmed in Africa like the missing pieces of a puzzle, trying all the while to turn the whole business into a coherent story. A 160-minute version finally made it to the cinemas but failed to convince the critics. Audiences loved *Hatari!*, and the film became one of Paramount's biggest box-office successes.

German actor Hardy Krüger was so taken with Tanzania that he emigrated there after filming was completed. He bought Momella Farm on which *Hatari!* was shot, extended it into a safari lodge, and lived there for thirteen years. After his return to Germany, the hotel fell into disrepair. It was reopened in September 2004 as the **Hatari Lodge.**

The Other Kenya: Love and Politics

The clichéd image of adventurers and safaris has become a thing of the past. Films shot recently in Kenya portray a less glamorous image, highlighting the contrast between the country's natural landscapes and friendly inhabitants on the one hand, and the legacy of bitter poverty, violence, and political conflict on the other.

The Constant Gardener (2005) is a political thriller and tragic love story in one: Justin Quayle (Ralph Fiennes) is a British diplomat in Kenya whose best friend, Sandy Woodrow (Danny Huston), brings him the news that Justin's wife, Tessa (Rachel Weisz), has been found murdered. Although the British government forbids Justin to pursue the killer privately, he decides to take matters into his own hands. His research reveals that Tessa had uncovered a major conspiracy involving the pharmaceuticals industry and was likely killed for what she knew.

In *The Constant Gardener*, the film adaptation of the novel by John le Carré, Rachel Weisz plays an activist who uncovers a conspiracy to make money from illegal medical testing in Kenya.

Actor Hardy Krüger fell in love with the area near Mount Meru during the filming of *Hatari!* He moved to Tanzania after the shoot was finished.

recordings were impossible under these conditions, the actors exchanged completely improvised dialogues during the hunting scenes, with the real sound later synchronized in the studio. Filming also took place on the plains near Lake Manyara. The dramatic opening scenes featuring a rhino chase were shot in the fantastic landscapes of the **Ngorongoro Crater.**

The confusing plot centers on Sean Mercer (John Wayne) and his friends, including Pockets (Red Buttons), Kurt Muller (Hardy Krüger), and young blood Brandy de la Court (Michèle Girardon), a troupe that captures wild animals and sells them to zoos all over the world. Love and jealousy start to ruffle feathers when the worldly-wise photographer Anna Maria "Dallas" D'Allesandro (Elsa Martinelli) joins the gang of friends. Hawks

Following shoots in Berlin and London, the production team went to Kenya for the most important phase of filming. They set up camp in the private **Royal Nairobi Club** and began by shooting the scenes set in and around **Nairobi,** including those that take place on a golf course in **Karen,** at the weekly vegetable market in **Kiambu,** and in the slums of **Kibera,** where more than a million people live in dilapidated housing.

When filming in Nairobi had wrapped up, the team moved farther south to the village of **Ol Tapese** near the **Rift Valley** to film the scene in which Justin Quayle is pursued by baddies in a speeding Land Rover. From there, the team went on to **Lake Magadi.** Flamingoes and insects are the only visible forms of life around this lake, a phenomenal sight that glows pinkish-red in the desert. The scenes due to be filmed on Lake Turkana, which lies to the north, were actually shot here. Director Fernando Meirelles discovered Lake Magadi by chance when he was flying in to northern Kenya. **Lake Turkana** does make an appearance, however, in the scenes set in Camp Seven, a refugee settlement in southern Sudan.

The political situation and the lack of infrastructure made it impossible to film in the Sudan itself. Some of the crew stayed in tents set up in a kind of military camp in the village of **Loiyangalani** on the southern shore of Lake Turkana. Others fared better, spending their nights at the **Oasis Lodge,** a luxurious hotel situated in the stone desert complete with two swimming pools fed with water from natural springs. For the final shots, Fiennes and a small crew traveled to **Lokichoggio** on the border with Sudan. The scenes showing Quayle's arrival in Lokichoggio and some aerial views of the Kenyan-Sudanese border were taken from the plane.

In 2001, German film also discovered East Africa when Kenya served as a location for director Caroline Link's filmic version of Stefanie Zweig's autobiographical bestseller **Nowhere in Africa.** Rather than conveying the image of an artificial paradise, Link wanted to use an authentic location to take a close look at Kenya and its people.

The film deals with the fate of the Redlichs, a Jewish family that fled the Nazis in 1938 and emigrated to Kenya. Walter Redlich (Merab Ninidze) finds work in Kenya at Rongai Farm. His daughter Regina (Lea Kurka, later Karoline Eckertz) blossoms in her new surroundings: She learns the local language, develops an interest in area customs and traditions, and makes friends with Owuor (Sidede Onyulo), the cook. But for her mother, Jettel (Juliane Köhler), Kenya remains a mystery, a land whose language and social hierarchies are anathema to her. The situation puts undue strain on her marriage to Walter.

Nowhere in Africa tells the story of the Redlichs, a Jewish family that fled Nazi Germany in 1938. They emigrate to Kenya, but adjusting to their adopted home presents a new set of problems. The movie was awarded the Oscar for the Best Foreign Language Film in 2003.

Little Regina (Lea Kurka) quickly makes friends with the locals.

The initial shoot was supposed to capture the essence of Rongai, the Redlichs' first farm. The surroundings had to be almost desert-like so as to create an accurate on-screen impression, but also unwelcoming, so that the audience would be able to understand Jettel's belief that nobody would ever want to live here. The crew found an ideal spot in **Lolldaiga,** northwest of **Mount Kenya.** Since no accommodation was available there, the only possibility to house crew and actors was a tent camp. This presented logistical challenges, such as procuring water for the site, gasoline for forty vehicles, and the necessary generators. Wild elephants and lions lived in the camp's immediate vicinity, so leaving on foot was strictly prohibited.

Further scenes were shot in **Ol Joro Orok,** where the team reconstructed the Redlichs' second farmhouse. While dry desert conditions prevailed in the Rongai area, Ol Joro Orok had to appear green and fertile, even though Caroline Link would only use the location for shots filmed in and around the farm. The field scenes and those in the farmworkers' village were captured at the third main location, **Mukutani,** a village some 25 miles (40 kilometers) northeast of **Lake Baringo.** The way in was such

a rough ride that the crew was forced to build its own road to ensure comfortable access. The team also planted large fields of maize – crops that had to achieve three different stages of ripeness during the shoot – to create an authentic impression of the passage of time.

About 700 people live in Mukutani, above all Pokots, former nomads who have settled along the River Mukutani. Many of them had never seen white people before the film crew arrived. Nevertheless, the village council of elders agreed to let Caroline Link film a Pokot night ceremony, in which Jettel and Regina take part. More than 400 Pokots in their own traditional costumes participated in the scene. Link later expressed her admiration

In *The White Masai*, Carola (Nina Hoss) develops a deep connection to Kenya – and to the proud Samburu warrior Lemalian (Jacky Ido).

for the acting talent and enthusiasm of the Pokots, most of whom had never seen a television or been to the movies.

For reasons of authenticity, one of the original locations from the book had to be replaced by a completely different place. The famous Norfolk Hotel situated on the outskirts of Nairobi, which had served as an internment camp for German women and children during World War II, no longer had the country atmosphere that it exuded in old photographs. Caroline Link chose to film these scenes instead in the Outspan Hotel in **Nyeri,** a northern provincial city. The myriad efforts to get things right were amply rewarded: *Nowhere in Africa* won the 2003 Oscar for Best Foreign Language Film.

Yet another German director found herself en route to Kenya four years later to film an autobiography: Hermine Huntgeburth shot the unusual love story of Swiss native Corinne Hofmann and a Masai man on location in Africa. **The White Masai** (2005) was based on the book of the same name, a bestseller first published in 1998.

Although the director changed the names of the protagonists for her film, she followed the autobiographical account very closely. At the end of her holiday in Kenya, Carola (Nina Hoss) gets to know the Samburu warrior Lemalian (Jacky Ido) and falls head over heels in love with him. On the spur of the moment, she cancels her return flight and goes looking for Lemalian. After a dramatic journey through the African wilderness, she ends up in Maralal, where she finds him. Carola follows the Masai to his village, Barsaloi, and marries him. While still fascinated by her husband's culture, the life they embark upon

Most scenes in *The White Masai* were shot at the original locations from the book. Samburu families worked with the crew as extras.

is marked by deprivation. Most scenes were shot at the original locations from the book, such as **Nairobi** and **Maralal.**

The director chose not to film in Barsaloi itself, so as not to confront Corinne Hofmann's Samburu family with the filming, or force them to confront the past. Instead, she chose **Wamba** north of Samburu National Game Reserve, an isolated spot not far from the village where Hofmann had lived for fifteen years. Here the film crew constructed a Masai village and the mission station run by the Italian padre Bernardo (Antonio Prester), with traditional Samburu families living in the film camp as extras. A tribe closely related to the Masai that also speaks the same language, the Samburu built their own huts based on the specifications of the set designers, who had to guarantee sufficient light for indoor shoots. The huts were lived in before filming began to lend them the necessary patina of real village life.

During the filming of *The White Masai,* the film crew lived in the isolated Kenyan steppes of Wamba, north of Samburu National Game Reserve.

CENTRAL AFRICA

HEART OF DARKNESS By Anja Hauenstein

Uganda, Rwanda, and the Congo: This is the heart of Africa, or, as Joseph Conrad called the part of it that was colonized by Belgium, "the heart of darkness." There is little in the way of tourism and safari-romanticism in this region of green hills, coffee plantations, mist-covered rain forests, and broad, mighty rivers. Instead, civil wars ravage the region, and travelers don't dare venture out into the immensely beautiful landscapes. Some hardy filmmakers have demonstrated their determination to film here for the sake of authenticity: Kevin Macdonald, for example, in *The Last King of Scotland* (2006), starring Forest Whitaker – a film that deals with the darkest period of Uganda's recent history, the reign of terror under Idi Amin. Terry George braved on-location filming, too, to shoot *Hotel Rwanda* (2004), a movie about the Rwandan genocide of the mid-1990s.

Things were different back in 1950 when John Huston decided to shoot **The African Queen** in Uganda and what was then the Belgian Congo. Huston had always been fascinated by the idea of going on an elephant shoot, and this became the driving force behind his decision to shoot *The African Queen* (1951) – based on C.S. Forester's novel of the same name – almost exclusively in Africa. The film is set during World War I. After the death of her brother, a missionary named Rose (Katharine Hepburn) is forced to flee the Germans with the rough-and-ready captain Charlie Allnut (Humphrey Bogart in an Oscar-winning performance) in his decrepit boat, the *African Queen*. On their

perilous journey downriver, the ill-matched pair get to know each other better and fall in love despite all odds.

To find a suitable river, Huston set out in an airplane, covering 25,000 miles (40,200 kilometers) before he finally set up camp near the village of **Biondo** on the **Ruiki River** in the Congo. It was here that he would shoot all the film's stunning opening scenes. The film crew constructed the village of Kungdu, complete with church, on the shores of **Lake Albert** in **Port Butiaba** on Uganda's border with the Congo. The reed-infested lake on which Rose and Charlie attack a German battleship is a smaller body of water in the northern part of **Murchison Falls National Park.** The real *African Queen* can still be admired: She's moored at the Holiday Inn in Key Largo, Florida.

The film crew put up with crocodiles, attacks by ants and boars, worms in their food, poisonous snakes in the camp, malaria, and dysentery – nor were there sanitary services of any kind. In 1987, Hepburn wrote a book on the difficult shoot that she sarcastically titled *The Making of The African Queen: Or, How I Went to Africa with Bogart, Bacall and Huston and almost Lost My Mind.* Huston's unrelenting desire to hunt elephants proved greater than all the adversities encountered during filming. He bullied everyone with his obsession for weeks on end, leaving stars and crew to wait in the wilds or endure changes of venue only to discover that the director had disappeared into hunting grounds, legal or illegal. Screenwriter Peter Viertel was enraged at Huston's behavior and left before the end of shooting. He

Some filmmakers have insisted on working in Africa for the sake of authenticity, like Kevin Macdonald, director of *The Last King of Scotland* starring Forest Whitaker as dictator Idi Amin. In *Gorillas in the Mist*, the story of the unusually brave zoologist Dian Fossey is framed by Rwanda's Virunga volcano ridge, west of Ruhengeri. John Huston wanted to go on an elephant hunt, so he decided to shoot *The African Queen* almost exclusively in Africa.

expressed his frustration with the filmmaker's outrageous safari circus antics in the novel *White Hunter Black Heart,* filmed by Clint Eastwood in Zimbabwe in 1990.

In the spring of 1967, a young zoologist named Dian Fossey traveled to Africa to study the behavior of mountain gorillas in the border region between Rwanda, the newly independent Congo, and Uganda. She befriended the animals, gave them names, and laid out a cemetery near her hut where she buried anthropoids that had been shot by hunters. In 1985, Fossey was murdered in her corrugated iron hut on Mount Visoke.

Three years after her death, director Michael Apted filmed her life story based on the autobiography that she had written in 1983. His film, **Gorillas in the Mist** (1988), with Sigourney Weaver in the role of Fossey, was shot in the native habitat of the remaining 650 mountain gorillas, the **Parc National des Volcans** in **Rwanda.** The park covers roughly 50 square miles

(125 square kilometers) and is situated in the northwest of the country in the border area with Congo and Uganda. The crew set up base camp at an altitude of about 8,530 feet (2,600 meters) on the slopes of the **Virunga volcano ridge** a few miles west of **Ruhengeri.** The Karisoke Research Center, where Dian Fossey lived and worked, is situated at an altitude of 11,810 feet (3,600 meters), high enough to challenge the crew to an epic trek each day to get to the film shoot. The Rwandan government allowed the team to film for one hour a day; only six members of the film team were permitted to get close to the animals. A behavioral biologist taught Sigourney Weaver how to emulate the gorillas' body language and sounds, and kept radio contact with her via an earplug during shooting to coach her on behavior among the gorillas. While most scenes were shot with the real gorillas in cameo roles, actors in gorilla costumes sometimes had to take their place for reasons of practicality.

149

ON THE TRAIL OF AN EMPIRE By Greg Langley

India has been independent for more than sixty years, but in the minds of Western audiences, it is still firmly part of the Raj, the nearly 200 years of British colonial rule that ended in 1947. Except for blockbusters in which the subcontinent features as one exotic backdrop in a collage of international action locations, Western films shot in India have tended to be pith-helmet dramas focusing on the days when much of the world map was pale pink, the hue that denoted the holdings of the British Empire.

The fascination is understandable. The history of this distant outpost of "the Empire on which the sun never sets" added yet another complex layer to an enigmatic land whose otherness is so compelling. The cultural, racial, and sexual tensions that resulted from the era of British dominion also provided intense storylines for such films as *Shakespeare Wallah* (1965), *Bombay Talkie* (1970), *Gandhi* (1982), *Heat and Dust* (1983), and *A Passage to India* (1984), while the vast landscape seduces the camera with rich vistas and staggering contrasts.

Stretching from the snowcapped peaks of the Himalayas in the north to the tropics of Kerala in the south, and from the sacred Ganges that gives life to the land to the arid, golden sands of the northwest's Thar Desert, the great triangle of subcontinent thrust into the Indian Ocean offers the camera exotica and incomparable variety. In remote Dharmsala in Northern India, Steven Spielberg filmed François Truffaut, Jerry Garcia of the Grateful Dead, and an endless plain of villagers pointing to the skies in *Close Encounters of the Third Kind* (1977). Roland Joffé shot the slums of Calcutta for *City of Joy* (1992), while David Niven made an appearance in the city for railway scenes in *Around the World in Eighty Days* (1956). Screen adaptations of Rudyard Kipling's novels have taken Hollywood to India, too: Director Victor Saville shot scenes with Errol Flynn around Jaipur and Bundi for *Kim* (1950), while Stephen Sommers took cast and crew to the Majestic Fort in Jodhpur in the northwestern state of Rajasthan for sequences in *The Jungle Book* (1994).

A significant force these days beyond the scope of Western forays to India is Bollywood, that curious portmanteau of Hindu cinema. Its various ethnic spinoffs continue to produce more films every year than its American counterpart in the Hollywood hills. Known as *masala* movies, these are melodramatic efforts with formulaic tales and lashings of singing and dancing that are in themselves a cultural journey through the land. In the past these films have played to the Indian diaspora, but the success of films such as *Monsoon Wedding* (2001) and *Bride & Prejudice* (2004) have brought the form to a wider, international stage.

An Epic Tour of India with *Gandhi*

"If you are a minority of one, the truth is the truth," stated Mohandas Karamchand Gandhi. Richard Attenborough's film focuses on the powerful convictions of the lawyer who led the nonviolent revolts against the British in the years following World War I. Ben Kingsley, the then thirty-seven-year-old

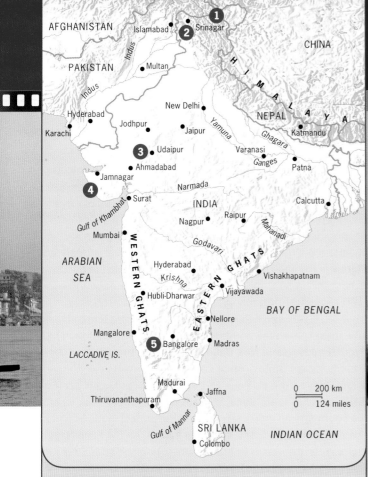

India has long fascinated moviegoers, from Rudyard Kipling's tales of British colonial rule in *Kim* starring Laurette Luez and Errol Flynn (above) to scenes of life along rivers like the Ganges (left), as in Roland Joffé's *City of Joy*.

Top landscape film locations

1. Ladakh, Himalayas: **The Razor's Edge, Samsara**
2. Lake Dal, Srinagar: **Heat and Dust, The Razor's Edge, Passage to India**
3. Lake Palace, Lake Pichola, Udaipur: **Octopussy**
4. Porbandar waterfront: **Gandhi**
5. Savandurga: **A Passage to India**

actor who made his film debut in the title role of *Gandhi* (1982), described the film as the "last true epic." Shot almost entirely in India, the film won eight Oscars and was created before the era of computer generated images – the claustrophobic crowds feature thousands of real extras.

The film opens at the funeral of Gandhi and sets the tone for what follows. Filmed on January 31, 1981, on the thirty-third anniversary of Gandhi's funeral, the sequence features a crowd of some 300,000, the most extras used in any film scene. Moving from **Rashtrapati Bhavan,** the Viceroy's Palace in **Delhi** and home to the president of India, the monumental funeral procession flows slowly through the grieving throngs down the broad **Rajpath** to the towering **India Gate.**

It was director Attenborough's lifelong dream to bring the story of the impassioned political and spiritual leader to the screen. He began in 1962 and, after eighteen years of negotiations, finally commenced filming in 1980. With a budget of $22 million, Attenborough could afford to be lavish with details. He shot as many scenes as possible on the location of the real events, allowing the biopic to undertake an epic journey through India: from **Mumbai** (Bombay) to **Patna** and then to Delhi and **Porbandar,** Gandhi's birthplace. The assassination scene was filmed where Gandhi was shot, in the gardens of **Gandhi Smriti** (formerly Birla House) at **5 Tees January Marg, New Delhi,** now

Ben Kingsley as *Gandhi*, sitting on the Porbandar waterfront. The great man reflects on the forces about to be unleashed against the British.

an official memorial and open to the public. A stone tablet marks the spot where the great man fell.

Gandhi is as much about India itself as it is about the ardent pacifist. Throughout, Attenborough shows the people of India as they accompany or cheer on the little man with a big walking stick. Gandhi journeys from the vast city of Bombay to **Calcutta,** scenes in which the spectacular countryside dominates the tale. The crashing surf of the **Porbandar** waterfront features in the background as Gandhi talks to journalist Vince Walker (Martin Sheen), hinting at the elemental force about to be unleashed against the British. Huge crowds greet his arrival at **Motihari Station** in the ancient city of Patna, while the protest at the Dharasana Salt Works, the culmination of the legendary 200-mile (320-kilometer) "salt march" of 1930, was shot in Mumbai.

In all, eighty-seven different settings were used for the film's 189 scenes; even the South African scenes were shot in India. **Hyderabad House** in **New Delhi** stands in as the office of General Christiaan Smuts (Athol Fugard), who meets Gandhi and acknowledges the success of the Indians' campaign against discriminatory laws. **Pune,** southeast of Mumbai, was where the South African mosque scene and the protest in the Imperial Theatre were filmed. The **Aga Khan Palace,** on the **Pune Nagar Highway,** is the venue where Gandhi was interned during the Quit India Movement in 1942. It is there that his wife, Kasturba, (played by Rohini Hattangadi in the film) died; today the palace is a memorial. The final location used in India for *Gandhi* was **Udaipur,** where the train scenes were staged, including the rooftop discussions with Charlie Andrews (Ian Charleson). The young English clergyman is, for all his good intentions, clearly a misplaced foreigner, a feeling the audience senses as he gazes uncomprehendingly at the broad plains of India.

Goa's Hippie Trail

"They should have left him alone," ran the tag line for ***The Bourne Supremacy*** (2004). The sequel to *The Bourne Identity* (2002) finds former CIA agent Jason Bourne (Matt Damon) and his girlfriend, Marie (Franka Potente), living in **Goa,** once a Portuguese colony. Located on the Arabian Sea in India's southwest, Goa was once famed as a hippie haven and is still popular with an eclectic group of travelers attracted by sandy beaches, swaying coconut palms, and a life of unregulated leisure. This made it, according to Patrick Crowley, one of the film's producers, the ideal setting for author Robert Ludlum's fictional character to drop out of the rat race.

But far from enjoying the carefree *sossegarde* lifestyle for which the region is known, Bourne is haunted by nightmares. At night he awakens and gazes out at the peaceful oceanfront

Director Richard Attenborough dances on a train during filming. The Golden Temple in Amritsar appears in the film, as does Delhi: Gandhi steps from a car on the Rajpath; his funeral procession passes the Viceroy's Palace.

The beaches of the former Portuguese colony of Goa host action-packed scenes from *The Bourne Supremacy* starring Matt Damon as Jason Bourne and Franka Potente as Marie, the love of his life.

on **Palolem Beach** in **Canacona**. His bad dreams prove all too real when Russian hit man Kirill (Karl Urban) tracks him down. After returning from an energetic training run past colorful fishing ketches littering the waterfront, Bourne identifies Kirill, so the couple quickly flee. Bourne's jeep races through the narrow streets of the capital city of **Panjim** with Kirill in pursuit, then speeds inland onto endless Goan red roads. The car spins out of control and plunges over a narrow bridge into the murky river near **Sinquerim Beach** in **Northern Goa**. Only Bourne survives. He emerges to resume his identity, with the film's action shifting to Moscow and Berlin where he seeks answers and revenge.

Other films shot in Goa include *The Sea Wolves* (1980) and the Hollywood/Bollywood hybrid *Bride & Prejudice* (2004). *The Sea Wolves* features a group of pensionable actors including Gregory Peck, David Niven, and Patrick Macnee playing "middle-aged, boozing, pot-bellied" British businessmen who undertake a commando-style operation in the stunning waters of **Goa Harbor.** *Bride & Prejudice,* a film by Gurinder Chadha of *Bend It Like Beckham* (2002) fame, gives Jane Austen's classic novel a *masala* treatment. Lalita (Aishwarya Rai) and Darcy

Aishwarya Rai conjures her best "come-hither" look as Lalita in *Bride & Prejudice*. Jane Austen's classic novel gets a *masala* treatment when the wide-eyed beauty and Darcy (Martin Henderson) give love a go in Goa.

(Martin Henderson) make an unlikely pair who are nonetheless forced to give love a chance in Goa. Most of the beach action in the Goan sequence takes place at **Benaulim** in the region's idyllic south. The spectacular **Golden Temple** is used to indicate action taking place in **Amritsar;** the location also features in *Gandhi* when General Reginald Dyer (Edward Fox) orders his troops to fire on unarmed civilians.

Octopussy in Udaipur

The palaces and the lakescapes of **Udaipur** in central India serve up the James Bond adventure *Octopussy* (1983) in typically exotic style. Agent 007 (Roger Moore) travels to **Lake Pichola** in Rajasthan, passing via the **Taj Mahal,** actually located

Why is Roger Moore smiling? Perhaps because these elephants were not the only good-lookers in Udaipur during the filming of the Bond flick *Octopussy*.

Bond's adventures take him to the opulent Lake Palace Hotel, a marble complex on an island that is the lair of Octopussy and her seductive cohorts.

hundreds of miles away in Agra. Bond resides at the opulent, historic **Shiv Niwas Hotel** while trying to come to grips with the seductive diamond smuggler Octopussy (Maud Adams). After a wild rickshaw ride through the labyrinthine old town of alleys, bazaars, and 250-year-old lakeside *haveli* mansions, he arrives at **Jag Niwas,** known today as the **Lake Palace Hotel.** The great marble complex that dominates a lake island and seems to float on the tranquil waters is the lair of Octopussy and her seductive cohorts. The **Monsoon Palace,** located on a distant mountaintop, serves as the retreat where Bond is held captive by the villainous Kamal Khan (Louis Jourdan). Scenes from **Heat and Dust** (1983), a Merchant-Ivory produc-

Judy Davis plays young Adela in *A Passage to India*. The rocks of Savandurga loom menacingly as she arrives by elephant on a fateful trip to see the caves.

tion, were also shot in this area, although much of the action featured southern **Hyderabad.**

Landscapes of Repressed Desires

Repressed sexuality breaks free in David Lean's epic **A Passage to India** (1984), a film based on E.M. Forster's book of the same name. The novelist set the tale of young Englishwoman Adela Quested (Judy Davis) in the fictional city of Chandrapore – a place modeled on **Bankipur,** a suburb of **Patna** in the northwestern state of **Bihar.** Director Lean – of *Lawrence of Arabia* (1962) and *Doctor Zhivago* (1965) fame – decided to film mostly in and around **Bangalore** in southern India so he could shoot the old Swiss steam locomotives that run on the World Heritage-listed **Nilgiri Mountain Railway,** as well as the caves at **Savandurga.** Most scenes, including the bazaar sequences, were filmed on sets created on the grounds of the **Bangalore Palace** in the city center. The famous shot in which Adela cycles through the fields and finds ancient Indian erotic figures was also filmed on a back lot, with the Tantric statues based on those in temples at the World Heritage site of **Khajuraho** in northern Madhya Pradesh.

Scenes of prim and proper conduct were filmed on the manicured lawns of the **Bangalore Club, Field Marshal K.M. Cariappa Road.** Originally created in 1868 for exclusive use by British troops, the club is the perfect backdrop to the Billiard Room "God Save the Queen" sequence, the endless teas, and the scene in which Dr. Aziz (Victor Banerjee) is refused admittance. Audiences get their first view of fictional Chandrapore when the Imperial Indian Mail train arrives. The station in the scene is **Dodballapur,** 25 miles (40 kilometers) north of Bangalore, while the Chandrapore Church is actually **St. Thomas's,** located in the hill station of **Ootacamund** (renamed Udhagamandalam) some 130 miles (210 kilometers) southwest of the city. The covered terrace and pool at Mr. Fielding's house, where Adela meets the locals over tea, was shot at the **West End Hotel** on **Race Course Road,** although the pool in which Professor Godbhole (Alec Guinness) and Adela dangle their feet has since been filled in.

Lean also uses the lush tropical scenery of the Nilgiri Mountain Railway – also known as the Blue Mountain Railway – during the expedition to the Marabar Caves. Particularly distinctive is the **Adderley Viaduct** over the **Bhawani River,** northwest of Kallar.

Forster based his Marabar Caves on caverns located 45 miles (72 kilometers) from Bankipur. Due to the prevalence of bandits there, Lean chose two locations near Bangalore to stand in. The scene in which Dr. Aziz and Adela arrive at their base camp by elephant before exploring the lower caves was shot in the moonscape of **Savandurga,** where local stonemasons hacked out "entrances" to make up for the area's lack of grottoes. The

and would also use Srinagar for filming: In the scenes after his acquittal, Dr. Aziz retreats to the city and opens a small hospital next to the **Jhelum River.** The eighteenth-century **Hari Parbat Fort** and the spire of the **Shah Hamdan Mosque** appear in these sequences. Dr. Aziz's houseboat is moored near **Nishat Gardens** on Lake Dal, scenes of tranquility that reflect his finally having found a place of peace and refuge.

Himalayan landscapes of the Ladakh region of Kashmir, such as the Nubra Valley (left) with its monasteries, feature in *The Razor's Edge* starring Bill Murray.

filming then jumps 25 miles (40 kilometers) to **Ramanagaram** for the upper caves, where Adela finally "succumbs" to the exotic atmosphere of India.

Serenity in the Himalayas

In Western films, the **Himalayas** are where lead characters go to find enlightenment – even if they have to settle for something less. For Larry Darrell (Bill Murray) in **The Razor's Edge** (1984), the second film adaptation of W. Somerset Maugham's classic novel, the destination was the historic capital of Kashmir, **Srinagar,** and the **Ladakh** region in eastern Kashmir. The monastery scenes were shot at **Thiksey Monastery** in Ladakh, while **Lake Dal** in Srinagar formed a photogenic backdrop for the meditative rambles that helped soothe Darrell's tortured soul. During filming, director John Byrum met up with David Lean in a nearby restaurant. Lean was scouting locations for *A Passage to India,*

Other films shot in the region include *Samsara* (2001), a love story about a sixth-century monk named Bodhidharma who inspired Zen Buddhism in China. Although it won many international awards, the film is perhaps best known for its Kamasutra sequence featuring a *saree* hung from a wooden beam. **Thiksey Monastery** makes an appearance in the film, as do the monasteries of **Hemis, Mhato,** and **Shergole,** and the villages of **Stagmo, Mhato** and **Shey.** In *Heat and Dust* (1983), the filmic version of Ruth Prawer Jhabvala's Booker Prize-winning novel, the bungalow where Olivia (Greta Scacchi) lives with her husband is at the hill station of **Gulmarg.** At the end of the film, Anne (Julie Christie), who is investigating the scandalous life of her great-aunt (Scacchi), retreats to Kashmir. Her destination is a *shikara*, or houseboat, on the waters of **Lake Dal.**

Samsara is best known for its Kamasutra scene featuring a *saree* hung from a wooden beam, and also for its stunning shots of monasteries like Shergole.

CHINA AND MONGOLIA

KUNG-FU FIGHTING & NOMADS´ TALES

By Anja Hauenstein

China is *the* emerging power in the Far East, a vast country with a total surface area of nearly 3.86 million square miles (10 million square kilometers), of which two thirds are barely inhabited – or not at all. The world's third-largest country after Russia and Canada is possessed of spectacular landscapes, and the variety is astounding, ranging from the deep canyons of the Yangtze River to the wide plains of the Taklamakan Desert, and from the craggy peaks of the Yellow Mountains to the fairy-tale limestone mountains of Guilin. Yet for most people in the West, the People's Republic remains an unknown land. It comes as no surprise that Chinese films were largely unknown in the West until just a few years ago. The first film was shot in China a century ago, and 7,000 movie productions have followed since, yet their influence on the film industry outside China has been negligible. Films such as *Raise the Red Lantern* (1991) and *Farewell My Concubine* (1993) are the notable exceptions.

Martial Arts Epics: Deserts and Bamboo Forests

China's first truly big international box office success was **Crouching Tiger, Hidden Dragon** (2000). The pictorially overwhelming movie about love, betrayal, and revenge enchanted viewers with its wonderful landscape shots and its graceful adaptation of the martial arts genre. The film team traveled the length and breadth of the country to work in some of the planet's most inhospitable regions. Director Ang Lee began filming with scenes that look back in time at the love story that brought Jiao Long (Zhang Ziyi) and Luo Xiao Hu (Chen Chang) together. To achieve the desired effect, the film crew spent a month living in tents in the **Gobi Desert** in the **Xinjiang Province** in west China. Landscape highlights such as the **Flaming Mountains** near **Turpan** and the **Taklamakan Plateau** dominate these images of a world made of stone, sand, and endless horizons. The crew then moved west to the border with Kazakhstan, four hours' drive from Urumchi and at the edge of the **Taklamakan Desert.** This landscape, so reminiscent of Mongolia's vast grass steppes, was the setting for the final scenes of forbidden love amidst glaciers, waterfalls, and yurt tents.

Continuing its journey, the film crew traveled on from the extreme west to the south of the country. Ang Lee filmed the concluding scenes in the **Huangshan Mountains** – also known as the **Yellow Mountains** – where Jiao Long plunges into the fog. The mountain range is famous for its jagged peaks that rise out of the clouds and for its deep canyons. The acrobatic fight scene between Jiao Long and Li Mu Bai (Chow Yun-fat) was shot in the **bamboo forest of Anji.** More than 130 million bamboo trees grow in this vast forest in Zhejiang Province to the

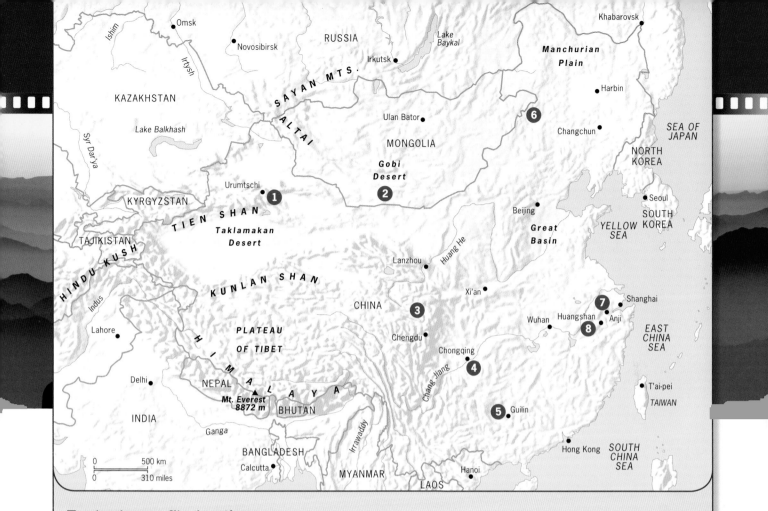

Top landscape film locations

1. Taklamakan Desert and the Flaming Mountains near Turpan, Xinjiang Province, China: **Crouching Tiger, Hidden Dragon, Hero**
2. Southern Gobi Desert, Mongolia: **The Story of the Weeping Camel**
3. Jiuzhaigou Natural Reserve, Sichuan Province, China: **Hero**
4. Bamboo forests near Chongqing, Sichuan Province, China: **House of Flying Daggers**
5. Limestone peaks near Guilin, Guangxi Province, China: **The Painted Veil**
6. Hulun Buir steppes, Inner Mongolia: **Urga**
7. Bamboo forest of Anji, Zhejiang Province, China: **Crouching Tiger, Hidden Dragon**
8. Huangshan Mountains, Anhui Province, China: **Crouching Tiger, Hidden Dragon**

southwest of Shanghai. Transposing the already complex fight choreography into the supple tree tops some 20 feet (30 meters) above the ground posed a particular challenge and involved a system of cranes, wires, and towing ropes. The effort paid off: In its first week alone, the film attracted more viewers in the U.S. than any other foreign film in history. *Crouching Tiger, Hidden Dragon* also garnered four Oscars, including those for Best Foreign Language Film and Best Cinematography.

Western audiences are crazy about Chinese films and their elaborate martial arts scenes. Epics such as *House of Flying Daggers* (far left) and *Crouching Tiger, Hidden Dragon* (left) were filmed in settings like the mist-cloaked Huangshan Mountains (above).

Another Chinese martial arts epic achieved similar success two years later. **Hero** (2002) tells the story of four warriors whose mission is the same: to kill the King of Qin. Director Zhang Yimou and his film crew of 300 traveled around China in search of the most suitable locations for the four-episode drama. Like Ang Lee, Zhang Yimou chose the **Taklamakan Desert** as a setting for several scenes. The team journeyed to the northwest of China, setting up camp in the old oasis town of **Dunhuang** in Gansu Province. From time to time, the crew had to brave frightening thunder and lightning and even the odd sandstorm on its daily three-hour trek into the desert for filming – and face the return each evening under similar conditions. The subsequent filming location, on the shallow **Arrow Bamboo Lake** in the **Jiuzhaigou Natural Reserve** in Sichuan Province, proved no easier. The crew filmed among the pine forests, waterfalls, and lakes here, including the scene at the **Nuorilang Waterfalls** and the elegantly executed fight on the mirror-like surface of the lake. Underwater currents mar the water's surface in the afternoon, so shooting on the bamboo-fringed lake could only take place in the morning if the effect was to be achieved. After three weeks, the director was finally satisfied with the scenes.

Perhaps the most memorable fight scene of all pits Flying Snow (Maggie Cheung) against Moon (Zhang Ziyi) in an ancient oak grove in **Inner Mongolia.** The sequence was scheduled for filming when the fall colors were at their most intense – one of the film assistants was charged with the single duty of staying at the location ahead of filming to observe the leaves. As

In *Hero*, Broken Sword (Tony Leung) and Flying Snow (Maggie Cheung) fight it out at the Nuorilang Waterfalls in Jiuzhaigou Natural Reserve.

soon as the trees turned that perfect golden hue, the whole crew hotfooted it northwards. These breathtaking landscape shots played a significant role in the film's Oscar nomination for Best Foreign Language Film and were the icing on the cake for director Zhang Yimou: "Viewers may not remember the storyline one or two years after seeing the film, but they will remember certain scenes: two women in red gowns dancing through the air in a sea of golden leaves. They'll also remember the sad combat between two men, whose swords clash over the glassy surface of a lake, flying over the water like dragonflies. These images will stay and I'm proud of that."

Zhang Yimou directed another martial arts love story two years later entitled **House of Flying Daggers** (2004). The film centered on the rebel uprising during the Tang dynasty in ninth-century China and was filmed largely in Ukraine. The long sequence in which the policeman, Jin (Takeshi Kaneshiro), and the blind dancer, Mei (Zhang Ziyi) flee their pursuers was shot in China, however, in the extensive **bamboo forests near Chongqing** in Sichuan Province.

Successes like these encouraged Western directors to take their film projects to China. John Curran made his way to the Middle Kingdom for **The Painted Veil** (2006), the film adaptation of the eponymous novel by W. Somerset Maugham. The story of a disappointing marriage takes English couple Kitty (Naomi

Watts) and Walter (Edward Norton) from London to **Shanghai** in the 1920s. When Walter discovers that Kitty is having an affair, they undertake a self-destructive journey to China's deep south, where a horrendous cholera epidemic is ravaging the populace. In search of a spot that would "appear both enchanting and frightening," Curran singled out an unusually beautiful range of limestone mountain scenery near **Guilin** on the **Li River**. The little village of **Huang Yao** close to Guilin was chosen to represent the town of Mei-tan-fu in the film.

Nomads on the Steppes of Mongolia

China's northern neighbor, bucolic Mongolia, only recently gained a foothold on the film location circuit. Although the movies shot in Mongolia have not enjoyed the same commercial success as those made in China, the "Land of Large Skies" with its endless steppes, mighty mountains, and deep blue lakes is regarded by many as the last untouched territory in Asia. In **Urga** (1991), shot in the steppes of **Hulun Buir** in **Inner Mongolia** – an autonomous region of the People's Republic of China – director Nikita Mikhalkov succeeded in filming a stirring story about modern civilization and its destructive influence on the lives of nomads. A broken television marks the end of *Urga*, a scene that would be reprised twelve years later in **The Story of the Weeping Camel** (2003). The opening scenes show a group of nomads enthusiastically watching satellite TV. Mongolian director Byambasuren Davaa, who submitted the movie as her student presentation to the Munich University of Television and Film, has garnered international attention for her work with this chronicle of a family of nomads living in the Gobi Desert with a herd of camels. One of their camels rejects its bright white newborn, and only a song and the strains of a violin can bring the mother to nurture her calf.

The co-director and cameraman, Luigi Falorni, spent two weeks traveling through the **southern Gobi Desert** in search of

A magical tale about nomadic life, *The Cave of the Yellow Dog* was filmed against the grasslands of northwestern Mongolia.

the protagonists. Finally they found what they were looking for: A family that owned enough camels to increase the likelihood of one's rejecting its calf. Set against the barren, unwelcoming background of the unforgiving, stony steppes, the story of the unwanted baby animal seemed even more moving. The unusual filmic study of nomadic life was honored with an Oscar nomination for Best Documentary.

Following this success, Byambasuren Davaa returned to her homeland to pursue the production of her first feature film. **The Cave of the Yellow Dog** (2005) tells the story of a young girl determined to keep a wild puppy against her father's will. Again, the director spent a long time looking for the right family: nomads with small children who were willing to be shadowed by a film team for the duration of several weeks. Shooting finally got underway in July 2004. The five-person crew flew to the Mongolian capital of **Ulan Bator** and then hopped in a jeep and drove to the northwest for two days until they reached the Batchuluun family yurt in the boundless steppes of the Mongolian highlands.

FROM **APOCALYPSE NOW** TO **THE BEACH**

By Claudia Hellmann

If the films shot in Southeast Asia are to be taken at face value, then this is a region of extremes. On the one hand, these movies feature a dropout's idyll of secluded coves and wonderful beaches, as seen in films such as *The Beach* (2000). Showcased, too, are adventures played out against exotic backdrops, as in the James Bond movie *The Man with the Golden Gun* (1974) and *Lara Croft: Tomb Raider* (2001). A nostalgic yearning for the colonial era often takes center stage, as in *Indochine* (1992), *The Lover* (1992), and *Anna and the King* (1999). The horror of the Vietnam War has drawn many directors to conjure battle scenes in dense jungles, as in *Apocalypse Now* (1979), *Platoon* (1986), and *The Deer Hunter* (1978). The image of Southeast Asia in the movies lies somewhere between beauty and terror – or perhaps it inhabits both ends of the spectrum.

Only a handful of films shot in Southeast Asia were made at the locations they are supposed to represent. Hardly any Vietnam War movies, for example, were actually shot in Vietnam.

James Bond made the island of Koh Ping Gan and its unusual limestone cliffs world famous.

The political situation there long made it expedient to choose locations in neighboring countries. Landscapes such as jungles, beaches, rice paddies, and unusual rock formations did not have to be genuine to satisfy Western viewers, and the stereotypical landscapes of Southeast Asia remained interchangeable for a long time. Only recently has importance been attached to authenticity of place, spurring filmmakers to use original locations – even in Cambodia, long regarded as taboo.

Thailand: Dream Beaches and Dark Abysses

Beautiful landscapes, low production costs, a well-developed infrastructure, and an indigenous film industry have made Thailand a veteran among film locations in Southeast Asia. The country has often stood in for its neighbors, Vietnam and Cambodia. Oliver Stone went so far as to reconstruct an Indian setting for his epic movie *Alexander* (2004) in the northern province of Ubon Ratchathani. When it comes to depicting Thailand as itself,

Top landscape film locations

1. Mae Hong Son Province, Thailand: **Air America**
2. River Kwai, Sai Yok National Park, Thailand: **The Bridge on the River Kwai**
3. "James Bond Island," Phang Nga Bay, Thailand: **The Man with the Golden Gun**
4. Phuket island, Thailand: **The Killing Fields, Good Morning, Vietnam, Bridget Jones: The Edge of Reason**
5. Phi Phi Leh island, Thailand: **The Beach**
6. Temple of Angkor, Cambodia: **Lara Croft: Tomb Raider, Lord Jim**
7. Ninh Binh, Vietnam: **Indochine, The Quiet American**
8. Halong Bay, Vietnam: **Indochine**
9. Baler Bay, Philippines: **Apocalypse Now**
10. Pagsanjan River, Philippines: **Apocalypse Now, Platoon**

and as a less than perfect place, the authorities get nervous. That is why all the versions of Anna Leonowens's famous story of an English governess who traveled to Siam at the end of the nineteenth century to take care of King Mongkut's children, and with whom the ruler promptly fell in love (or so Hollywood would have us believe), have been forbidden in the kingdom itself, where it is feared that they could damage the monarch's reputation. Both *Anna and the King of Siam* (1946) and the musical remake *The King and I* (1956), which starred Yul Brynner and won five Oscars, were American studio productions. The more recent version of *Anna and the King* (1999), with Jodie Foster in the main role, was filmed in Malaysia.

Sometimes one blockbuster can thrust an unknown location into the spotlight. One such place that has since become a movie pilgrimage site is **Phang Nga Bay** between Phuket and Krabi, where bizarrely formed and bushy limestone rocks rear up out of the water. This is where James Bond (Roger Moore) seeks out the evil Scaramanga (Christopher Lee) in **The Man with the Golden Gun** (1974). Nowadays, Scaramanga's hideout, formerly known as the island of **Koh Ping Gan,** is generally referred to as **James Bond Island. Ko Tapu,** or "needle hill," is a striking limestone rock just off the island, a pincushion for the antenna with which Scaramanga threatens the world. The exciting motor-boat scenes in **Bangkok** were actually shot on site in sweltering heat in the famous *klongs*, the canals with floating markets. James Bond (Pierce Brosnan) returned to Koh Ping Gan in **Tomorrow Never Dies** (1997) for a couple of scenes. This time Phang Nga stood in as the famous Halong Bay in Vietnam.

Daniel Cleaver (Hugh Grant) and Bridget Jones (Renée Zellweger) get to know one another better on the island of Phuket. Scenes were filmed at the luxurious Banyan Tree resort, as well as on the beach in Nai Yang.

The area around Phuket also served as Cambodia for the brutal drama **The Killing Fields** (1984), which tells the story of the American journalist Sydney Schanberg. After the fall of Phnom Penh and seizure of power by the guerrilla leader Pol Pot in the 1970s, Schanberg (Sam Waterston) is unable to prevent his native interpreter and friend Dith Pran (Haing S. Ngor) from falling into the hands of the Khmer Rouge. In **Bridget Jones: The Edge of Reason** (2004), on the other hand, Phuket makes a stunning appearance as a vacation paradise – at least until Bridget's (Renée Zellweger) brief stay in prison at the end of her dream holiday. In the second part of this successful comedy, Bridget decides to bid farewell to rainy London and travels to the luxurious beach resort of **Banyan Tree** in Phuket with playboy Daniel Cleaver (Hugh Grant). The beach scenes were shot in **Nai Yang**. The scene in which Bridget and Daniel enjoy a romantic dinner overlooking the sea was shot on a specially constructed set in the 200-year-old Muslim town of **Ko Panyi,** originally built on stilts in **Phang Nga Bay.**

No film has been more successful in propagating the image of Thailand as a vacation paradise with turquoise water,

secluded coves, and white sands than **The Beach** (2000). The cliché holds true even though the film is based on a contradiction: the illusive and obsessive search for an untouched Garden of Eden. Richard (Leonardo DiCaprio) travels to Thailand as a backpacker who dreams of finding adventure off the beaten track. Bangkok's backpacker mile, Khao San Road, was reconstructed along Prachacheun Road and Maharat Road in **Krabi.** When Richard chances upon a map showing a lonely island, he starts out on his search for paradise accompanied by a French couple. The scenes in which the three seekers complete their journey to the mysterious island by swimming across a body of water were shot near **Bamboo Island** and **Mosquito Island,** not far from Krabi.

When they finally arrive on the small island, they must jump down a waterfall to reach their destination. Filming took place at **Haeo Suwat Falls** in **Khao Yai National Park** just north of Bangkok. After they take the plunge, the place of their dreams unfolds before their eyes. A circular cove, almost completely closed in by rocks, is home to "the beach," a stretch of powdery white sand fringed by swaying palms. The three newcomers receive a friendly welcome from the colony of dropouts settled here. The filmmakers had looked in Malaysia, Australia, and the Philippines to locate a beach that would do justice to its central role in the film before finding a suitable location in Thailand. They chose the uninhabited island of **Phi Phi Leh** to the southwest

Boats ferry tourists to Maya Bay and the island of Phi Phi Leh where Leonardo DiCaprio starred in *The Beach*.

of Krabi, also the site of a rather forgettable pirate film called *Cutthroat Island* (1995), starring Geena Davis. The beach itself is actually on cliff-ringed **Maya Bay** on the west coast of the island. Further cliffs were added using computer animation so that the beach appears completely cut off from the ocean. But not all changes were carried out after the fact. Environmental lobbyists protested vehemently against the shoot because the beach, which is located within the confines of Phi Phi Leh Nature Reserve, was styled to perfection using machinery that threatened to disturb the area's ecological balance.

Thailand has served again and again as a substitute location for films set in Vietnam. Only three years after the end

Like many other films about the Vietnam War, *The Deer Hunter* was shot on location in Thailand.

ful radio show. The lesser known **Air America** (1990), with Mel Gibson and Robert Downey Jr. as pilots who are secretly operating from Laos and get caught between two fronts, was shot in **Mae Hong Son Province** in the northwest corner of Thailand. The lush tropical forests and hilly landscapes can be seen in many of the aerial shots, such as those in which Robert Downey Jr. is flown over the sleepy provincial capital dangling from a rope.

The Philippines: Jungle Backdrop for Vietnam Films

Some of the most important Vietnam War films ever made were shot in the Philippines. The hazardous shoots for **Apocalypse Now** (1979) turned out to be a major challenge for Francis Ford Coppola and his crew. Coppola once said during an interview: "We were in the middle of the jungle! There were too many of us, we had too much money, and after a while we all went crazy." The fact is that the money dried up as one catastrophe followed another, ranging from a heart attack suffered by the starring

"Good morning, Vietnam!" Robin Williams is Adrian Cronauer, an Air Force disc jockey whose unstoppable mouth makes him a hero with the troops.

of the Vietnam War, director Michael Cimino traveled there to film the Vietnam scenes for **The Deer Hunter** (1978), which won five Oscars. The troubling episodes in which Michael (Robert De Niro), Nick (Christopher Walken), and Steven (John Savage) are forced to play Russian roulette in a Vietnamese POW camp were shot on the **River Kwai** in **Sai Yok National Park** in the province of Kanchanaburi. **The Bridge on the River Kwai** (1957), David Lean's famous film about Allied prisoners of war used as forced labor in the construction of a railway line during World War II, was not shot on the River Kwai at all, but filmed in its entirety in Ceylon, now Sri Lanka. Other Vietnam films shot in Thailand include **Good Morning, Vietnam** (1987) with Robin Williams as the Air Force disc jockey who goes to Saigon – actually **Bangkok** and **Thalang** on **Phuket** – and rapidly gains an enthusiastic fan base among the troops for his disrespect-

Helicopters swooped over Baler Bay in *Apocalypse Now*.

A trip into the heart of darkness in *Apocalypse Now:* The jungle camp where Captain Willard (Martin Sheen, right) tracks the ominous Colonel Kurtz (Marlon Brando) was filmed near Pagsanjan Falls in the Philippines, today a popular tourist destination.

actor to a hurricane that destroyed the set. Shooting took more than two years. Hollywood jokingly dubbed the film "Apocalypse Later," but against all odds, the film was completed.

Coppola transposed Joseph Conrad's novella *The Heart of Darkness* into the era of the Vietnam War. Captain Willard (Martin Sheen) is ordered to assassinate the renegade Colonel Kurtz (Marlon Brando), who has set up his own army in the middle of the Cambodian jungle, over which he presides like a self-anointed god. On his journey into the heart of darkness, Willard is confronted with terrible and bizarre situations, such as the episode in which Lieutenant Colonel Kilgore (Robert Duvall) bombards Vietnamese coastal villages from a helicopter to the strains of Richard Wagner's *Ride of the Valkyries* so that his surfer soldiers will be able to catch the best waves. He comments on the grotesque situation with the legendary line, "I love the smell of napalm in the morning." This scene was shot in **Baler Bay,** a lush stretch of forest on the wild eastern coast of Luzon, and has since become a surfing spot. Coppola rented the helicopter from the Philippine armed services, but because President Marcos's troops were busy fighting rebel forces at the time, the helicopter was often requisitioned for real combat and remained unavailable for days at a time.

Willard's most dangerous trip takes him up river through enemy territory accompanied by a patrol boat. These scenes were shot in **Pagsanjan** on the River Pagsanjan, also known as the Magdapio River, to the southeast of Manila. Here, hundreds of Philippine workers were hired to construct Colonel Kurtz's jungle realm from blocks of clay. The entire local Ifuago tribe was taken on as extras to play Kurtz's followers. From time to time, it looked as though Coppola was losing control over his vast project in the Philippine jungle, especially when an overweight Marlon Brando turned up and there was no script for his scenes, and the actor was forced to improvise. Yet a masterpiece was born of the chaos, and the film won two Oscars.

In 1986, Charlie Steen followed in his father's footsteps when he also traveled to the Philippines to a shoot a Vietnam film. In Oliver Stone's **Platoon,** Sheen plays a naive recruit who volunteers for service in Vietnam and finds himself fighting for survival in the dense jungles. Once again, it was the jungles near **Pagsanjan** and in the province of **Cavite** that stood in for the bitterly contested Vietnam battlefields close to the Cambodian border. Key scenes such as the fateful meeting between Sergeant Elias (Willem Dafoe) and Sergeant Barnes (Tom Berenger) were shot on **Mount Maquiling** near Los Baños. The coastal town of **Puerto Azul,** a seaside resort famous for its black sandy beaches, was the location for many sequences.

Oliver Stone, who wove many of his own experiences as a young soldier in Vietnam into *Platoon*, returned to the Philippines a few years later for the opening scenes of **Born on the Fourth of July** (1989). Ron Kovic (Tom Cruise) signs up to fight, but when he is severely wounded and finds himself in a wheelchair, he becomes a dedicated opponent of the war. The scene in which Ron's unit is ambushed was shot close to **Fort Ilocandia** in the province of Ilocos Norte to the southwest of Laoag City. The sand dunes are situated by **Paoay,** also in Ilocos Norte.

Peter Weir's film **The Year of Living Dangerously** (1982) is proof that the Philippines have represented Southeast Asian locations other than Vietnam as well. Mel Gibson plays Guy Hamilton, an Australian reporter working in 1960s Indonesia, who is alerted by a local photographer to the rebellion against

Tom Berenger and Willem Dafoe are bitter adversaries in Oliver Stone's *Platoon*. The movie won four Oscars, including Best Picture.

President Sukarno. Filming took place in Manila and high up in the mountains near the beautiful rice terraces of **Banaue,** where Guy searches for weapons being delivered to the communists.

The rice terraces of Banaue in the Philippines stand in for Indonesia in *The Year of Living Dangerously* starring Sigourney Weaver and Mel Gibson.

Vietnam: Secretive Beauty

Represented in movies by nearly every other Southeast Asian country, Vietnam itself has appeared on the big screen infrequently but memorably. The film that most successfully brought the real Vietnam to audiences was doubtless *Indochine* (1992), Régis Wargnier's pictorially overwhelming epic that was awarded an Oscar for Best Foreign Language Film. The movie was shot on location in Vietnam and Malaysia. Frenchwoman Eliane (Catherine Deneuve), born in the French colony of Indochina, manages a rubber plantation with her father and her

adopted Vietnamese daughter, Camille (Linh Dan Pham). The vast, late nineteenth-century Blue Mansion on the Malaysian island of **Penang,** the property of millionaire Cheong Fatt Tze, stands in for their villa. When Camille falls in love with the young officer Jean-Baptiste (Vincent Perez), with whom her mother is having an affair, the whole edifice of privileged life comes crashing down. Jean-Baptiste is banned to Devil's Island, a remote military outpost where poor farmers from the north of the country are sold each month to plantation owners from the south at a slave market. In the film, the island of **Hon Oan,** not far from Hong Gai, stands in for Devil's Island. Despite the sadness of the place, the fairy-tale images of junk rigs with their rust-red

Indochine made the most of the natural beauty of Halong Bay with fairy-tale images of junk rigs sailing between the limetone cliffs.

The rice paddies and cliffy outcroppings of "dry Halong Bay" near Ninh Binh in northern Vietnam provided a rural setting for scenes in *Indochine* and *The Quiet American* with Michael Caine in the main role.

sails negotiating their way through the rocks and islands into a mist-covered bay are nothing short of breathtaking. These scenes were shot in the famous **Halong Bay** in the northeast of Vietnam, where some 3,000 islands and bizarrely formed limestone rocks are dotted around a broad inlet.

At first, Camille seems to have accepted her fate and agrees to an arranged marriage, with the wedding ceremony filmed in the imperial palaces at **Hue.** But then, to Eliane's great consternation, Camille sets out to find Jean-Baptiste. She travels with a farmer's family on her arduous way to the north of the country, and becomes acquainted with the miseries of rural life. These scenes, as well as those of Camille and Jean-Baptiste's escape, were shot to the southeast of Hanoi, between the rice paddies and limestone rocks of the "dry bay" near **Ninh Binh** and the ancient capital of **Hoa Lu.**

The idyllic landscapes close to Ninh Binh were featured on film once again a decade later when Phillip Noyce shot **The**

Quiet American (2002), a movie version of the eponymous novel by Graham Greene. At the beginning of the 1950s, the jaded English journalist Thomas Fowler (Michael Caine) is living and reporting in Saigon. His comfortable life is suddenly upended when he gets to know an idealistic American (Brendan Fraser) who falls in love with Fowler's young Vietnamese girlfriend, Phuong (Do Thi Hai Yen). At the same time, the country is sliding into crisis as the French colonial powers find themselves increasingly beset by communists from the north. At the beginning of the film, Fowler says: "I can't say what made me fall in love with Vietnam – that a woman's voice can drug you; that everything is so intense. The colors, the taste, even the rain." The haunting portrait that Noyce paints of Vietnam is just that – intense. Shooting took place not only in the rural area around **Ninh Binh,** but also in **Hanoi,** in the old harbor city of **Hoi An** on the Thu Bon River, and naturally in Saigon itself, officially called Ho Chi Minh City today.

Cambodia: the Temple of Angkor

Cambodia is anything but a filmmaking country. The war and the regime of terror exercised by the Khmer Rouge have left deep scars on the land. The tourist industry is still its infancy, and the film industry lags even further behind, not least because large parts of the country still remain

Lord Jim starring Peter O'Toole and Daliah Lavi was the first film to be shot in the elaborate stone temples of Angkor.

The jungle seems to be reclaiming this temple at Ta Prohm, but not before Lara Croft (Angelina Jolie) can discover a secret burial chamber within.

of focusing on great monuments such as the Temple of Angkor, Dillon chose to showcase the country's diversity. Shooting took place in **Phnom Penh,** in the temple of **Phnom Chisor** to the south of the capital, whose ruins bear a certain resemblance to Angkor, in **Battambang** with its grand colonial architecture, and in the popular coastal resort of **Kep** close to the Vietnamese border. The atmospheric final scenes were shot in the south of Cambodia at **Bokor Hill Station,** a French settlement built on a slope outside the town of Kampot in the 1920s and known for the elegant Bokor Palace Hotel & Casino, but deserted today.

inaccessible due to land mines. A handful of films have been shot in Cambodia, and their locations are remarkable. Thirty-five years after **Lord Jim** (1965) was shot on location, with Peter O'Toole in the starring role, a film crew set up its headquarters in Cambodia to shoot the fantastic temple site of Angkor.

The famous historic site, the capital of the Khmer empire from the ninth to the fifteenth centuries, would serve as an important location for the film version of a video game, **Lara Croft: Tomb Raider** (2001). Although there were protests against the filming of action sequences in a temple that dates back to the twelfth and thirteenth centuries, the Cambodian government anticipated an increase in tourism as a result of the movie. They were right: The number of visitors rose by 30 percent in the wake of the film.

In search of two halves of a mysterious plaque that have been hidden at opposite ends of the world, Lara Croft (Angelina Jolie) sets out for the temple ruins of Angkor, where she does battle against stone monkeys and a huge, eight-armed deity that suddenly comes to life. She descends by parachute onto the temple of **Phnom Bakheng,** right next to the southern gate of the ancient city of Angkor. Further scenes were shot at **Ta Prohm,** situated just to the northeast of the main temple of Angkor Wat, where Lara falls into a hidden burial chamber. The temple ruins of Angkor, situated in the middle of the jungle and decorated with huge faces, were deliberately left untouched after their discovery by European archaeologists. Fig trees and the large roots of kapok trees grow everywhere as the jungle moves in to reclaim its territory.

After *Tomb Raider,* **City of Ghosts** (2002) was the second Hollywood blockbuster filmed on location in Cambodia. Matt Dillon's directorial debut tells the story of an insurance broker who follows his crooked mentor, Marvin (James Caan), to Cambodia and gets involved in his dubious machinations. Instead

Natascha McElhone stars alongside Matt Dillon in his directorial debut, *City of Ghosts*. Filming locations in Cambodia included Phnom Penh and the deserted casino at Bokor Hill Station.

167

26

AUSTRALIA

ON LOCATION "DOWN UNDER" By Luke Brighty

Australia is best known for white sandy beaches, dense green rain forests, the turquoise waters along the Great Barrier Reef, and the interior's red, dusty outback plains. The Great Southern Land and its harsh, beautiful locations have inspired filmmakers for years, inviting

them to experience one of the world's most perfect back lots made up of stunning and varied landscapes stretched across six states and two territories.

Take the majestic and lush scenery of Kakadu National Park in the Northern Territory, one of the settings for Peter Faiman's hit movie *Crocodile Dundee* (1986), starring Paul Hogan. It could not be more different from the arid desert landscapes of the Red Centre, used extensively as a backdrop in another box office success, Stephan Elliott's outrageously funny feel-good movie *The Adventures of Priscilla, Queen of the Desert* (1994). The rich flora and fauna of Victoria's Hanging Rock Reserve featured in Peter Weir's eerie *Picnic at Hanging Rock* (1975) offer a stark contrast to the desolation and post-apocalyptic locations

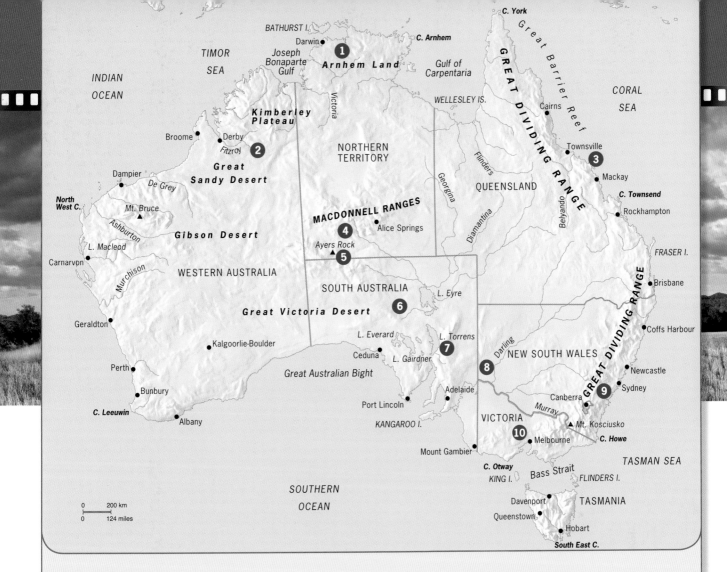

Top landscape film locations

1. Kakadu National Park: **Crocodile Dundee & Crocodile Dundee II**
2. Wolfe Creek Meteorite Crater National Park: **Wolf Creek**
3. Whitsunday Passage: **Dead Calm**
4. Kings Canyon, Watarrka National Park: **The Adventures of Priscilla, Queen of the Desert**
5. Ayers Rock: **A Cry in the Dark**
6. Moon Plain, a.k.a. Breakaways Reserve, near Coober Pedy: **Mad Max Beyond Thunderdome, Red Planet, Pitch Black**
7. Nilpena Station, Flinders Ranges: **Rabbit-Proof Fence**
8. Broken Hill and Silverton area: **Mad Max 2: The Road Warrior, Razorback, Mission: Impossible II, Dirty Deeds**
9. Robertson, Southern Highlands: **Babe, Babe: Pig in the City**
10. Hanging Rock Reserve: **Picnic at Hanging Rock**

From the farmland beauty of New South Wales, to Aboriginal rock art in Kakadu National Park, and beyond, Australia's landscapes have long inspired filmmakers. The stunning and varied vistas stretch across six states and two territories to include white sandy beaches, lush green rain forests, the turquoise waters of the Great Barrier Reef, and the interior's red, dusty outback plains. Skilled crews and first-class moviemaking facilities have helped cement Australia's reputation as a good place for making movies.

seen in *Mad Max 2: The Road Warrior* (1981), the George Miller cult film shot in the Silverton area of New South Wales.

Over the last decade, Australia has attracted major international productions to its shores, and not only because of a favorable exchange rate and government incentives. The near-perfect quality of the natural light and spectacular locations have played an important role, as have skilled crews and first-class movie-making facilities that have helped cement Australia's reputation as a vibrant and expanding film center worthy of any overseas competition. Sydney's Fox Studios, Warner Roadshow Studios on the Gold Coast, and Central City Studios in the Melbourne Docklands have played host to numerous movies. Besides a constant output of quality moviemaking, the Australian Film Industry has much to be proud of. In 2006, Australian Cinema celebrated a centenary of filmmaking that began with *The Story of the Kelly Gang* (1906) directed by Charles Tait, an Australian and British box office hit that holds the distinction of being the world's first full-length feature film.

This little pig makes it big in the movie *Babe*.

New South Wales: Australia's Moviemaking Capital

Seventy percent of Australia's film and television production is based in New South Wales, much of it specifically in Sydney. With one of the most photographed harbors in the world, Sydney offers a landscape in an urban setting that is epic in its appeal. Its natural beauty has been immortalized in dozens of films such as *Mission: Impossible II* (2000). In addition to the stunning backdrops that the city provides, the state of New South Wales beyond the metropolis serves as a valuable resource for filmmakers in search of sweeping settings. Just over an hour and a half's drive south of Sydney on the M5 motorway are the **Southern Highlands,** made famous by a pair of movies that turned a talking piglet called Babe (voice of Christine Cavanaugh) into a star. The action for **Babe** (1995) and its sequel **Babe: Pig in the City** (1998) occurs on a farm located just outside **Robertson,** a quiet little village surrounded by rolling green hills that boasts spectacular views across the coastal plain to the rolling surf of the Pacific Ocean.

Before work began on Arthur and Esme Hoggett's (James Cromwell and Magda Szubanski) homestead, the acreage rented by the production company had to be landscaped and developed as there were no roads leading to the set nor facilities for water, gas, or electricity. An original farmhouse was made up to look like a character with a face. Two giant sheds, corrals, and a barn were then designed and constructed. All that remains of the Hoggett farmhouse today is a pile of timber: A strong windstorm destroyed the sets but spared the stone walls that the owners of the farm had left in place.

Before *Babe* placed New South Wales on the map by directing film fans to a sleepy corner of the Southern Highlands, a transsexual and two drag queens with a school bus full of sequined costumes, glitter, shoes, and seventies pop music were attracting a different kind of attention. **The Adventures of Priscilla, Queen of the Desert** (1994) kicks off with Bernadette/Ralph (Terence Stamp), Mitzi/Tick (Hugo Weaving), and Felicia/Adam (Guy Pearce), three bored "drag" performers who quit the stage circuit in the big city to take their show to Alice Springs, where a two-week paid gig awaits.

After purchasing a bus christened "Priscilla," the trio enjoy a royal send-off from the front of the **Imperial Hotel** in Erskineville and head for the Australian outback, leaving behind Sydney and its iconic Opera House and Harbour Bridge. When they arrive in **Broken Hill** in New South Wales, Bernadette, Mitzi, and Felicia stop off for a night at **Mario's Palace** on Argent Street, a classic 1800s pub with an iron lace balcony and intriguing outback scene murals painted by an Aboriginal artist on every wall. A good amount of filming took place inside the hotel, including the

The other star of *Babe* is the agricultural life of the Southern Highlands. In the film, an orphaned pig learns to herd a flock of sheep.

Three drag queens take their school bus full of sequined costumes, glitter, shoes, and seventies pop music on the road from the big city to the outback. Here the well-dressed stars of *The Adventures of Priscilla, Queen of the Desert* pose in front of Kings Canyon, a chasm located in Watarrka National Park.

bar area. Before settling in, the "girls" decide to go shopping and step off the bus onto **Argent Street** all dolled up and in exaggerated drag, much to the bemusement of the locals.

The lonely settlements of the outback surrounded by desolate, unforgiving landscapes add an otherworldly element to adventure films. **Broken Hill,** a mining town that celebrated its centenary in 1988, and neighboring ghost town **Silverton** have served as backdrops in music clips, documentaries, commercials, and movies since 1967. More recently, they appeared in *Mad Max 2: The Road Warrior* (1981), *Razorback* (1984), *Mission: Impossible II* (2000), *Red Planet* (2000), and *Dirty Deeds* (2002). The sandstone and brick **Silverton Hotel** has a wealth of history and a great collection of movie photographs, in particular memorabilia that would interest **Mad Max 2** fans. One of the cars used in the movie is still parked outside.

The opening scene in which nomadic drifter Max Rockatansky (Mel Gibson) is chased by Wez (Vernon Wells) was shot on the road out past Silverton, towards the **Mundi Mundi Plains Lookout,** as was the climactic semitrailer wreck scene. The location where Max first meets the Gyro Captain (Bruce Spence) and falls for the Gyrocopter trap is **Stephen's Creek.** More filming took place on the stretch of road leading to **Menindee Lakes** and at the base of one of three hills known as **"The Pinnacles"** on the outskirts of Broken Hill, a site where the compound set housing the fuel supply was built. Max spies on it and its residents from the top of the middle hill. The oil refinery is destroyed in a massive explosion when the community abandons the compound and makes a dash for freedom to escape a bike gang that is after the gasoline. Nothing remains of the compound site today but a few scars that can be seen from the top of The Pinnacles.

The Northern Territory: Chasing Kangaroos and Wrestling Crocodiles

After breaking down with their bus in the middle of nowhere and being rescued by Bob (Bill Hunter), the drag queens in *The Adventures of Priscilla, Queen of the Desert* make a short dogleg into South Australia before motoring on up into the Northern Territory. Following a smash hit show at **Lassiters Casino** in Alice Springs, Bernadette, Mitzi, and Felicia take a side trip to **Kings Canyon,** a mighty chasm located in **Watarrka National Park.** Swatting at flies as they begin their climb, the drag queens finally make it to the top of the rock and, dressed in full frock, they enjoy the magical moment, soaking up the sight before them in what can only be described as a dazzling scene that is beautifully underscored by the topographical drama surrounding them.

Mel Gibson is the avenging road warrior Max Rockatansky in *Mad Max 2.* The ghost town of Silverton in the outback has served for decades as an otherworldly element in adventure films.

In *Kangaroo Jack,* shot around Alice Springs and Ayers Rock, a couple of American kids chase a wild kangaroo throughout the outback. They must recover the money that the animal has taken – or answer to the mob.

The Northern Territory, an untamed province of contrast and color, is almost the size of France, Italy, and Spain combined. Travelers the world over flock there to experience the wonders of a land famous for ancient Aboriginal sites, the prolific wildlife of Kakadu National Park, the impressive gorges at Katherine, and the central deserts surrounding Alice Springs, a base from which to explore the famous monolith Uluru, also known as Ayers Rock. **Alice Springs** has played host to many international productions over the years. The outback town and surrounding area became the setting for ***A Cry in the Dark*** (1988), a.k.a. ***Evil Angels,*** a controversial and true story brought to the screen by director Fred Schepisi. During a family camping trip at Ayers Rock in August 1980, Lindy and Michael Chamberlain's (Meryl Streep and Sam Neill) baby daughter Azaria went missing. A dingo allegedly took the sleeping infant from a tent and killed it, resulting in a case that attracted copious media attention. Much of the filming for the movie took place at **Ayers Rock,** Australia's number-one tourist attraction and most sacred Aboriginal site, and up north in **Darwin.** Cast and crew sometimes had to endure temperatures of up to 113 degrees Fahrenheit (45 degrees Celsius). The final days of shooting were spent battling a freak desert storm.

Kangaroo Jack (2003), another movie shot around Alice Springs, tells the story of a couple of Americans, Charlie (Jerry O'Connell) and Louie (Anthony Anderson), who pursue a wild kangaroo throughout the outback; they must recover money belonging to mob boss Sal Maggio (Christopher Walken) from

Meryl Streep and Sam Neill play the parents of a missing baby in *A Cry in the Dark*. Filming took place at the famous red monolith of Ayers Rock.

a jacket that the animal has taken off with. Director David Mc-Nally considered the rugged outback landscape to be another character in the movie, and made it his mission to show the world just how fantastic the geography out there is. The weather on location, however, was less than fantastic, fluctuating from freezing in the morning to scorching hot at midday and back to polar conditions in the evening. Because scouts couldn't find a suitable location for a chase scene, production designer George Liddle had to create a rocky gorge in a quarry near Alice Springs. When the production relocated to Fox Studios in Sydney, the gorge and a lagoon were recreated on a sound stage using molds taken from actual rock faces as well as sand and vegetation that matched the sites on location.

A trip to the Northern Territory wouldn't be complete without a visit to **Kakadu National Park,** the setting for *Crocodile Dundee* (1986) and its sequel, *Crocodile Dundee II* (1988). Located 90 miles (150 kilometers) east of Darwin, Kakadu National Park is a natural wonder that stretches 60 miles (100 kilometers) to

the western border of **Arnhem Land.** The vast park gets its name from the Aboriginal word *Gagudju,* the name of the area's first tribe. **Ubirr Rock,** one of its many highlights, offers an impressive 360-degree view of the flood plains below and is the spot where Mick Dundee (Paul Hogan) points out to Sue Charlton (Linda Kozlowski) the watering hole in the distance where he wrestled a crocodile.

Like Ubirr, **Nourlangie** is known for its outstanding Aboriginal art work. At the base of the rock lies **Anbangbang Billabong,** a location made famous by the shaving scene in *Crocodile Dundee* where Mick shows off to Sue by substituting his impressive-looking knife for a razor blade. Just as famous are the **Gunlom Falls** and plunge pool at **Waterfall Creek Nature Park,** a particularly beautiful area and popular swimming spot featured in a

scene in which Mick, having cooked a goanna, settles for baked beans instead, and where Sue narrowly escapes a crocodile attack. On the outskirts of the park, along the Stuart Highway, is **Adelaide River Inn,** home to Charlie the water buffalo. In an amusing scene, Mick Dundee challenges the animal when they come face to face on a dirt road and it refuses to move out of the way. He hypnotizes it and leaves Sue in awe after succeeding in getting the beast to lie down at the side of the road. When the gigantic animal passed away in 2000, its remains were stuffed and are now on display at the bar in the inn.

Paul Hogan poses in Kakadu National Park (left), the setting for *Crocodile Dundee.* He hugs a croc by the plunge pool at Waterfall Creek Nature Park.

Shot in **Ramingining** and in the **Arafura Swamp and Wetlands** region of northeastern Arnhem Land, Rolf de Heer's *Ten Canoes* (2006) is an Australian production filmed entirely in an indigenous Aboriginal language with an English voice-over by actor David Gulpilil that makes good use of landscape locations. The movie tells the story of a young man, Dayindi (Jamie Gulpilil), who covets one of his older brother's wives during an egg-gathering trip and learns right from wrong through an ancient tale that his older sibling, Minygululu (Peter Minygululu), relates to him. The footage depicting canoe making and goose-egg gathering is in black and white, and was shot this way as a tribute to photographers such as anthropologist Dr. Donald Thomson, who worked in Arnhem Land in the mid-1930s. The main story, however, is set in mythical times and is in color.

While filming in the landscapes of the Northern Territory brought visual intensity and increased depth of meaning to the film, it also proved quite a challenge for the cast and crew. At one point, Ralph de Heer was standing waist deep in a swamp with ten crocodile spotters on set armed with guns, ready to spring into action. Leeches and mosquitoes added to the fun and made shooting in the wild an unforgettable experience.

Instead of gazing at Whitsunday Passage from the safety of Whitehaven Beach (above), John (Sam Neill) and Rae (Nicole Kidman) Ingram brave the open waters and a dangerous stranger in the eerie thriller *Dead Calm*.

Queensland: Oceans and Jungles

To most travelers, Queensland conjures up images of pristine beaches, turquoise waters, beautiful corals, and watersport activities. The **Great Barrier Reef,** one of nature's masterpieces, extends more than 1,250 miles (2,000 kilometers) from New Guinea in the north to the Sunshine Coast in the south. The underwater spectacle of colorful animal and plant life is simply breathtaking and offers some of the world's best snorkeling and diving opportunities. Sailing around the Great Barrier Reef is a perfect way to experience both the aquatic life and above-water vistas, which include the resort islands scattered along the Queensland coast.

Set against this idyllic backdrop is Philip Noyce's eerie suspense thriller **Dead Calm** (1989), based on the novel by Charles Williams that Orson Welles attempted to adapt to the big screen in 1970. Trying to escape the painful memory of the loss of their son in a car accident, the Ingrams, John (Sam Neill) and Rae (Nicole Kidman), take to the open waters of the Great Barrier Reef in their private yacht. After a few days at sea, they come across a mysterious young man, Hughie Warriner (Billy Zane), the only survivor of a damaged, drifting schooner whose entire crew has perished. As the terrible truth unfolds, the stranger gains control of the Ingrams's yacht, kidnaps Rae, and leaves John stranded on the sinking schooner fighting to keep it afloat. The exteriors of both boats were real; however, interiors were sets built in a studio. Most of the filming was done in the

The harsh side of South Australia: Mining town Coober Pedy, one of the world's top opal centers, is located in one of the hottest and driest regions in the state. Its unforgiving landscapes feature in *Mad Max Beyond Thunderdome* with Mel Gibson. The chase scenes make good use of Breakaways Reserve (above).

Whitsunday Passage because the reef provided a breakwater just below the surface, creating a natural water tank.

Dean Semler, the movie's cinematographer, uses the landscape as another element of the storyline, just as he did in films such as *Mad Max 2* (1981) and *Dances with Wolves* (1990). The aerial photography of the wide open spaces between the vessels and endless seascape cleverly brings into focus one of the main ingredients of fear: isolation. *Dead Calm* introduces international audiences to a whole new setting, exchanging the vast expanse of dusty, red outback often featured in Australian cinema for the tranquil yet potentially threatening waters of Australia's eastern seaboard.

Painting an altogether different picture of Queensland is Terrence Malick's **The Thin Red Line** (1998), which, although set on the island of Guadalcanal in the South Pacific, was filmed in **Port Douglas, Mossman, Cairns, Bramston Beach,** and in the rain forests of north Queensland. Due to logistical reasons –

one of them being that Guadalcanal could not sustain a movie crew – the filmmakers decided to scout out locations in Australia. **Daintree,** with its jagged mountains, steep escarpments, and lush rain forest, became the backdrop to Malick's World War II movie depicting a group of men who develop a strong bond while fighting the Japanese advance into the Pacific. The huge vines and creepers hanging from the canopy in great festooning arcs, the remarkable fan palms, strangler fig trees, and giant towering tree trunks filled in beautifully for the intended jungle location. The film's impressive flora and fauna seem almost to spring out of a nature documentary, and their beauty provides a stark contrast to the graphic scenes and countless moments of violence. *The Thin Red Line* features an impressive cast including Sean Penn, Jim Caviezel, Ben Chaplin, Nick Nolte, and John Cusack. John Travolta, Woody Harrelson, and George Clooney make cameo appearances both at the beginning and at the end of the movie.

South Australia: Green Valleys and Lunar Landscapes

South Australia comprises two very distinct areas: The verdant south is famous for its wine-growing **Clare** and **Barossa Valleys,** seen in *"Breaker" Morant* (1980) and *Wolf Creek* (2005), and cosmopolitan **Adelaide,** a location central to the film *Shine* (1996), starring Geoffrey Rush as Australian piano virtuoso David Helfgott. The other half of the Festival State, the arid northern region, encompasses the Flinders Ranges and outback mining towns such as **Coober Pedy.**

The rural property of **Nilpena Station,** 24 miles (39 kilometers) northwest of **Parachilna** in the **Flinders Ranges,** served as

The mountains, escarpments, and rain forests of Daintree in north Queensland were the backdrop to the film *The Thin Red Line*. Terrence Malick's World War II drama boasts an excellent cast including Sean Penn (far left).

The Flinders Ranges region (top) provided one of the settings for Phillip Noyce's *Rabbit-Proof Fence*. The film tells the true story of three Aboriginal girls who walk 930 miles (1,500 kilometers) on their journey home.

one of several locations featured in Phillip Noyce's heartrending **Rabbit-Proof Fence** (2002). This critically acclaimed film tells the true story of three Aboriginal girls, Molly Craig (Everlyn Sampi), Daisy Kadibill (Tianna Sansbury), and Gracie Fields (Laura Monaghan), who, after being taken from their families, make an extraordinary journey home by walking 930 miles (1,500 kilometers) along a rabbit-proof fence. The filmmakers shot scenes in nearby **Lake Torrens,** a salt lake 155 miles (250 kilometers) long also seen in *Gallipoli* (1981), and **Leigh Creek.** The three sections of mountains that make up the Flinders Ranges produce some of the outback's most spectacular scenery, a landscape mirror to the almost impossible task the girls have set themselves of covering an incredible distance on foot. The area may look familiar to movie audiences as it has been used in productions such as *Sunday Too Far Away* (1975), *Holy Smoke* (1999), *The Tracker* (2002), and more recently in *Stealth* (2005), for which the mountain ranges stood in for a naval air test range in the U.S. state of Nevada.

Coober Pedy, one of the world's leading opal centers, is probably also one of the hottest and driest regions in South Australia. Not surprising, then, that the town's residents spend so much of their time living in underground dugouts. Even churches have been built below ground to escape the dust storms and scorching temperatures that reach their peak during the summer months. A real dugout belonging to a local character and legend by the name of Crocodile Harry was used as Jedediah's home in George Miller's **Mad Max Beyond Thunderdome** (1985), shot extensively around Coober Pedy. The chase scenes made good use of **Moon Plain,** also known as the **Breakaways Reserve,** a 15-square-mile (40-square-kilometer) block of low mounts that resembles Mars. These same striking rock formations, buttes, and jagged hills have provided an otherwordly backdrop for *The Adventures of Priscilla, Queen of the Desert* and sci-fi movies *Red Planet* (2000) and *Pitch Black* (2000). Although the *Mad Max* settlement of Bartertown was a set built in a brick pit in Sydney's Olympic Park, much of the surroundings of Bartertown were filmed in the Breakaways area.

Victoria: Snowy Mountains and Swift Rivers

Picture an idyllic spot such as a reserve with a picnic area and a large rounded hillock in the middle to climb and explore. Add blue skies and sunshine and you have the perfect setting for a day's outing. Or so you would think. In **Picnic at Hanging Rock** (1975), the film based on Joan Lindsay's novel, a group of schoolgirls mysteriously go missing while climbing the rock on a St. Valentine's Day outing. Peter Weir's period piece was beautifully filmed by Oscar-winning cinematographer Russell Boyd at Victoria's **Hanging Rock Reserve,** a few miles northeast of Woodend. Although some people falsely believe the story to be true, Hanging Rock Reserve hasn't anything spooky about it. Walking around the base of the lava rock formation is a popular activity and climbing to the summit takes just under an hour.

But Victoria isn't just about flatland and hills. Much of the state is occupied by the Great Dividing Range, which stretches along the east coast and ends west of Ballarat, one of several locations north of Melbourne featured in *Ned Kelly* (2003), the bushranger movie starring Heath Ledger, the Aussie actor who garnered international acclaim in *Brokeback Mountain* (2005). Victoria is also known for its high country and snowfields, a backdrop for George Miller's **The Man from Snowy River** (1982), starring Tom Burlinson. Based on the classic Banjo Paterson poem of the same name, the movie was shot in several areas of the **Snowy Mountains** including **Mansfield** and **Merrijig.** Craig's Hut, part of the original set located at the end of an access track off Mount Stirling's Circuit Road, was left a smoldering ruin following a bush fire in December 2006. Despite the extensive damage to the set, one of Victoria's most popular tourist attractions, there are plans to restore the hut to its former glory.

Western Australia: Deserts and Craters

Just as Crocodile Dundee sparked the imagination of movie enthusiasts the world over by promoting Australia's larrikin spirit and fantastic landscapes, Greg McLean's *Wolf Creek* (2005), the hit film about a maniac preying on unsuspecting backpackers heading into the dauntingly isolated Australian outback, drew gore-seeking audiences to movie theaters in droves. Despite struggling to get off the ground financially, the movie grossed roughly three times its budget when it opened in the U.K. and has since garnered several awards.

The film is loosely based on a number of backpacker crimes such as the Ivan Milat abductions and the story of Peter Falconio, a British tourist who disappeared in Barrow Creek while traveling with his girlfriend, Joanne Lees, in July 2001. In Wolf Creek, three young backpackers, played by Cassandra Magrath, Kestie Morassi, and Nathan Phillips, begin their great adventure on the delightful beaches of **Broome** in Western Australia and journey through the **Kimberley** area to **Wolfe Creek Meteorite Crater National Park,** where their car breaks down and their watches mysteriously stop.

They are "rescued" by Mick Taylor (John Jarratt), a happy-go-lucky outback character who offers to tow the kids back to his desert camp so he can fix their car. Little do they know what horrors await. Wolfe Creek, the second-largest meteorite crater in the world, is 90 miles (145 kilometers) from **Halls Creek** via the Tanami Road. Location trivia fans will note that the "e" in the word Wolfe was dropped and digitally removed from maps and signs in the film.

Sigrid Thornton, Tom Burlinson, and Victoria's high country in *The Man from Snowy River.*

Another movie that captures the feeling of remoteness and isolation in plot and in landscapes is **Japanese Story** (2003). Sue Brooks's emotional film tells the story of a geologist, Sandy Edwards (Toni Collette), who reluctantly agrees to play tour guide to visiting Japanese businessman Hiromitsu Tachibana (Gotaro Tsunashima), who is keen on exploring the remotest areas of the **Pilbara Desert.** The film analyzes the complexity of both characters, divided by cultural differences and a language barrier, a study reflected effectively in the barren locations. Filming at the various sites was a mammoth endeavor and required seeking townships that offered enough infrastructure to support a cast and crew of sixty. Permits had to be obtained to film both at BHP's iron and ore mine in **Newman** and on hard-to-access land belonging to the Aboriginals. Filming in the Pilbara was no piece of cake, but the incredible landscapes and spectacular results made dealing with red dust, dirt, heat, and physical stress worthwhile.

In *Wolf Creek*, three backpackers head for horror in the isolated outback of Western Australia. The adventure begins on the beaches of Broome, but their car breaks down at Wolfe Creek Meteorite Crater National Park. The trouble begins when a man offers to tow them back to his desert camp...

27

NEW ZEALAND

A CINEMATOGRAPHIC WONDERLAND

By Luke Brighty

Because of its incredible scenic variety within a relatively small area, New Zealand has become an immensely popular film location. The country is divided into two main parts, the North and South Islands, and also boasts numerous smaller offshore isles. The main islands offer a diversity of landscapes hard to equal, well beyond what a country roughly two thirds the size of the U.S. state of California would be expected to offer. Dense rain forests, majestic mountains, impressive volcanoes, glaciers, lakes, rivers, and magnificent coastlines – black-sand beaches on the west coast and a golden or white variety in the east – embellish New Zealand's wealth of wonderful visual experiences.

New Zealand's awe-inspiring landscapes and pleasant climate produce a haven for outdoor shooting. Kiwi locations have appeared in movies and documentaries as far back as the 1920s, when the local film industry was in its infancy. In recent years, blockbusters like *The Chronicles of Narnia – The Lion, The Witch and the Wardrobe* (2005), *King Kong* (2005), and *The Lord of the Rings* trilogy (2001-2003) have trained the spotlight on New Zealand, highlighting its stunning scenery. Movies such as *Perfect Strangers* (2003) and *Whale Rider* (2002) have taken audiences to some of the most remote corners of the country. Famous films have done wonders for New Zealand's tourism industry, with international visitors flocking to the land of the long white cloud in search of Middle Earth, Skull Island, and Narnia's magical world.

North Island: From Auckland to the Center

Auckland and its sparkling harbor, best known as the venue of the America's Cup races, are one of two main filming hubs on the North Island, the other being Wellington. The sprawling city's Henderson Valley Studios have been home to productions such as *Boogeyman* (2005), *The Chronicles of Narnia* (2005), *In My Father's Den* (2004), *The Last Samurai* (2003), *Whale Rider* (2002), *The Piano* (1993), and the TV series *Hercules: The Legendary Journeys* (1995-1999).

Mount Taranaki stands in for Mount Fuji in Edward Zwick's *The Last Samurai*.

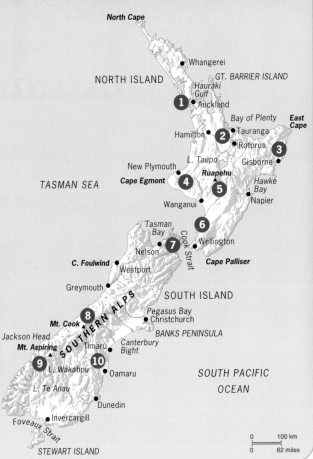

The *Lord of the Rings* trilogy starring Elijah Wood as Frodo Baggins trained the spotlight on New Zealand, highlighting its stunning scenery.

The Pevensie children arrive at the station in *The Chronicles of Narnia*. Below: Monte Cecilia House, a Catholic refuge in Hillsborough, features as the mansion with the wardrobe that is their portal to a magical land.

Top landscape film locations

1. Karekare Beach: **The Piano**
2. Matamata: **Lord of the Rings** trilogy
3. Whangara, Eastland Region: **Whale Rider**
4. Mount Taranaki, Egmont National Park: **The Last Samurai**
5. Mount Ruapehu, Tongariro National Park: **Lord of the Rings: The Two Towers**
6. Kapiti Coast: **Lord of the Rings: The Fellowship of the Ring, King Kong**
7. Marlborough Sounds: **Perfect Strangers**
8. Mount Gunn, Franz Josef Glacier: **Lord of the Rings: The Return of the King**
9. Deer Park Heights: **Lords of the Rings** trilogy
10. Elephant Rocks: **The Chronicles of Narnia**

Although much of **The Chronicles of Narnia** (2005) was filmed on sets at Hobsonville Air Base in West Auckland and at Henderson Valley Studios, some exterior shooting took place at **Monte Cecilia House,** a Catholic refuge located in **Hillsborough,** Auckland. The grounds of Professor Kirke's (Jim Broadbent) mansion and the house with the wardrobe that is the portal to Narnia were used in many scenes. **Woodhill Forest** was transformed into the dreaded White Witch's (Tilda Swinton) camp.

Jane Campion's masterpiece *The Piano*, starring Holly Hunter as mute Scottish pianist Ada McGrath, was filmed at Karekare Reserve. The black-sand beach on which Ada's piano is unceremoniously deposited, then subsequently abandoned by her new husband, Alisdair (Sam Neill), is Karekare Beach.

Shot in the same region, in the **Waitakere Ranges,** was Jane Campion's masterpiece ***The Piano*** (1993), starring Holly Hunter as mute Scottish pianist Ada McGrath. After having been sold to a man on the other side of the world by her father, Ada is shipped to New Zealand, where she starts a new life for herself and her young daughter, Flora (Anna Paquin). Their arrival by sea was filmed at the **Karekare Reserve,** and the black-sand beach on which Ada's piano is unceremoniously deposited, then subsequently abandoned by her new husband, Alisdair (Sam Neill), is **Karekare Beach.**

Jane Campion chose the setting for its inhospitable look: The vast imposing cliff faces, wild surf, and gloomy stretch of sand lent the scene a powerful sense of foreboding. Filming also took place in the nearby forest. Exteriors of George Baines's (Harvey Keitel) and Alisdair Stewart's homes were shot in **Warkworth.** The Karekare area has also appeared in other productions such as ***Xena: Warrior Princess*** (1995-2001), a series that put **Karekare Falls** to good use in several of its episodes. More *Xena* filming took place on a ridge that separates Karekare Bay from Union Bay. Other locations on the west coast include Piha Beach, Pukekowhai Point (with its very distinctive profile, cliffs and cave), Bethells Beach (with Ihumoana Island as a backdrop), Erangi Point, Bethells Valley, Lake Wainamu, Wainamu Stream and dunes, and Woodhill Forest, inland from Muriwai Beach. As one travels south of Auckland to the **Waikato region** of the North Island, the landscape suddenly becomes very Eng-

lish, with rolling green hills, country lanes, and paddocks. The area thrives on agriculture – the fertile basin is served by the Waikato River – and horse breeding. It is easy to see why Peter Jackson fell in love with **Matamata** when scouting locations for Hobbiton. Apart from a slight makeover that required some landscaping and planting of crops and flowers, the private **Alexander Farm** was ideal for building the sets that became the homes of Frodo Baggins (Elijah Wood) and his wee mates in the *Lord of the Rings* movies.

On the east coast some 20 miles (30 kilometers) north of **Gisborne** lies **Whangara,** the location heart of Niki Caro's ***Whale Rider*** (2002). The highly acclaimed novel and movie tell the story of Paikea (Keisha Castle-Hughes), a young girl who must prove herself worthy of becoming the next leader of her tribe by winning her grandfather's (Rawiri Paratene) approval. The Eastland Region where the film was shot is famous for its dramatic coastal scenery, winegrowing, and aboriginal Maori heritage. The house where much of the filming took place can be visited on a three-hour guided tour departing from Gisborne Visitor Information Centre.

Central North Island displays an incredible choice of landscapes all within a short drive of one another. Located south of **Taupo** is **Tongariro National Park,** the oldest such preserve in New Zealand and a region centered on three active volca-

Jane Campion chose Karekare Beach as a location for its inhospitable look: The cliffs, wild surf, and gloomy sands lend the scene a sense of foreboding.

noes: Tongariro, Ngauruhoe, and Ruapehu, the menacing-looking Mount Doom in the *Lord of the Rings* movies. The scenery is ever-changing, from lakes to forests, from fields to steep bluffs and strange rock formations. The highest of the North Island's peaks is **Mount Ruapehu** at 9,177 feet (2,797 meters). It is on this volcano, at **Iwikau Alpine Village** near Whakapapa Ski Field, that the Mordor scenes in *The Lord of the Rings: The Two Towers* (2002) were filmed. **Meads Wall** beside **Pinnacle Ridge** is where Sam and Frodo capture Gollum. Other rocky outcrops in the area depicted the wastelands of Emyn Muil as the Hobbits made their way to Dagorland, then on to the Black Gates. Also located on the edge of Tongariro National Park is **Ohakune,** the location for Ithilien Camp where Sméagol caught and ate a fish. The exact spot is up the **Turoa Ski Field Road,** level with Mangawhero Falls. As many of the sites used to create Mordor are hard to reach, the best way to enjoy them is by helicopter tour out of Ohakune.

Enjoying similar exposure to Tongariro's Mount Doom on the silver screen, **Mount Taranaki** in **Egmont National Park** stood in for Mount Fuji in Edward Zwick's ***The Last Samurai*** (2003). Tom Cruise plays the disenchanted American soldier Nathan Algren, a man whose life is changed forever when he is captured in the aftermath of a Japanese army charge against Samurai rebels. **New Plymouth** on the west coast served as a base for cast and crew, and scenes involving a nineteenth-century army parade and Samurai learning how to use rifles were shot on **Pukekura Park**'s cricket ground. The filmmakers had tents and flags brought in and added a Japanese palace façade to the Bellringer Pavilion. The Yokohama port scenes were filmed on a set in the waterfront area while the foggy battle scene in which Nathan is captured by the enemy was shot in **Mangamahoe Forest,** a short drive from downtown New Plymouth. The final battle was staged on a farm overlooking the Kaitake ranges near Mount Taranaki. Some 30 miles (50 kilometers) northeast of New Plymouth lies **Uruti Valley,** site of the remote Samurai village where Captain Algren recovers from his wounds and learns about the locals and their culture.

More than 125 miles (200 kilometers) from the New Plymouth region are more sites important to ***The Lord of the Rings: The Fellowship of the Ring*** (2001). Four different rivers portrayed the majestic River Anduin, but the main location here is the **Rangitikei River** south of Taihape near Ohotu. It is crossed by a bridge popular with bungee jumpers that is renowned as the best spot from which to view the gorge below. Another filming site is situated nearby, where the Moawhango and Rangitikei rivers meet. Also appearing in several Anduin scenes were the **Hutt River,** which flows from its source in the

Whangara in the Eastland Region is the location heart of Niki Caro's *Whale Rider.* The movie tells the story of the Maori girl Paikea (Keisha Castle-Hughes).

Southern Tararua Ranges to Petone, and the **Waiau River** on South Island. The **Waitarere Forest,** south of Foxton, stood in for Trollshaw Forest and Osgiliath Wood. In the latter, Frodo (Elijah Wood), Sam (Sean Astin), and Sméagol (Andy Serkis) make their way through the forest after leaving Faramir (David Wenham). This location is on the **Kapiti Coast,** an area near Wellington that was also used by Peter Jackson in **King Kong** (2005). The waters on the Kapiti Coast as well as the Cook Strait feature in the ocean scenes. Filming of the *Venture* steamship on its way to Skull Island took place between **Raumati Beach** and **Kapiti Island,** a wildlife reserve and bird sanctuary.

Otaki Gorge Road near Otaki, an hour's trip north of Wellington, also featured in *The Fellowship of the Ring* and is especially memorable because of the scene in which Gandalf the Grey (Ian McKellen) leads the young Hobbits away from the Shire. The **Otaki River gorge** and the surrounding scenery fit beautifully with Tolkien's description of the countryside on the outskirts of the Shire. Film fans heading

Otaki Gorge Road near Otaki, north of Wellington, features in *The Fellowship of the Ring,* and is especially memorable for the scene in which Gandalf the Grey (Ian McKellen) leads the young Hobbits away from the Shire.

The Otaki River gorge (below) and the surrounding scenery fit beautifully with author J.R.R. Tolkien's description of the countryside on the outskirts of the Shire.

south to Wellington from Otaki can stop at **Queen Elizabeth Park** near Paraparaumu where battle scenes from *The Lord of the Rings: The Return of the King* (2003) were filmed in the fields in front of Minas Tirith. There isn't much to see at the site of the Battle of the Pelennor Fields as many of the shots involved blue-screen backgrounds. Still, location hunters can stroll through the paddocks where a dead Mûmak war elephant once lay.

Over the Rimutaka Ranges and southeast of Otaki is **Feath-erston,** a town that earned notoriety in 1943 when Japanese prisoners of war rioted in a nearby camp. More recently, **Fern-side,** one of the country's finest historic homes, put Featherston on the map when its gardens and ornamental lake were trans-formed into Lothlorien, home of the elves of Galadhrim in *The Return of the King.* The scenes of Sméagol and Déagol's fight beside the Gladden Fields were filmed here, and the gardens served as the woods where Frodo gets help and advice from elf queen Galadriel (Cate Blanchett). The filmmakers worked their magic on Fernside's white bridge, turning it into the mystical-looking bridge of Lothlorien featured in the farewell scene.

Nearby in the foothills of the Tararua Ranges is spectacular **Kaitoke Regional Park,** a magnificent natural setting of bush-clad hills, riverside glades, and beech forests. Of the four walks that lead into the park from Pakuratahi Hutt Forks, the most popular is the **Ridge Track.** In addition to splendid views of the Hutt Valley, the walk leads to a flat, grassy, sheltered area and significant location from the *Lord of the Rings* trilogy: the Elven

Peter Jackson (left) poses on the Hobbiton set. Exteriors were shot at Alexan-der Farm. The volcanic landscape of Tongariro National Park (above) appears in the *Lord of the Rings* trilogy, providing the setting for Mount Doom.

the surrounding natural river system. A short trip from the Riv-endell site to **Harcourt Park** brings you to the place where the gardens of Isengard were filmed, scenes in which Gandalf rides Shadowfax to meet with Saruman (Christopher Lee) at the Tower of Orthanc and Saruman's Orcs fell trees to fuel his forge.

In and Around Wellington: Capital Locations in the South

Wellington, Peter Jackson's hometown, is New Zealand's capi-tal. Located at the southern tip of North Island, the city is sur-rounded by rugged hills and a sweeping harbor and is close to beaches, valleys, vineyards, and splendid scenery along the coastlines. Much of the filming of the *Lord of the Rings* trilogy and *King Kong* was done in Wellington at Jackson's Camper-down Studios and Weta Workshop, a state-of-the-art post-production facility, both located in the suburb of Miramar.

Although most of **King Kong** was filmed in a studio environ-ment, some exterior shooting did take place at various locations in and around the Wellington region. The *Manuia,* a tuna fishing vessel that was converted into the *SS Venture,* the ship that

Refuge of Rivendell. Complex sets were erected here, buildings, towers, and walkways carefully designed to fit in amongst the trees. The bedroom where Frodo recovers from his knife wound was built on a large set featuring an artificial waterfall and riv-ers; these were fed by water brought in by tanker and carefully poured into an enclosed structure to avoid leaking chlorine into

Naomi Watts is Ann Darrow and Adrien Brody is Jack Driscoll in Peter Jackson's epic *King Kong*. The Kapiti Coast (below) as well as the Cook Strait feature in the ocean scenes. Filming of the *Venture* steamship on its way to Skull Island took place between Raumati Beach and Kapiti Island.

took the great ape from Skull Island to New York, was berthed at **Miramar Wharf** on Cobham Drive, the location for the pier scenes. A near full-size model of the ship was constructed on the studios' back lot. Filming for Skull Island took place mainly at **Lyall Bay,** although a giant wall keeping the ape confined to his pen was erected above the Massey Memorial near **Shelly Bay.** New York in the 1930s was built on a backlot at **Seaview** in the Hutt Valley.

Mount Victoria, one of Wellington's most popular tourist destinations, is a prominent hill that offers a spectacular bird's-eye view of the city and the harbor. Its forests and landscape were used as a location for the Outer Shire in *The Lord of the Rings: The Fellowship of the Ring.* Several Hobbiton Woods scenes were filmed here, including the Hobbits' discovery of mushrooms on a steep bank and their lucky escape from the evil Nazgûl riders of Mordor. A disused quarry on Mount Victoria became the Rohirrim encampment of Dunharrow. **Cape Palliser,** southeast of Wellington, is home to the majestic **Putangirua Pinnacles,** a set of "earth pillars" formed 120,000 years ago by erosion. Following the stream bed upstream is probably the most spectacular way to visit the outlandish natural landscape and see the location where Legolas (Orlando Bloom) told the story of the Army of the Dead while riding up the Dimholt Road in *The Return of the King.*

South Island: From Nelson to Narnia

Nelson, located at the northern tip of South Island, also played a prominent part in the *Lord of the Rings* movies. Many props for the films were created by local artisans, including the famous "one" ring crafted by goldsmith Jens Hansen. The Nelson region has three National Parks that feature a variety of superb locations, from golden sandy beaches to gorgeous mountain lakes. **Mount Olympus** in **Kahurangi National Park** provided the setting for Eregion Hills and the rough country south of Rivendell while **Mount Owen** stood in for the Dimrill Dale hillside where the Hobbits exit the Mines of Moria. The

park is home to many of the oldest rocks in New Zealand, some of them in remote areas best seen from the air with the help of Nelson Helicopters. **Chetwood Forest,** where Aragorn (Viggo Mortensen) and the Hobbits fled after their stay at Bree, was **Takaka Hill** on the border of the park. This is, with its ghostly trees and rocky marble outcrops, the only place outside Italy where such formations exist.

On the northeastern side of the island, located in the **Marlborough Sounds,** is **Puketea Bay,** an area that recommended itself for the filming of ***Perfect***

Strangers (2003). Director Gaylene Preston's story of obsessive love stars Sam Neill as the perfect stranger and Rachael Blake as Melanie, the woman he charms and takes back to his home on a remote and inaccessible island. Most of the action takes place on the wild and treacherous west coast and is amplified by the powerful seascape that is so typical of this part of South Island. The sequences in which the actors are out at sea were thankfully filmed in the calmer, less treacherous waters of the east coast. More filming took place near **D'Urville Island,** an area of great beauty inhabited by blue penguins and seabirds, of native forests and regenerating bush, and waterways that lead to the outer sounds.

The stranger's shack is located in **Meybille Bay** – the director's childhood home – just north of the startling pancake-shaped limestone rocks of Punakaiki in Paparoa National Park. **Constant Bay,** just before Charleston, is an untamed stretch of coast that provided the seascapes for the tumultuous love affair. The little horseshoe-shaped bay was once a prosperous area: Both Little Beach and Nine Mile Beach were so heavily excavated for gold that Constant Bay is now too shallow to operate safely as a harbor. Once a thriving gold-mining town known as Crescent City, **Greymouth** is the main hub of the west coast's Westland District and provides a good, central base for exploring the region. The exterior of the pub and the fishing docks in *Perfect Strangers* were filmed here, while suitable interiors were found up north, in **Westport.**

Magical Heights: The Southern Alps and the Central Districts

The mountains of South Island act as a barrier to storms moving to the east, a geographic feature that serves to halt weather fronts and initiate rainfalls on the western side of the island. For this reason, the west coast is among the rainiest places in the world, rich in lush rain forests and glaciers. The **Franz Josef** and **Fox Glaciers** belong to the Southwest New Zealand World Heritage area, and still flow almost to sea level, making them unique relics of the last Ice Age. Deep blue lakes, clear streams, and untamed yet accessible wilderness surround them. Part of the mountain range is **Mount Gunn,** which appears in the famous "Lighting of the Beacons" scene in *The Return of the King.* Sent by Gandalf, Pippin lights the beacon atop Minas Tirith. After all the beacons atop the peaks of the White Mountains have been lit in turn, Aragorn sees the last one from his vantage point outside the Golden Hall in Edoras.

The untamed west coast and powerful seascape form an ideal frame for drama in *Perfect Strangers*.

South Island's central **Canterbury District** boasts some of the film world's most dramatic scenery, as captured in both the *Lord of the Rings* trilogy and *The Chronicles of Narnia.* Arthur's Pass National Park, the third oldest national park in New Zealand after Tongariro and Egmont, is well known for its stunning landscapes of mountains, glaciers, waterfalls, fields of alpine flowers, and deep native forests. Linking Canterbury and Christchurch by road and railway is **Arthur's Pass** itself, the main crossing of the Southern Alps. **Castle Hill,** located between Darfield and Arthur's Pass, displays formations of soft limestone boulders, reminiscent of a dilapidated stone castle. These striking sculptured rock forms attract a constant flow of visitors and photographers. Nearby **Flock Hill Station,** with its vast number of climbable rocks, was the site of the great battle for Narnia between the army of the great lion Aslan (voice of Liam Neeson), led by the boy king Peter (William Moseley), and the White Witch's forces. The craggy ranges of Flock Hill featured in the final image showing the majestic animated Aslan roaring from the cliff top.

South of the Selwyn District of Canterbury, **Ashburton District** provides filmmakers with some of the best scenery in New Zealand. Large forests, majestic mountain ranges, snow-fed rivers, and colorful plains are just some of the fantastic natural resources on offer. **Mount Sunday,** a sheer-sided hill in the middle of the **Rangitata River Valley,** an hour's drive west of Methven, was the set for Edoras, the fortress city of the Rohan people, and King Théoden's (Bernard Hill) hall of Meduseld in *The Two Towers* and *The Return of the King.* Nothing remains of the set, but the rocky spur located in the middle of an expansive river plain surrounded by the towering Southern Alps is a remarkable sight and well worth a visit. The area is best viewed from nearby Mount Potts Station.

In neighboring **Mackenzie District,** the countryside changes again, this time to brown grass plains and deep turquoise glacial lakes. Sitting amidst the Mackenzie Basin and contrasting starkly with the surrounding landscapes is New Zealand's highest mountain, **Mount Cook,** also known as **Aoraki.** Just down the road from Mount Cook and Aoraki National Park is **Twizel,** backdrop for the opening sequence of *The Two Towers,* where Aragorn, Legolas, and Gimli (John Rhys-Davies) pursue the Orcs. It is also the site of the Battle of the Pelennor Fields and the Eastemnet Gullies in *The Return of the King.* The Ride of the Rohirrim, where Théoden leads the charge into the Orc army, was staged on the **Ben-Ohau Station,** and ranks as the largest cavalry charge ever filmed in motion-picture history. The golden plains framed by the snowcapped peaks of the Ered Nimrais (the **Ohau Range**) made for a perfect backdrop. The scenes of Gandalf and Pippin (Billy Boyd) crossing a stream on their way to Minas Tirith and of Gandalf riding out to repel the Nazgûl from Faramir and his rangers were also shot here.

The Roaring East Coast

Much of the filming of *The Chronicles of Narnia* took place near **Oamaru.** The area around Duntroon features limestone outcropped valleys overlooking the Maerewhenua River. Millions of years ago, this area was under water, and when the sea receded it left behind limestone hulks on the sandy ground. Among the more peculiar formations are the ancient **Elephant Rocks** that appear like giant animals grazing the flat, dark land. Eighty red-and-gold tents, all handmade from silk designs manufactured in Auckland, were set up between the boulders, and the area became Aslan's Camp, where the children first meet the great lion.

From the *Lord of the Rings* series: the Remarkables (top), where Aragorn guides the Fellowship (middle). Mount Sunday (left) hosts Edoras, the Rohan city, while Twizel (below) provides a dramatic backdrop for sorcery.

South of the city of **Dunedin** is the **Catlins region** made famous by *The Chronicles of Narnia*. The computer-generated Cair Paravel, the castle where the Pevensie children are crowned rulers of Narnia, was set atop the spectacular cliff top of **Purakaunui Bay.** The wilderness of the Catlins Coast consists of dense southern rain forest, dramatic headlands, waterfalls, and an abundance of wildlife, including seals, sea lions, penguins, and dolphins. The Southland Scenic Route that runs from Dunedin to Invercargill is a photographer's paradise.

The Stunning Lake District

The reservoir at **Poolburn Dam** in **Central Otago,** a popular recreational area situated on the Ida Valley side of the Rough Ridge Range, was the location used for the lakeside Rohan village where Morwen (Robyn Malcolm) sent her children to safety in *The Lord of the Rings: The Two Towers*. The terrain and lake are easily recognizable as the site where the Orc attack took place and from which the refugees fled.

Lake Wanaka in the **Otago region** is New Zealand's fourth largest lake, a popular resort area bounded by high peaks on its western shore. The snowcapped Southern Alps that frame the lake doubled as a backdrop in ***The Fellowship of the Ring*** for Gandalf's flight to Rohan after he is rescued from the top of the Tower of Orthanc by Gwaihir, the Windlord, just as Saruman is about to throw him over. The drive from Wanaka to Queenstown on meandering State Highway 89 takes you through scenic **Cardrona Valley,** famous for its world-class resort and ski slopes. At the summit of Cardrona Road are expansive views over the River Anduin, site of the Pillars of the Argonath and Dimrill Dale. Another kilometer downhill brings you to the Ford of Bruinen and Amon Hen, nestled on the shore of Nen Hithoel in the far distance.

Close to Queenstown is **Arrowtown,** a settlement that developed almost overnight during the 1862 gold rush, and the **Ford of Bruinen,** located on the **Arrow River** upstream from the town. This is the location of the scene in which Arwen Evenstar (Liv Tyler), pursued by the Black Riders, carries a dying Frodo across the river on Asfaloth, her Elven steed. The Gladden Fields scenes where Isildur (Harry Sinclair) was attacked by Orcs from the Misty Mountains were shot beside the river on a path with curved, overhanging trees. Scenes of the Ford of Bruinen in flood were filmed on the **Shotover River** at **Skippers Canyon,** a short way from Arrowtown. Nearby Coronet Peak Ski Fields lookout proffers breathtaking views of the **Remarkables Mountains** that doubled as Dimrill Dale; it is down these slopes that Aragorn leads the Fellowship to Lothlorien after their ordeal in the Mines of Moria. These also featured as the Misty Mountains of Mordor and the digital background for Minas Tirith.

The White Witch swings her sword among the strange rocks of Flock Hill Station. Young Peter readies for battle at Aslan's Camp near Elephant Rocks.

Queenstown, a breathtaking sportsman's paradise, also draws *Lord of the Rings* fans. **Deer Park Heights,** a nearby 800-hectare park and working farm, offers several filming sites to visit: those representing Rohan, the mountain wall where Aragorn exited the Paths of the Dead, Gandalf's journey to Minas Tirith, and the large rock wall from which the Warg scout jumped and killed Háma (John Leigh). The scenes in which Gimli was thrown from his horse to the amusement of Eowyn (Miranda Otto), the cliff face Aragorn was dragged over, the place where Eowyn provided Aragorn with his tasty stew, the site where the Wargs and Riders of Rohan clashed, and the lake the Rohirrim Refugees walked past as they fled Edoras – they're all here.

Looking back towards Queenstown over **Lake Wakatipu** from the West Summit Lookout, a familiar panorama presents itself: This is where Aragorn, Legolas, and Gimli see the corsair ships sailing up the Anduin. There are many more *Lord of the Rings* regions to visit, such as Glenorchy, the Fjordland National Park, Mavora Lakes, and Te Anau, which provided locations for Isengard, Lothlorien, and Amon Hen, as well as Nen Hithoel, Silverlode River, and Fangorn Forest. For more coverage, fans should buy a copy of *The Lord of the Rings Location Book* by Ian Brodie, a well-written guide for visitors to New Zealand.

INDEX OF FILMS

20,000 Leagues Under the Sea 51, 54, 55
2001: A Space Odyssey 9
39 Steps, The 76, 77, 80
50 First Dates 37–39

A

Adaptation 26, 27, 34
Adventures of Priscilla, Queen of the Desert,
  The 4, 168–171, 176
African Queen, The 139, 148
Against All Odds 42, 43
Aguirre: The Wrath of God 46, 47
Air America 161, 163
Alamo, The.. 7, 13
Alexander 127, 135, 160
Alice in the Cities 94
All the Pretty Horses 7, 13
Allan Quatermain and the Lost City of Gold.. 141
Amistad 60
Among Giants 67
Anna and the King 160, 161
Apache Gold 121
Apache's Last Battle 121
Apocalypse Now 160, 161, 163, 164
Apocalypto....................................... 43, 45
Arizona 10
Around the World in Eighty Days 150
Asterix & Obelix: Mission Cleopatra 131
Avanti! 108

Bananas 60
Beach, The...............................4, 160–162
Bear, The 110
Beat the Devil 103, 108, 109
Big Blue, The...................................... 123, 124
Big Easy, The 29
Big Jake 45
Big Sky, The 6, 21
Big Trail, The...................................... 11, 21
Birds, The 18
Blue Crush 37, 41
Blue Hawaii 37–39
Bombay Talkie 150
Bon Voyage 88
Bonnie and Clyde 13
Boogeyman... 178
Born Free 140
Born on the Fourth of July 164
Bourne Identity, The 123, 124, 152
Bourne Supremacy, The 152, 153
Boy on a Dolphin 122, 123
Braveheart 76–79
Bride & Prejudice 150, 153
Bride, The 88
Bridge on the River Kwai, The 161, 163
Bridges of Madison County, The 188
Bridget Jones: The Edge of Reason 111
  161, 162
Brokeback Mountain 6, 24, 176
Buffalo Bill 11
Burden of Dreams 47
Butch Cassidy and the Sundance Kid........ 7, 11

Cinema Paradiso 116
City of Ghosts... 167
City of Joy 150, 151
City Slickers.. 7, 14
Clearing, The... 33
Cliffhanger 103, 110
Close Encounters of the Third Kind 6
  21, 150
Cocktail 51, 52
Cocoon 55
Color Purple, The 26, 27, 31
Comancheros, The 10
Comedian Harmonists 97
Constant Gardener, The................... 139, 144
Contact 51, 60, 61
Creature from the Black Lagoon 27, 35
Crocodile Dundee 168, 169, 173
Crocodile Dundee II 169, 173
Crouching Tiger, Hidden Dragon 4
  156, 157
Cry in the Dark, A 169, 172
Cutthroat Island 163

D

Da Vinci Code, The...........................63, 64, 67
Damned, The 97, 99
Dances with Wolves 4, 6, 19, 175
Darling Clementine, My 8, 9
Dead Calm 169, 174, 175
Deadwood Coach, The 11
Dear Diary 119
Death in Venice 97
Deep, The 51, 59
Deer Hunter, The 160, 163
Deliverance 26, 27, 30
Die Another Day 71
Dilwale Dulhania Le Jayenge 101
Dirty Dancing 4, 27, 32, 33
Dirty Deeds 169, 171
Dirty Rotten Scoundrels 84
Django... 92, 93
Doctor Zhivago 83, 92, 154
Don Juan DeMarco 39
Don't Come Knocking 9
Down by Law 26, 27, 29
Dr. No 51, 52, 53
Duellists, The 88

B

Babe 169, 170
Babe: Pig in the City 169, 170
Babel 127, 129

C

Cabaret.. 95
Caddyshack 35
Cape Fear 35
Captain Corelli's Mandolin 122, 123
Casablanca 118, 127
Casino Royale 51, 57, 103, 113
Cast Away 189
Cattle Queen of Montana 6, 23
Cave of the Yellow Dog, The...................... 159
Caveman 44
Challenge, The 100
Chariots of Fire 77, 80, 81
Cheyenne Autumn 10
Chimes at Midnight 93
Chitty Chitty Bang Bang 95, 96
Chocolat 85, 89
Chronicles of Narnia – The Lion, The Witch and
  the Wardrobe, The 5, 178, 179, 185–187

Francesca Johnson (Meryl Streep) and Robert Kincaid (Clint Eastwood) fall in love in *The Bridges of Madison County* (1995). Locations include Roseman and Holliwell bridges near Winterset, Iowa.

E

Easy Rider..................................... 4, 7, 8, 29
Edge, The.. 6, 25
El Cid 93

Life will never be the same: In *Cast Away* **(2000), Tom Hanks is a FedEx manager who is stranded on a tiny isle in the South Seas. The movie was shot mostly on the island of Monuriki, Fiji.**

El Dorado 10
Elizabeth 64
Endless Summer, The 41
English Patient, The 5, 68, 103, 104, 137
Englishman Who Went Up a Hill But Came
    Down a Mountain, The 63, 73, 74
Entrapment 81
Ever After 88, 89

F

Far and Away 83
Far Country, The 25
Far from the Madding Crowd 62, 63, 70
Femme Fatale 85
Field, The 82, 83
Fight for the Matterhorn 100
First Knight 74
Fistful of Dollars, A 92, 93
Fitzcarraldo 4, 46, 47
Flipper 57
Fog, The 18
For a Few Dollars More 92
For Whom the Bell Tolls 16, 17
For Your Eyes Only 51, 55
    57, 111, 123, 125
Forrest Gump 5, 9, 26, 27, 33, 34
Fort Apache 9
Four Feathers, The 127, 131
French Kiss 85
French Lieutenant's Woman, The 71
Fried Green Tomatoes 5, 26, 27, 30, 31
From Here to Eternity 37, 38
From Russia with Love 75
Frontier Hellcat 121
Fugitive, The 27, 32
Fun in Acapulco 44

G

Gandhi 150–152
Gaslight 118
Geierwally 99
Geronimo 7, 10
Giant 12
Ginostra 119
Girl from Paris, The 85–87
Gladiator 126–128, 130, 131
God Created Woman, ... And 84, 85
Godfather, The 4, 103, 114, 115
Godfather: Part II, The 103, 114, 115
Godfather: Part III, The 103, 115
Godzilla 37
Gold Rush, The 7, 16
GoldenEye 51, 60, 61, 101
Goldfinger 101
Gone With the Wind 26, 27
Good Morning, Vietnam 161, 163
Good Woman, A 103, 108, 109
Good Year, A 85, 86
Good, the Bad and the Ugly, The 92, 93
Gorillas in the Mist 139, 149
Gosford Park 64
Great Escape, The 96
Greed 17
Guns of Navarone, The 123, 125

H

Hamlet 77, 81
Hannibal 33
Harry Potter film series 4, 44
    63, 64, 76, 77
Hatari! 139, 143, 144
Heat and Dust 150, 151, 154, 155
Heaven 97, 103–105
Heaven's Gate 6, 23
Heidi 100, 101
Help! 56
Herbstmilch 95, 97
Hercules: The Legendary Journeys 178
Hero 157, 158
Hideous Kinky 126, 127, 133, 134
Hierankl 97
High Sierra 7, 16
Highlander 77, 79
Highlander III 79
Hofrat Geiger 99
Hombre 10
Hop-Along Cassidy 16
Horse Whisperer, The 6, 22, 23
Hotel Rwanda 148

House of Flying Daggers 157, 158
How Stella Got Her Groove Back 50–52
Howards End 63, 64

I

In My Father's Den 178
India 99
Indiana Jones and the Last Crusade 9
Indochine 5, 160, 161, 165, 166
Inn of the Sixth Happiness, The 63, 73
Instinct 54
Iron Horse, The 11
Island of Dr. Moreau, The 51, 59
It Started in Naples 106

J

Jane Eyre 67
Japanese Story 177
Jeremiah Johnson 7, 11
Jesus of Nazareth 130
Jewel of the Nile, The 127, 128, 130
Johnny English 72
Jungle Book, The 150
Jurassic Park 36, 37
Jurassic Park III 37

K

Kangaroo Jack 172
Kaos 118
Killing Fields, The 161, 162
Kim 150
King and I, The 161
King Arthur 83
King Kong 37, 40, 178, 179, 182–184
King of the Road 94
King Solomon's Mines 139–141
Kingdom of Heaven 93, 127, 131, 135
Knockin' on Heaven's Door 95
Kundun 5, 126, 127, 131, 133

L

L'Avventura 103, 115, 116, 118
Ladies in Lavender 63, 72, 73
Lady from Shanghai, The 44
Lara Croft: Tomb Raider – The Cradle
    of Life 123, 124, 160, 161, 167
Last King of Scotland 148, 149
Last Movie, The 46, 47
Last of the Mohicans, The 5, 27, 32
Last Samurai, The 5, 178, 179, 181
Last Temptation of Christ, The 127
    131, 132

INDEX OF FILMS

Lawrence of Arabia 74, 83, 92, 93, 127–130, 154
Legends of the Fall 6, 25, 54
Leopard, The 103, 116
Letters from Iwo Jima 190
Libertine, The 66
Licence to Kill 44
Life of Brian 136, 137
Lion in Winter, The 74, 86
Live and Let Die 53, 54
Local Hero 77, 81
Loch Ness 81
Longest Day, The 85, 90
Lord Jim 161, 166, 167
Lord of the Flies 51, 60
Lord of the Rings: The Fellowship of the Ring, The 105, 179, 181, 182, 184
Lord of the Rings: The Return of the King, The 105, 179, 181, 184–186
Lord of the Rings: The Two Towers, The 105, 179, 181, 185–187
Lost World: Jurassic Park, The 36, 37
Lover, The 160
Lucky Luke 14
Ludwig 95, 97
Lust for Life 87
Luzhin Defence, The 112

M

Macbeth 75, 77, 81
Mad Max 2: The Road Warrior 169, 171, 175
Mad Max Beyond Thunderdome 4, 169, 175, 176
Madness of King George, The 65
Magnificent Seven, The 43, 45
Malèna 116
Man and a Woman, A 90
Man Called Horse, A 45
Man from Laramie, The 14
Man from Snowy River, The 176
Man Who Shot Liberty Valance, The 10
Man Who Would Be King, The 127, 130
Man with the Golden Gun, The 160, 161
Mask of Zorro, The 45
Maverick 16
Medicine Man 43, 45
Midsummer Night's Dream, A 104
Mighty Aphrodite 115
Misfits, The 7, 12
Missing, The 7, 14
Mission Impossible II 169–171

Mission, The 49
Mississippi Burning 26–28
Mogambo 139, 142
Monsoon Wedding 150
Month by the Lake, A 112, 113
Monty Python and The Holy Grail 76, 77, 80
Moonraker 49
Morocco 127
Motorcycle Diaries, The 4, 48, 49
Mountain Calls, The 100, 101
Mountain of Destiny 110
Much Ado About Nothing 103–105
My Dog Skip 28
Mystery of the Marie Celeste, The 71

N

Name of the Rose, The 95, 96
Nell 26, 27, 32
Never Say Never Again 56, 57
Night of the Iguana, The 42–44
No More Mr. Nice Guy 94, 95
North by Northwest 15
Nowhere in Africa 138, 139, 145, 147

O

O Brother, Where Art Thou? 27, 28
Ocean's Twelve 103, 112
Octopussy 151, 153, 154
Oedipus Rex 130
Old Man and the Sea, The 59
On Her Majesty's Secret Service 101
Once Upon a Time in the West 9, 92
Open Water 57
Orpheus 87
Out of Africa 4, 138, 139

P

Painted Veil, The 157, 158
Papillon 51, 54
Paris, Texas 12
Passage to India, A 150, 151, 154, 155
Passion of the Christ, The 78
Patch Adams 33
Pearl Harbor 37, 40, 41
Perfect Strangers 178, 179, 184, 185
Perfume: The Story of a Murderer 87, 93, 97, 104
Piano, The 5, 178, 179, 180
Picnic at Hanging Rock 168, 169, 176
Picnic on the Grass 88
Pink Panther 111

Pirates of the Caribbean: At World's End 58
Pirates of the Caribbean: Dead Man's Chest 51, 58, 59
Pirates of the Caribbean: The Curse of the Black Pearl 51, 58
Pitch Black 169, 176
Place in the Sun, A 7, 16
Platoon 160, 161, 164
Plein soleil 107
Point Break 37, 41
Postman, The 103, 108, 118, 119
Predator 44
Pride & Prejudice 62–66
Prince of Tides, The 5, 26, 27, 34

Q

Quiet American, The 161, 166
Quiet Man, The 82, 83

R

Rabbit-Proof Fence 169, 176
Raiders of the Lost Ark 37, 39, 137
Rapa Nui 191
Razor's Edge, The 151, 155
Razorback 169, 171
Rebecca 18
Red Planet 169, 171, 176
Remains of the Day, The 62, 64
Ride the Wild Surf 41
Rio Bravo 10
Rio Conchas 10
Rio Grande 10
River of No Return 6, 25

An elegant anti-war statement: Director Clint Eastwood and actor Ken Watanabe on the beach of the Japanese island of Iwo Jima, where the movie *Letters from Iwo Jima* (2006) was filmed.

River Runs Through It, A 4, 6, 22, 23
River Wild, The 23
Robin Hood: Prince of Thieves 63
  69, 85, 88
Rockers 51
Rocky 79
Romeo + Juliet 45
Room with a View, A 64, 103, 105
Run Lola Run 97, 104
Ryan's Daughter 82, 83

S
Samsara 151, 155
Sandpiper, The 7, 18, 19
Saving Grace 72
Saving Private Ryan 83, 85, 90
Schindler's List 68
Schlafes Bruder 99
Sea Wolves, The 153
Searchers, The 7, 9
Secret Garden, The 68
Secret of Roan Inish, The 83
Sense and Sensibility 63–66
September Affair 106
Sergeant Rutledge 6, 9
Seven Years in Tibet 48, 49
Shadowlands 63, 75
Shakespeare Wallah 150
Shane 6, 21, 23
She Wore a Yellow Ribbon 9
Sheltering Sky, The 4, 5
  126–128
Shirley Valentine 123, 124
Sideways 7, 15
Sissi film series 98, 99, 109
Six Days Seven Nights 37, 40
Smile Orange 51
Snows of Kilimanjaro, The 139, 141
Sodom and Gomorrah 130
Solino 94
Son of the Sheik, The 126
Sound of Music, The 4, 98, 99
South Pacific 37, 38
Spartacus 17, 92
Spessart Inn, The 94, 95
Splash 55
Stagecoach 4, 7, 8
Stalingrad 97
Star Trek V: The Final Frontier 16
Star Wars 7, 17, 136, 137
Star Wars Episode I – The Phantom
  Menace 136, 137

Star Wars Episode II – Attack of the
  Clones 112, 113
Star Wars Episode III – Revenge of the
  Sith 101
Stealing Beauty 105
Story of the Weeping Camel, The 157
  159
Stromboli 103, 118
Summer Lovers 122, 124
Suspicion 18

T
Talented Mr. Ripley, The 103, 107
Tall Men, The 45
Tarzan and the Slave Girl 138
Tarzan's Adventure in New York 35
Tarzan's Secret Treasure 35
Ten Canoes 173
Terra Trema, La 115
Tess 91
The Harder They Come 51
Thelma & Louise 4, 7, 9
Thieves Like Us 28
Thin Red Line, The 175
Thunderball 51, 55–57
Time to Kill, A 28
To Catch a Thief 85
Tomorrow Never Dies 88, 161
Tora! Tora! Tora! 37, 40, 41
Trader Horn 138
Tragedy of Othello: The Moor of Venice,
  The 126, 127, 134, 135
Train Robbers, The 45
Treasure Island 72
Treasure of Silver Lake 120, 121
Treasure of the Sierra Madre, The 43
Tristan + Isolde 83
Troy 42, 43
True Grit 7, 20
Truman Show, The 35

U
Under the Tuscan Sun 4, 102, 103
Unforgiven 24
Urga 157, 159

V
Vacances de Monsieur Hulot, Les 86
Vertigo 7, 18
Very Long Engagement, A 85, 91
Vier Mädels aus der Wachau 99
Vikings, The 90, 91

W
Wagon Master 10
Walk in the Clouds, A 15
Wer früher stirbt, ist länger tot 95, 97
Whale Rider 178, 179, 180, 181
What Dreams May Come 23
White Hell of Pitz Palu, The 100, 101
White Masai, The 139, 146, 147
Wide Sargasso Sea 51

The logistics involved in filming *Rapa Nui* (1994) on Easter Island, 2,200 miles (3,540 kilometers) off the coast of Chile, challenged cast and crew. Jason Scott Lee (top) stars as the warrior Noro.

Wild Bunch, The 43, 45
Wild Things 35
Willow 75
Winchester '73 10
Wind That Shakes the Barley, The 83
Winnetou and Shatterhand in the Valley of
  Death 121
Winnetou: The Desperado Trail 121
Winter Sleepers 95, 97
Wolf Creek 169, 175, 177
Wrong Move 94
Wuthering Heights 62, 63, 68
Wyatt Earp 7, 14

X
Xena: Warrior Princess 180

Y
Y tu mamá también 43, 44
Year of Living Dangerously, The 164, 165

Z
Zabriskie Point 7, 17
Zorba the Greek 122–125

CREDITS

THE AUTHORS

Claudia Hellmann is an American Studies specialist and freelance journalist who works for various travel and cultural publications. She discovered her passion for film in L.A. and New York.

Claudine Weber-Hof is an architectural historian who specialized in city history during her studies at Georgetown University and the University of Virginia. She is a freelance editor and journalist.

THE PHOTOGRAPHER

Cornwall native David John Weber chose cities and landscapes as his focus during his studies with the New York Institute of Photography. His great love is shooting photo essays of the Alps, just south of his adopted home of Münsing, Germany.

PHOTO CREDITS

Front cover, top: Joe Gough; center and bottom: David John Weber; back cover, top and bottom: David John Weber; center: Eric Isselée; film stills on the cover: Cinetext Bild- und Textarchiv GmbH, Frankfurt am Main. Film stills and posters in this volume were provided by Cinetext Bild- und Textarchiv GmbH, Frankfurt am Main. Also from Cinetext: 72 t., 112 t.l., 114 c., 152 t.; 152 b.; 177 t.l.; 177 b.l.; 181 b.r.

David John Weber: 4 t.l.; 5 t.r.; 6 t., 11 b., 18 t., 22 b., 64 b.r., 65 t.r., 66 b.r., 76 b.; 78 t.; 79 c.; 89 c.; 102 t.; 104 b.r.; 107 t.; 110-111 t.; Volkmar Janicke: 35 b.l., 39 b.r., 60 t.l., 82 b.; 144 t., 153 t.r.; 154 t.l.; 155 b.l.; 168 b.l. and b.r.; 170 b.; 171 b.; 176 t.l.; 177 b.r.; Luke Brighty: 178 t.; 179 b.r; 180 b.; 182 b.; 183 b.l.; 184 b.l.; 185 b.
The Bahamas Ministry of Tourism: 50 t; Bigstockphoto.com: Wes1972uk/ Jane Edwards: 82 t.r.; Professorgb/ Greg Boiarsky: 88 b.l.; David Martyn/ David Hughes: 90 b.r.; darrenmbaker/ Darren Baker: 104 t.; Mayday/ Paul Hill: 109 t.r.; Bigpressphoto/ Dee Reiiss, 113 t.; PaulCowan/ Paul Cowan: 125 t.l.; Smr 78/ Stroie Mihai Razvan: 125 b.; Chimney Rock Park: 32 b.r.; Dreamstime.com: Javarman: 160 t.; Jiewwan: 156 t.r.; Saba11: 117 b.; El Dorado County, Jill E. Nauman: 16 c.; Fin Photo, Claudia Pellarini: 55 t., 56 b.r.; Flickr.com: Andrea Fiore (www.andreafiore.com): 116 o.; Peter Fuchs: 119 r.; Crisanto Guadiz: 164 t.c.; G. Lützig: 96 b.l.; Mauro Pedretti: 46 t.r.; Neil Stapleton: 115; Michael R. Swigart: 45 c.; Mircea Turcan: 42 t.; Fotolia.de: Michael Joest: 95 b.l.; Georgia Department of Economic Development: 30 b.l.; Groombridge Place: 65 b.; Hatari Lodge: 143 t., 143 b.l.; Anja Hauenstein: 5 t.l., 135 t., 141 b., 166 c.l.; Claudia Hellmann: 20 t.l., 31 t.l., 34 b.r., 132 t.l.; Dieter Hellmann: 108 t.r., 162 b.l.; Istockphoto.com: Rachel Acheson: 155 t.l.; Allgood Media: 59 c.r.; Ken Babione: 19 t.r.; Roberta Bianchi: 105 b.l.; Mark Billings: 159 b.l.; BMPix: 81 t.; Frank Boellmann: 33 b.l.; Mark Bond: 69 b.; Rob Bouwman: 103 t.; Mark Breck: 123 t.r.; Dustin Brunson: 10 c.; Canimedia: 118 t.; Chrisds: 71; Richard Clarke: 165 t.r.; Sue Colvil: 69 c.; Constantgardener: 25 b.r.; Kris Coppieters: 183 t.r.; Mike Dabell, 67 b.; Deejpilot: 152 c.; Thomas de Buman: 174 t.l.; Dan Eckert: 17 b.l.; Alexandru Florescu: 124 b.; Michael Foy: 167 t.l.; Joe Gough: 168 t.; Yves Grau: 148 t.r.; Jeff Hackett: 22 t.r.; Robert Hardholt: 140 r.; Graham Heywood: 132 c.; David Hughes 87 b.l.; Eric Isselée: 138 t.r.; Anthony Jager: 17 c.r.; Mark Jensen: 38 t.l.; Angela Jones: 94 t.r.; Jeroen Kloppenburg: 76 t.; Adam Korzekwa: 134 t.l.; Boleslaw Kubica: 146-147 b.; Peter Kunasz: 20 t.r.; Lanny19: 17 t.r.; Benjamin Lazare: 84 t.; Jakob Leitner: 165 b.l.; Lilly3: 85 t.; Henryk Lippert: 11 t.r.; Cyrille Lips: 87 t.; Manu10319: 91 b.; Andrew Martin: 70 b.r.; Amy Matthews: 102 b.; Bruce McKenzie: 66 c.; Carlos Munoz: 106 t.; Mike Norton: 9 t., 21 t.l.; S. Greg Panosian: 86 b.l.; David Pedre: 122 t.l.; Phdpsx: 21 c.r.; Karen Low Phillips: 90 t.; Pomortzeff: 131 c.r.; Henry Price: 36 t.l.; Matej Pribelsky: 172 b.; Horst Puschmann: 124 t.l.; Stephen Rees: 72 b.; Giovanni Rinaldi: 107 b.r.; Fanelie Rosier: 88 t.l; Matthew Rowe: 40 b.r.; Wolfgang Schoenfeld: 48 t.; Harris Shiffman: 175 t.r.; Jon Tarrant: 174-175 b.; Texasmary: 75 t.; TexPhoto: 61 c., 61 b.; Chee Kong See Thoe: 185 t.; Laura Thomas: 60 b.l.; Alan Tobey: 34 t.r., 150; Uriel Ulam, 80 c.; Lillis Werder: 109 t.l.; Ingmar Wesemann: 96 t.; Don Wilkie: 25 t.l.; John Woodworth: 63 b., 68 b.l.; 126 t., 129 b.; YinYang: 15 c.r.; IFA: Noton: 73; Jon Arnold Images, 136; Island Outpost, Villa Goldeneye: 53 c.l.; Kasbah du Toubkal: 132 b.r.; New Mexico Tourism Department: 13 b.r.; photograph by Jim Stein: 14 b; One&Only Ocean Club: 57 b.r.; Round Hill Hotel: 50 b.l.; Schilthornbahn AG, 3800 Interlaken: 100 t.; Schloss Fuschl: 98 t.l.; Donnie Sexton/ Travel Montana: 23 c.; South Dakota Tourism: 19 c.r.; Texas Tourism, Kenny Braun: 12 b.; Travel Alberta: 24 c.

CONCEPT

Claudia Hellmann and Claudine Weber-Hof with support from Gerhard Grubbe, Grubbe Media GmbH, Munich, Germany

EDITORIAL COORDINATION Dr. Birgit Kneip
MANUSCRIPT EDITED BY Peter Meredith, Severna Park, Maryland
PRODUCTION EDITING BY Danko Szabó, Munich, Germany
TRANSLATION OF PARTS OF THE MANUSCRIPT FROM GERMAN TO ENGLISH Eve Lucas, Berlin, Germany, and Elizabeth Schwaiger, Pecton, Canada

GRAPHIC DESIGN, CONCEPT & LAYOUT
VOR-ZEICHEN, Munich, Germany, Marion Sauer and Johannes Reiner, www.vor-zeichen.de

CARTOGRAPHY Astrid Fischer-Leitl, Munich, Germany
PRODUCTION Bettina Schippel
LITHOGRAPHY Repro Ludwig, Zell am See, Austria
PRINTING AND BINDING Printer Trento, Trento, Italy

Our full listing:
www.bucher-publishing.com